www.wadsworth.com

wadsworth.com is the World Wide Web site for Wadsworth and is your direct source to dozens of online resources.

At *wadsworth.com* you can find out about supplements, demonstration software, and student resources. You can also send email to many of our authors and preview new publications and exciting new technologies.

wadsworth.com
Changing the way the world learns®

FIRST EDITION

Writing for Psychology
A Guide for Students

Mark L. Mitchell and **Janina M. Jolley**
Clarion University of Pennsylvania

Robert P. O'Shea
University of Otago, Dunedin, Otago, New Zealand

THOMSON
™
WADSWORTH

Australia • Canada • Mexico • Singapore • Spain
United Kingdom • United States

THOMSON

———✦———™

WADSWORTH

Publisher: Vicki Knight
Editorial Assistant: Monica Sarmiento
Marketing Manager: Lori Grebe
Marketing Assistant: Laurel Anderson
Advertising Project Manager: Brian Chaffee
Project Manager, Editorial Production: Paul Wells
Print/Media Buyer: Barbara Britton

Permissions Editor: Kiely Sexton
Production Service: Shepherd, Inc.
Copy Editor: Francine Banwarth
Cover Designer: Kim Rokusek
Cover Printer: Webcom Limited
Compositor: Shepherd, Inc.
Printer: Webcom Limited

For more information about our products, contact us at:
Thomson Learning Academic Resource Center
1-800-423-0563
For permission to use material from this text, contact
us by: **Phone:** 1-800-730-2214
Fax: 1-800-730-2215
Web: http://www.thomsonrights.com

Library of Congress Control Number: 0155085549

ISBN 0-155-08554-9

Wadsworth/Thomson Learning
10 Davis Drive
Belmont, CA 94002-3098
USA

Asia
Thomson Learning
5 Shenton Way #01-01
UIC Building
Singapore 068808

Australia/New Zealand
Thomson Learning
102 Dodds Street
Southbank, Victoria 3006
Australia

Canada
Nelson
1120 Birchmount Road
Toronto, Ontario M1K 5G4
Canada

Europe/Middle East/Africa
Thomson Learning
High Holborn House
50/51 Bedford Row
London WC1R 4LR
United Kingdom

Latin America
Thomson Learning
Seneca, 53
Colonia Polanco
11560 Mexico D.F.
Mexico

Spain/Portugal
Paraninfo
Calle/Magallanes, 25
28015 Madrid, Spain

CONTENTS

CHAPTER **1**

What Every Student Should Know About Writing Psychology Papers   1

CHAPTER **2**

Writing Term Papers   23

CHAPTER **3**

Writing Research Reports and Proposals   47

CHAPTER **4**

Finding, Reading, Citing, and Referencing Sources   89

CHAPTER **5**

Making Your Case: A Guide to Skeptical Reading and Logical Writing   131

CHAPTER **6**

Writing the Wrongs: How to Avoid Gruesome Grammar, Putrid Punctuation, and Saggy Style   149

CHAPTER **7**

Preparing the Final Draft 179

Your professor has asked you to use this book to guide you in writing a paper. In response, you may be asking yourself three questions:

1. Why is my professor asking me to write a paper?
2. Why is it important to write a good paper?
3. How can this book help me?

In the next few sections, we will answer these questions.

Why Teachers Assign Papers

Your term papers and research reports show that you can find out things on your own. Ideally, your papers will show that you have learned enough from your teacher that you can now become your own teacher. Specifically, you can

- find relevant material in journals,
- read and understand complex material,
- evaluate what you read,
- organize both your notes and your thinking about what you read, and
- create new knowledge by pulling together information from several different sources and critically analyzing that information.

Your papers also show that you are capable of carrying out complex assignments. A good paper shows that you can

- make a case using evidence,
- express ideas clearly,
- get things done on time,
- balance independence with following directions,
- produce a professional looking product, and
- please your teacher, supervisor, or client.

Finally, a good paper reflects well on your fairness, honesty, and intellectual integrity. You display fairness, honesty, and intellectual integrity by

- including evidence that goes against your position,
- giving proper credit to others for their ideas,
- giving proper credit to others for their words, and
- giving proper credit to others for their help.

Why You Should Write a Good Paper

Most students would find it useful to impress a teacher or a potential employer with their ability to learn on their own, their ability to get things done, and their academic integrity. Psychology students have even more reasons to write well. As a psychology student, one of your goals is to learn how to describe and explain people's thoughts. As a writer, you are trying to describe and explain your own thoughts. By writing carefully, not only will you discover your own thoughts (as one person said, "How can I know what I think until I see what I say?"), but you will also learn to evaluate your own thinking. You will see where your thinking is logical, where it is biased, where it is based more on faith than on evidence, and where it is slightly disorganized—and you will use those insights to improve your thinking.

Successful writing also requires that you understand and control the mind of the reader. Indeed, King (2000) argues that writing is almost like telepathy—your vision is sent into a reader's mind. At a more practical level, you want to control the behavior of the reader. That is, you want the reader (your professor) to give you a good grade.

How This Book Can Help You

This book is full of tips, checklists, and practical advice to improve your writing. You will get so much insight into how professors look at papers that you should be able to grade—and correct—your paper before it reaches your professor. To be more specific

- Chapter 1 will help you understand what teachers look for in papers so that you will avoid the most common errors that students make, regardless of what kind of paper you are writing.

- Chapter 2 is full of tips that will help you write better term papers. If you are writing a term paper, you will want to study Chapter 2's sample paper and take advantage of its checklist.

- Chapter 3 has practical advice that will help you write better research reports. If you are writing a research report, you will want to study Chapter 3's sample paper and take advantage of its checklist.

- Chapter 4 helps you find the references you need and shows you how to make sense of them after you have found them. Then, it helps you avoid two common student mistakes: (a) not citing sources correctly and (b) not referencing sources correctly.

- Chapter 5 helps you understand what professors mean by critical thinking. After reading Chapter 5 (a) you will be more likely to find flaws that others made in their research and in their arguments, and (b) you will be less likely to make those mistakes in your research and in your arguments.

■ Chapter 6 contains a review of basic grammar. It also contains some tips on how to write well. You will probably consult this section when you are editing the next-to-final draft of your paper. You may also find the definitions of grammatical terms helpful in trying to decipher the American Psychological Association (APA) *Publication Manual.*

■ Chapter 7 will be useful as you prepare to print out the final draft of your paper. Following the formatting tips in that chapter will ensure that your paper makes a good first impression.

■ Appendix A points out the key differences between APA copy style (the format of an unpublished manuscript submitted for review) and APA final-form style (the format of a published article). If your professor asks you to use APA final-form style, Appendix A will be invaluable. By highlighting the formatting rules that published articles follow, it will help you use a published article as a model for your paper. If your professor asks you to use APA copy style, Appendix A will still be valuable. Specifically, because Appendix A highlights the differences between published articles and unpublished manuscripts, it will help you avoid errors caused by modeling the formatting you see in published articles. For example, you will know that although published articles are single-spaced, your unpublished manuscript should be double-spaced.

■ The web site for this book (http://www.writingforpsychology.com) contains many useful resources, including

   ■ screen shots that show you exactly how to set up your word processor to make it work for you,

   ■ templates that you can use so that your paper will be correctly formatted,

   ■ practice quizzes that you can take, and

   ■ sample papers that you can grade.

Formatting Tricks We Use That You Should Not

Like many writing guides, we have divided chapters into sections, numbered each section, and put each section's number in the section's heading. Section numbers consist of two or three digits separated by periods; the first digit specifies the chapter, the others refer to the section within that chapter. When you have a specific question about how to write your paper, these section numbers will help you quickly find the answer to your question. However, *you should not use numbers in the headings of your term papers or research reports.* (To learn how to use headings that conform to APA style, consult 7.2.3.)

We have also used formatting to help you easily spot examples. Brief examples are in a slightly different font from the one we normally use (Courier rather than Times Roman), and are indented more than regular text. When we are contrasting examples of correct and incorrect writing, we put

✔ a check mark next to good examples and

✘ an "x" next to bad examples.

To make it easy to spot the sample papers, we have set them in a "typewriter" font.

Finally, we use two techniques for drawing your attention to particular points: bullets and footnotes. However, when you write papers for psychology classes, *do not use bullets and do not use footnotes.*[1]

---

[1]Different fields have different views about footnotes. For example, if you are writing a term paper for a history class, your teacher will probably require you to use footnotes.

TO THE PROFESSOR

Thanks to all of you who have improved this book. By sharing with us what you did not like about student papers, we have been able to focus this volume on the main errors that student writers make. By providing concrete examples of these errors, we have been able to show—rather than merely tell—students what to do and what to avoid. As a result of your efforts, this book should help students find and correct errors in their papers before they hand them in so that you will get to read better quality papers. To be more specific, the goals of this book are to

1. Be student-friendly so that students can read the book on their own and still

   ■ adhere to the basics of American Psychological Association (APA) style;

   ■ refine critical thinking skills, library search skills, revising skills, editing skills, and proofing skills; and

   ■ avoid plagiarism.

2. Be professor-friendly by eliminating the need for you to provide students with multiple-page handouts about your assignment or spend an entire class period describing the assignment. By assigning this book, you will only need to provide your students with a general description of the project, a due date, a word limit, and any exceptions to our recommendations that you want to make.

Acknowledgments

This book is an adaptation of the fourth edition of Robert O'Shea's *Writing for Psychology: A Guide for Students*. Therefore, we owe a great debt to the individuals whose constructive comments shaped that successful book: Kypros Kypri, Lea McGregor Dawson, Lorelle Burton, Sue Galvin, Jamin Halberstadt, Cindy Hall, Neil McNaughton, Jeff Miller, David O'Hare, Ann Reynolds, Rob Thompson, Diana Rothstein, and 13 anonymous reviewers. This version of *Writing for Psychology: A Guide for Students*, owes a tremendous debt to English professor Darlynn Fink and Psychology professor Jeanne Slattery for their insights into teaching writing as well as for their editing skills, to History professor Robert Frakes (author of an excellent writing guide for History majors) for his insights into teaching writing, to award-winning journalist K. Lee Howard for his editing skills, to Philosophy professor Todd Lavin for his insights into teaching critical thinking, to Psychology professor Ruth Ault for her useful suggestions and mastery of APA style, to Publisher Vicki Knight for her skillful guidance, and to the following reviewers for their constructive comments: Marie Balaban, Eastern Oregon University; Michael Hulsizer, Webster University; Hal Miller, Brigham Young University; Moises Salinas, Central Connecticut State University; Vann B. Scott Jr., Armstrong Atlantic State University; Linda Mezydlo Subich, University of Akron; and Daniel Webster, Georgia Southern University. In addition, we would like to thank Paul Wells, our Production Editor at Wadsworth; Lori Grebe, the Marketing Manager for Psychology; Vernon Boes, the Creative Director; and Shepherd, Inc.

What Every Student Should Know About Writing Psychology Papers

1.1. Understanding Your Assignment

To write a good paper, you must meet your audience's expectations. In the end, the most important audience you must satisfy is yourself. At the moment, however, you may be more concerned about pleasing another audience—your professor. If, as you write your paper, you wonder whether your paper would please your professor, you may be surprised to learn that, as your professor reads your paper, your professor wonders whether your paper would please (a) you, (b) other professors, and (c) potential employers and graduate schools.

To meet the expectations of your professor and the audiences that your professor represents, you must know what those expectations are. Your professor may use written directions to spell out some of those expectations. However, even if your professor gives you written instructions, you will still need to do some work to make sure that you understand your professor's formatting and content requirements.

Most professors will want you to write your paper using American Psychological Association (APA) copy style, the style used for submitting a manuscript to a journal. APA copy style differs from what the final form of the published work will look like. This book will help you write in APA copy style. However, you need to pay attention to your professor's formatting instructions because you cannot assume that your professor wants you to follow APA copy style. For example, instead of requiring APA copy style, your professor may require *APA final-form* style—the reader-friendly format that you would see in a published article (to learn more about final-form style, see Appendix A). Even if your professor wants you to follow APA copy style, you still need to pay attention to your professor's instructions because your professor may impose formatting requirements that are more extensive than APA's. For example, your professor may require a special cover sheet or require that your paper be between 10 and 12 pages long.

Although you should know your professor's formatting requirements, it is more important that you know what type of assignment you have and what goals your professor has for the assignment. You should know whether you are writing a term paper in which you will review the literature (if so, you should consult Chapter 2) or whether you are writing a paper about a study that you either conducted or plan to conduct (if so, you should consult Chapter 3).

Once you know what type of assignment you have, you should try to find out your professor's goals for the paper. For example, if you are writing a term paper, your professor may state that the main goal of the assignment is for you to show that "you can find and summarize the relevant literature," that "you can analyze the strengths and weaknesses of studies," "that you can synthesize information from many sources to come up with an original conclusion," or that "you can write a paper in APA format."

Even if you understand your professor's main goals, you may still have questions about how to meet those goals. Part of the problem is that if your professor told you exactly how to write the paper, the professor would essentially be writing the paper for you. Part of the problem is that there are so many goals to achieve and so many rules to follow that your professor must use shorthand. For example, "appropriately referenced" is shorthand for the rules you will find in Chapter 4; "making a logical argument and informed criticisms" is shorthand for the rules you will find in Chapter 5; "grammatical and well written" is shorthand for following numerous grammatical rules, the most important of which are explained in Chapter 6; and "APA format" is shorthand for following the suggestions in Chapter 7. Another part of the problem is that, because many of your professor's goals for the paper are the same goals that almost all professors have, your professor may think those goals "go without saying." One reason that almost all professors have similar expectations is that almost all professors share certain underlying values—and those shared values affect what professors expect from a paper. As a result of those shared values, if you write a paper that your professor likes, other professors will probably like it too; and, if you a write a paper that your professor does not like, other professors probably will not like it either. Thus, if you do not understand your professor's expectations for a paper, chances are that the problem is not that you do not understand your professor's specific tastes, but that you do not understand academic values. Therefore, we will devote the next section to helping you understand academic values.

1.2 Understanding Academic Values

As you will see in the next sections, to be consistent with academic values, you should

- have the curiosity to find out what others have said, done, and thought;
- have the wisdom to learn from what others have said, done, and thought;
- have the honesty to give others credit when you use what you have learned from them, such as when you quote, paraphrase, or summarize what others have said;
- have the originality to come to a conclusion that is not merely a summary of what others have said, but rather is based—at least in part—on your own thinking;
- have the rationality to support your conclusion with logic and evidence; and
- have the fairness and objectivity (a) to acknowledge evidence that does not fit with your conclusion and (b) to acknowledge alternative explanations for the evidence that you present in support of your conclusion.

1.2.1 Be Informed

Professors value knowledge, learning, and tracing the history of an idea. Most professors want you to demonstrate these values by expressing well-supported and well-informed opinions. Therefore, before turning in your paper, find, study, and understand the relevant background material. (In section 4.1, we will show you some strategies for using the library and the Internet to get resources that both you and your professor will find worthy. In section 4.2, we will discuss strategies to help you digest the information you obtain.)

1.2.2 Make a Claim

Although your professor wants you to understand what others have done, your professor probably wants you to do more than quote or paraphrase what others have written. Rather than merely regurgitating the information you have found, use that information to support your claim. Ideally, your claim will be an original idea based on thinking about what you have read.

If you are writing a term paper, your claim will be a thesis statement. You will support that thesis statement by interpreting, analyzing, and synthesizing the information you have uncovered.

If you are writing a research paper, your claim will be a hypothesis. You will use the works of others to argue (a) that the hypothesis being tested is reasonable and interesting, (b) that the procedure used was a good way to test the hypothesis, and (c) that the results have certain implications.

1.2.3 Defend Your Claim

Not only must you make a claim, but you must also support it. However, you should not support it by asserting how strongly you feel that it is true. Instead, support your claim with evidence and logic. There are two basic approaches to using empirical evidence to support a claim (we will discuss using logic to support a claim in Chapter 5).

First, you can cite empirical evidence that others have obtained. For example, suppose you needed to establish that children of high socioeconomic status tend to be more resistant to conformity than children of low socioeconomic status. Empirical support would be that someone has tested children's resistance to conformity and found that children of high socioeconomic status tend to be more resistant to conformity pressure than children of low socioeconomic status. If you find that someone has done such a study, you can present that evidence. Your citation should include a description—in your own words—of the study, along with the last name(s) of the person(s) who conducted it, and the year in which it was published.

```
Brown (1978) tested 40 children in an Asch-type conformity
setting (Asch, 1956) and found that children from high
socioeconomic backgrounds were more resistant to conformity
than children from low socioeconomic backgrounds.
```

A full reference to each citation should appear in the reference list (see 4.4). The reference list enables the interested reader to find and read the original source. (To learn more about citing material in the body of your paper and referencing it in the References section, see Chapter 4.)

The second way to mount an empirical defense is to present evidence from a study you conducted. We will discuss how to report that evidence in Chapter 3.

Although you should present evidence to support your main point, you should try to be fair. You are not trying to win a debate: You are trying to find the truth. To be fair, discuss studies that seem to contradict your main point and identify weaknesses in studies that appear to support your main point.

1.2.4 Be Honest

Whereas being unfair may hurt your grade, being dishonest may lead to your expulsion from school. The two types of dishonesty that are most likely to lead to expulsion are falsifying data and plagiarism.

Falsifying data is either altering or inventing data. Most of your professors are deeply committed to seeking truth and most see data as a way to truth. Therefore, most of your professors would be outraged at anyone who falsified data. In short, do not falsify data: For most class projects, both the chances and the costs of getting caught are high.

Plagiarism involves passing off someone's words or ideas as your own. In most cases, if you were to plagiarize, the person plagiarized would be either a person you have come into contact with at your school or the author of a work you have read.

Working with other students is sometimes allowed. Even on individual assignments, your professor may encourage you to work with other students to share readings and to review each other's work. On group projects, your professor may require you to work with other students. However, unless your professor clearly says otherwise, when you turn in a paper with your name on it, that paper is supposed to be your work. To reiterate, your instructor will expect any assignment that you turn in to be independent of, and different from, every other student's paper. If the words or ideas of even a small section of your assignment are identical to another student's work, you—or that other student—may be accused of plagiarism.

Plagiarism is not limited to lifting passages or ideas from a classmate's paper. Plagiarism can sometimes result just from not giving people credit for something they said to you. For example, if a professor, study partner, classmate, or roommate gave you an idea that you used in your paper, you should give that person credit (to see how, see 4.3.3). If you do not give the person credit, you are guilty of plagiarism.

Often, when people think of plagiarism, they think of the easiest type of plagiarism to detect: plagiarism of words from a published work. For example, suppose you had the following text (taken from the 1974 APA Manual, p. 91).

> Psychologists have developed various approaches to
> therapeutic change, most involving one-to-one relationships
> between practitioner and client. However, for many people
> these therapies are unavailable, undesirable, or too
> expensive. So these people have often turned to popularized
> self-help techniques. (Mikulas, 1974, p. 91)

If you were to use the preceding paragraph in your paper, you would have to make it clear that you were quoting it.[1] Otherwise, you would be guilty of plagiarism. As a general rule, if you take three or more consecutive words from another author, you should place those words in quotation marks, cite the author, and list the page(s) of the quoted words. Thus, if you turned in the following passage, you would be guilty of plagiarism.

> ✗ Mikulas (1974) has stated that various approaches to
> therapeutic change have been developed.

You would be guilty of plagiarism because you would be using Mikulas's words without admitting that you were doing it. The five-word phrase "various approaches to therapeutic change" should have been surrounded by quotation marks, and the page number from which those five words were taken should have been cited.

Thus far, we have presented cases of stealing words. To see a case of stealing ideas without stealing words, imagine we wrote

> ✗ Most people find these therapies too expensive, undesirable
> or unavailable and so have turned to self-help techniques.

Although we paraphrased Mikulas's words, we would still be guilty of plagiarizing Mikulas's ideas. To avoid plagiarizing Mikulas's ideas, we should have made it clear that he—rather than we—originated them. If we did not want to quote Mikulas, an acceptable version of the whole text would be

> ✔ Mikulas (1974) noted that many people dislike current
> psychotherapies in which a single client is seen by a

---

[1]If it were a quote shorter than 40 words, you would cite the author, year, and page number, and you would surround the quotation with quotation marks. However, because the quotation is longer than 40 words, you should use the block quote format that APA prescribes for long quotes (see 4.7.2).

> single counselor. He gives their unavailability, expense,
> and lack of appeal as reasons. Mikulas suggests that many
> prospective clients have instead tried self-help
> techniques.

Note that here, to avoid plagiarism of words, we have used our own words as much as possible without changing the original meaning of Mikulas's passage. To avoid plagiarism of ideas, we have provided a citation for every sentence (Mikulas's name is in the first and third sentence, and "he" is used in the second).

1.2.5 Use Your Own Words

To make sure you do not plagiarize, you might be tempted to put most of your assignment in quotation marks. Resist that temptation. Your professor is interested in your thoughts about a topic, not in your ability to string others' words together with linking sentences. Indeed, your professor will probably not let you get away with having more than 50 words of quotation for every 1,000 words of your own.

One reason professors dislike quotation marks is that when you quote, the professor does not know whether you understand what you have quoted. Therefore, always try to paraphrase the author. There are only two conditions under which you should revert to using quotation marks: (a) You fear that your paraphrase is so close to the original passage (e.g., you have merely replaced a couple of words with synonyms) that you could be guilty of plagiarism; or (b) you fear that your paraphrase, because you disagree with the author's position, unfairly represents the position expressed in the original passage.

1.3 Understanding APA Style

As you have seen, your professor expects you to write a paper that

- draws on the work of others but proposes an original idea,
- cites the work of others but describes their work in your own words, and
- uses logic and evidence to build a case for an idea but addresses contradictory evidence.

You may think that meeting those demands would be enough to get a good grade. However, your professor will also require that your paper meet some style and formatting guidelines. A few of these guidelines may be specific to a certain assignment (e.g., a particular word limit). Most, however, will be the same no matter what psychology class you are taking. These style and formatting requirements are set out in the *Publication Manual of the American Psychological Association* (2001). In the next section, we will provide an overview of APA's requirements. (APA style requirements will be discussed in more depth in Chapter 6; APA formatting requirements will be discussed in Chapter 7.)

1.3.1 Ideals

APA style requires that grammar, spelling, and punctuation be perfect. Consequently, your professor will probably penalize you for each grammatical error, each spelling error, and each punctuation error. However, avoiding these errors in mechanics does not mean that you have met APA's standards for good writing. According to APA, good writing[2]

> must be precise in its words, free of ambiguity, orderly in
> its presentation of ideas, economical in expression, smooth
> in its flow, and considerate of its readers. A successful
> writer invites readers to read, encourages them to
> continue, and makes their task agreeable by leading them
> from thought to thought in a manner that evolves from clear
> thinking and logical development. (APA, 1974, p. 25)

If you think that meeting APA's requirements is easier said than done, you are right. Although Chapter 6 provides useful writing tips, writing well is a skill that must be attained like any other—through practice.

Apart from practice, the next best way to improve your writing is to read good writing. The more you read articles in psychological journals, the more you will be exposed to the works of authors who have met APA's writing standards. We do not mean that all published works are of high quality. Unfortunately, some are poorly written, hard to follow, and boring. Others are a pleasure to read: Imitate and study those. If you study how good writers make content readable, you should become a good writer.

1.3.2 Appropriately Personal Prose

One thing you will learn by studying good writers is that you can write in a professional, formal style without writing in a completely impersonal style. For example, although APA style essentially bans the use of the word "you," it does allow you to use the personal pronoun "I." The old rule that any "I" in a paper should be automatically deleted is no longer true. However, we do not mean that skilled scholars write in an extremely personal way. The focus of a paper should be on the ideas and findings of the paper, not on the author. Consequently, most skilled writers almost never use the phrases "I feel," "I think," or "I believe." Many of them never use the word "I." All of them will check sentences where they used the word "I" to see if the sentence would be better without the "I." They will take the "I" out of the sentence if they believe that the "I" is focusing the reader's attention on the writer when the reader's attention belongs elsewhere.

---

[2]The passage quoted from the *Manual* is longer than 40 words and therefore is not surrounded by quotation marks. Readers know the passage is quoted because it is indented and "blocked." In addition, note that the citation for a quotation contains not just the source and the year, but also the page number.

When writers remove an "I" from a sentence, they must find another subject to replace the "I." One strategy is to replace "I" with whatever was the target of the action in the original sentence. For example, rather than write, "I analyzed the data using a *t* test," an author could write, "The data were analyzed using a *t* test." Similarly, rather than writing, "I read the list to the participants," an author could write, "The list was read to the participants." Although skilled writers do use this strategy, it comes at a cost: They are breaking a rule of powerful writing by not letting the subject of the sentence perform the action that the sentence is supposed to describe. In other words, rather than using the stronger, *active voice*, in which the subject actively does something (e.g., "I hypothesized . . ."), writers are using the weaker, *passive voice*, in which the subject passively has something done to it (e.g., "It was hypothesized . . ."). In unskilled hands, the passive voice can sound clumsy and wordy (e.g., "It was hypothesized by me . . ."). Even in skilled hands, the passive voice should be used sparingly.

Fortunately, writers can replace "I" without using the passive voice. Rather than write, "The list was read to the participants," they may write, "The participants listened to the list." Rather than write, "It was hypothesized," they may write, "The hypothesis was . . ."

However, as we mentioned earlier, writers do not always have to replace the word "I." Skilled writers can use the words "I" or "we" when that is what they mean. In other words, skilled writers do not twist reality or grammar to avoid personal pronouns.

In the real world, people perform actions. For example, researchers make hypotheses, conduct studies, and come to conclusions. Skilled writers respect both (a) the fact that researchers perform actions and (b) the laws of grammar. Therefore, skilled writers may use verbs to describe researchers' actions and make the researcher performing the action the subject of the sentence. Such skilled writers may occasionally add an adverb (such as "occasionally," "slowly," "interestingly," and "thoroughly") to an action verb to describe how the researcher performed the action (e.g., "The researcher *thoroughly* debriefed the participants.").

Some less skilled writers, on the other hand, attempt to disown their own thoughts and end up violating the laws of grammar. For example, some authors write the adverb "hopefully" when they mean, "I hope." They write, "Hopefully, future research will use a more representative sample," when they should write, "I hope future research will use a more representative sample."[3] The problem is that they are using an adverb ("hopefully"), which is supposed to modify a verb, to do the work of a subject ("I") and a verb ("hope"). Similarly, less skilled writers may use the adverb "interestingly," when they mean, "I find it interesting that."

In the past, writers were encouraged to disown their own thoughts—even if that meant violating the laws of nature. For example, authors routinely pawned off their thoughts to nonliving entities, such as experiments (e.g., "this experiment will test the hypothesis") and papers (e.g., "this paper will argue" or "this paper will examine"). Currently, however, APA's position is that writers should not *anthropomorphize:* give human qualities to nonhuman entities.

---

[3]Alternatively, as an anonymous reviewer pointed out, they could write, "Future research should use a more representative sample."

To avoid both anthropomorphism and using "I," some authors attribute their actions to a role. For example, they might write, "It will be argued by the present author that" rather than "I will argue that." The price they pay for avoiding "I" is that they write a wordier and clumsier sentence. Other authors get into more serious trouble by attributing their actions to the researcher. For example, an author, instead of writing "I told the participant," will write, "The experimenter told the participant," leaving the reader to guess whether the author paid someone else to be the experimenter or whether the author is also the experimenter. Another, even more awkward technique for avoiding "I," is to replace "I" with "we." For example, the writer of a single-author paper, instead of writing "I hypothesized," writes, "We hypothesized," leading the reader to suspect that the author is either a plagiarist or a member of a royal family.

In short, you should not use "I" frivolously. Furthermore, as you will see later, you should never use "I" in a paper's Abstract (a summary of the paper, see 2.4). However, as a general rule, do not avoid using "I" if avoiding "I" would put you in conflict with the APA ideal of saying what you mean as clearly and simply as possible.

1.3.3 Simple Language

The APA ideal of saying what you mean as clearly and simply as possible applies not only to using simple, active sentences, but also to using simple vocabulary. To use vocabulary that complies with the APA ideal, you should obey two rules.

First, do not use fancy words or fancy phrases just to impress your professor. If you do, you will be disappointed. Your professor, rather than being impressed with your sentence, will probably see the sentence as pretentious, wordy, or unclear.

Second, do not banish technical terms from your paper. Your professor will expect you to show that you understand the field's key terms (a) well enough to use those terms to communicate clearly and efficiently and (b) well enough to make distinctions between related concepts. Thus, if you wrote a paper on behavior modification and never used the term "reinforcement," your professor would be disappointed. In such an assignment, your professor would probably expect you to use key terms in a way that showed that you understood key distinctions between related concepts, such as the distinction between negative reinforcement and punishment. In such an assignment, your professor would probably also hope that you would use key terms, such as "schedules of reinforcement," in a way that showed that your understanding of the effects of reinforcement was more sophisticated than "giving rewards increases behavior." In short, use technical terms when those terms help you express your ideas concisely and precisely.

1.3.4 Respectful Language

To write in APA style, you must not only use clear language, but you must also use respectful, inclusive language. Do not use language that might suggest that another group is less competent, less important, less moral, or less likely to occupy a certain role (e.g., professor) than your own. If you must differentiate among individuals on bases such as gender, race, disability, or age, then be accurate, specific, cautious, and respectful. To see what you should do, study the following examples of disrespectful language (italicized) and solutions:

✗ *Subjects* were 10 men and 10 *girls*.

✔ *Participants* ["subjects" is considered disrespectful because it does not acknowledge that individuals voluntarily participated in the study] were 10 men and 10 women [if you use "men" to describe male participants, then use the equivalent, parallel term "women" when describing female participants].

✗ *He* [the participant] was required to use *his* right index finger to press the response button.

✔ Participants were required to use their [using the plural is often a good way to avoid the problem of using the generic "he," a term that is sexist because it excludes women] right index fingers to press the response button.

✔ Participants were required to use the [when using a pronoun would be sexist or awkward, see if you can eliminate the pronoun] right index finger to press the response button.

✗ These results have important implications for the development of *man*.

✗ These results have important implications for human development.

Although you should use gender-inclusive language, you still have a duty to write clearly and smoothly. Thus, you would be penalized for using such clumsy—but non-sexist phrases as (s)he and he/she. Furthermore, inclusiveness should not come at the expense of accuracy. Thus, if all the participants were boys, you could write

✔ *Participants* were 10 boys. . . . *He* was required to use his right index finger to press the response button. . . . These results have important implications for male development.

Now, study an example of disrespectful language involving race (italicized) and a solution:

✗ Participants were 100 Whites and 100 *Non-Whites*.

✔ Participants were 100 Whites, 60 African Americans, and 40 Asian Americans. [Relative to the term "Non-white," the terms African Americans and Asian Americans are (a) more specific and (b) describe individuals in terms of belonging to—rather than being excluded from—a group.]

Next, carefully examine a case of disrespectful language involving individuals with disabilities (italicized) and a solution:

✗ Participants were 100 normals and 100 *schizophrenics*. [Labeling the group as schizophrenics both depersonalizes and dehumanizes them. They are individuals who have a condition, but they are not the condition. Avoid labels that focus on an individual's limitations or problems.]

✔ Participants were 100 people with no previously diagnosed psychiatric illness and 100 people diagnosed with schizophrenia.

Finally, consider an example of disrespectful language involving age (italicized) and a solution:

✗ Participants were 100 adults and 100 *elderly*. [The term "elderly" is out of favor: "Older adults" is now the preferred term.]

✔ Participants were divided into two groups based on age: a middle-aged group (ages 45-60) and an older group (ages 70-85).

1.4. Writing and Revising

1.4.1 Plan to Finish Early

Now that you understand what your professor wants, you need to produce it. Perhaps the greatest obstacle to meeting your professor's expectations is procrastination. Procrastination may prevent you from turning in the paper on time—and that can mean flunking the assignment. Most professors strictly enforce due dates. Few, if any, instructors will accept "pressure of other commitments" as an excuse for an extension. Most students have other commitments. Most students would do a better job if they were given more time. Therefore, it is unethical for professors to give you more time than other students without penalizing you (Keith-Spiegel, Wittig, Perkins, Balogh, & Whitely, 1993). If you fear you are going to run late, a visit to your professor will help you decide whether you are better off handing in a poorer paper on time or a better paper late.

You might believe that "I had some unexpected problems" is an acceptable excuse. It is not. Your professor expects you to know that Murphy's Laws apply to any major project:

■ Anything that goes wrong will have the worst possible outcome.

■ Anything that can possibly go wrong will.

■ It will go wrong at the worst possible time.

Therefore, do not expect to be exempt from the deadline just because you had some unusual problem at the last minute. Your professor expects you to have everything done at least 48 hours before the due date because, when applied to assignments, Murphy's Laws mean that 48 hours before the due date

■ your vital piece of equipment (computer, printer, disk, car, bicycle) will break down irreparably.

- any people vital to the assignment (typist, study companion, person commenting on your drafts, reference librarian, computer repair person, professor, head of department, head of the United Nations) will disappear.

- anything about you vital to the assignment will cease functioning (your hand will become paralyzed, your memory will go blank, your motivation will evaporate).

- all material vital to the assignment (your notes, photocopies, rough drafts, computer disks, the piece of paper with the assignment details on it, the library itself) will disappear.

Even if you meet the deadline, procrastination can hurt you. Waiting until the last minute can lead to sloppiness. Consider yourself lucky if your sloppiness leads to errors that hurt only your grade: spelling errors, grammatical errors, punctuation errors, and formatting errors. Sloppiness can lead to plagiarism—which can lead to expulsion.

Often, students do not realize how much they have been hurt by procrastination. They do not know about the sources they could have obtained through interlibrary loan. They are too tired and too rushed to evaluate their paper before they give it to the professor. They do not study the professor's comments on their paper when they get it back, and they do not know how much better they would have done had they spent more time revising, editing, and proofing.

To avoid the many problems that procrastination can cause, start work on any major paper at least three weeks before the due date.[4] Draw up a schedule (e.g., days 1 to 3 for reading, days 4 to 6 for producing a first draft, days 7 to 10 for showing the assignment to others, days 11 to 14 for producing the final draft, days 15 to18 for emergencies). Then, stick to your schedule.

1.4.2 Think, Search, Read, and Get Organized

Sticking to your schedule will not be easy. Even before you start to write, you may start to procrastinate. The problem is that getting started means doing five tasks that you may be uncomfortable doing:

1. choosing a topic;
2. developing a question or thesis statement that will guide you in searching, reading, summarizing, and evaluating articles;
3. finding relevant articles (for tips on using the library and computers to find relevant literature, see 4.1);
4. reading and critiquing those articles (see 4.2); and
5. taking, retaining, and organizing your notes on those articles.

Once you have accomplished these five tasks, you are almost ready to write the first draft. However, before writing the first draft, you should organize your thoughts.

---

[4]Five weeks would be better, especially if, at your school, getting materials through interlibrary loan takes three weeks.

One way to organize your thoughts is to use an outline. You may find it useful to outline your paper on the computer. Fortunately, almost all word-processing programs have tools that can help you outline your paper.

Another way to organize your thoughts is to make a diagram of your ideas.[5] (Your English teacher might call such diagramming "clustering," "concept-mapping," or "mapping.") You can use concept-mapping software such as *Inspiration*[6] to help you visualize how your ideas fit together.

Yet another way to organize your thoughts is to make a table. For example, you could make a two-column table in which the left column lists evidence for a certain idea and the right column lists evidence against a certain idea.

Finally, you could just jot down a list of points you want to include in your rough draft. Listing your key points is an easy way to help your first draft focus on the points you want to make.

1.4.3 Write Your First Draft

After you have organized your thoughts, start writing. Resist the biggest stumbling block in sticking to your schedule: talking yourself out of writing your first draft. Realize that almost any reason you give yourself for not writing is an excuse. You say you are waiting for inspiration? Do you really think it will knock on your door tomorrow? Almost all good writers let a schedule—not a muse—dictate when they write. You say you cannot possibly write because your own thinking on the topic is unclear? Do you really think a lightbulb is going to go on tomorrow to give you insight? It is much more likely that you will be lost until you start writing. By writing, you will start to realize what you are thinking. As one person said, "How can I know what I think until I see what I've written." As Howard and Barton (1986) put it, writing is "thinking on paper" (p. 1).

In your first draft, just get your ideas on paper. Do not worry about wording. As the saying goes, "Don't get it right, get it written." Your rough draft is just a starting point for your paper. It will help you understand your own thinking on the topic, and it will help you remember the points you wanted to make (Howard & Barton, 1986).

If you need some help getting started on your rough draft, engage in *free-writing*. To free-write, just write continuously (no pausing or editing allowed) for three minutes. Try to get down as many words as you can in those three minutes.

You may wish to free-write using the computer for any of the following reasons:

■ You can type faster and longer than you can write things out by hand.

■ You have voice recognition software on the computer that allows you to talk to the computer rather than type.

■ You like having the computer correct many of your spelling and grammatical mistakes.

---

[5]For more information on how to diagram ideas, see our web site (http://www.writingforpsychology.com).

[6]Information on how to order *Inspiration*, as well as additional information on concept-mapping, is available from our web site (http://www.writingforpsychology.com).

- You like being able to make corrections and minor changes on screen.

- You like how the computer makes it easy to move sentences and paragraphs.

- You find you can edit your free-writing better when the computer speaks it aloud to you.

- You find that you can edit your free-writing more easily when looking at a nicely printed, double-spaced copy of your writing rather than when looking at your messy handwriting.

1.4.4 Revise Your First Draft: Reorganize, Rethink, Reread, and Rewrite

As we have stated, your first draft is a rough draft. It is only the first of many steps in the writing process. In a way, writing is like going on a geological dig to produce a mineral exhibit for a museum.

When you start writing, you are digging around in your mind, hoping to find something useful. Much of what you dig out is stuff that you cannot use. Some of it is, like dirt, clearly worthless. Some of it seems valuable, but on further examination, is really fool's gold. Some of it is valuable, but it is not suitable for the particular collection you have been asked to create. As you dig, you will find that some spots are dead ends and should be abandoned; other spots, although promising, need to be dug into more deeply before they yield valuable material.

Once you find the right material, you still have work to do. You must lay out the individual pieces, categorize them, and figure out how to organize them into a suitable collection. As you try different configurations, you may realize (a) that you must cut some pieces from the collection because they are redundant, distracting, or do not fit, and (b) that you must acquire additional pieces to fill in the gaps in your collection.

Once you have a collection of pieces that you are excited about, you still need to do some work before viewers will share your excitement. You will have to clean up, cut, and polish each individual piece. You will have to add labels and text to help viewers appreciate what each piece is and how the pieces fit together. Finally, you will have to display the collection in a professional format so that viewers can fully appreciate the collection's beauty.

If the whole writing project is like the mineral collection project we just described, the rough draft corresponds to the early phase of the project: the "digging around" phase. That is, by using writing to talk to yourself, you have dug up some of your thoughts. When reading over the draft, you can extend this conversation with yourself (Howard & Barton, 1986)—and thus dig deeper—by saying things such as, "Yes, and it is also true that . . ." and "What I really mean to say here is . . ."

Once you have unearthed your thoughts, the next step is to organize those thoughts. To organize your thoughts, ask two questions of each paragraph. First, "What do I want this paragraph to do?" Second, "If I want the paragraph to accomplish that goal, is the paragraph in the right place?" As a result of asking these two questions, you may eliminate some paragraphs and move others.

Once you have moved and deleted material, you should outline your revised paper again. Even a glance at the outline may help you see that

■ you are not pleased with the order in which the ideas are presented;

■ ideas are included that do not relate to your main point;

■ certain ideas that you think are important have been either not included or not emphasized;

■ some assertions are made but are not supported by either logic or evidence;

■ your discussion of one idea or topic is much more thorough than your discussion of an equivalent topic; and

■ you have failed to make connections between related ideas.

As you struggle to rectify the problems in your thinking that were apparent by looking at the outline, you will refine your thinking. Specifically, you will

■ put your ideas in a more logical order;

■ ignore ideas and evidence that could distract you from your main point;

■ distinguish between important ideas and less important ideas;

■ develop support for unsupported assertions; and

■ see connections among concepts that you had not previously recognized.

Like re-outlining, rereading will help you refine your thinking—if you ask questions as you read (Howard & Barton, 1986). At the very least, ask the following two questions: "Does this make sense?" and "Do I have adequate support for this idea?"

Like re-outlining and rereading, rewriting also helps you refine your thinking. With each rewrite, you will find that you have more arguments, more support for those arguments, and that your paper is becoming more organized, more insightful, and more original. Thus, as you rewrite, you will probably find that (a) passages you quoted in your rough draft now make enough sense to you that you can put them into your own words; and that (b) the outline of your revised draft is more organized and more detailed.

In short, as a result of "talking to yourself," outlining what you have said, and questioning yourself, you should have a fair, focused, and properly sequenced set of arguments in support of your main point. At this point, it is time to stop writing to yourself and start writing for the people who will read your paper.

1.4.5 Help the Reader Navigate Through Your Paper

Once you are satisfied that your own thinking on the topic is clear, you can devote your next few drafts to making your thinking clear to your audience. Although the audience of your paper may number in the thousands, we will call your audience "the reader" for two reasons. First, it is more useful to picture a particular individual, such as a friend or your professor, reading your work and anticipating how that person will react than it is to picture an anonymous audience reading your work. Second, your audience may be a single reader—your professor.

A first step to making your thinking clear to the reader is to make the organization of your paper clear to the reader. You make your paper's organization clear to the reader by (a) adding short subheadings (often taken from the major headings of your outline) so that the reader does not read more than two pages without encountering a subheading, (b) adding topic sentences (often taken from your outline) to each paragraph, and (c) adding transitions between paragraphs (some of these transitions may be entire paragraphs that preview what the next few paragraphs are going to do). After you have tried to make the organization of your paper clear to the reader, you are ready for the real test: See if a friend can re-create your outline from reading your paper.

Once you are sure that a reader could follow the general outline of your paper, it is time to help the reader understand the individual paragraphs. Thus, in the next few drafts, you may work on refining your topic sentences. If the topic sentence is the paragraph's first sentence, ask, "Does the topic sentence provide a preview of the paragraph?" If the topic sentence is the paragraph's last sentence, ask, "Does the topic sentence provide a summary of the paragraph?"

Once you have good topic sentences, you have done much of the work of organizing your paragraphs. However, there are still four things you should do to improve the organization within each paragraph. First, you should split long paragraphs into two: No paragraph should be longer than a page. Second, if a sentence is not tied to the topic sentence, you should remove it from that paragraph. Third, if a sentence reiterates what another sentence in the same paragraph said, delete one of those sentences. Fourth, if it is not clear how two adjoining sentences relate to each other, you should consider using transition words (such as "consequently," "therefore," "however," and "although") to connect the sentences inside a paragraph with each other.

Once you have taken steps to prevent readers from getting lost between paragraphs and from getting lost between sentences, you should take at least three steps to prevent readers from getting lost within your sentences. First, see if you can eliminate, reword, or move tangential remarks. Usually, you can eliminate those tangential remarks that are set off from the rest of the sentence by parentheses, a pair of commas, or a dash. Second, shorten sentences that are longer than 40 words. Usually, you can split these longer sentences into two shorter sentences. Third, go back and look at pronouns such as "it," "they," "those," "these," and "this" that you are using to refer back to another word or idea. If your pronouns are not unambiguously pointing back to the right word or phrase, see 6.3.5.

Although you want to make each paragraph and sentence clear to the reader, there are at least two reasons you may fail to revise an unclear section. First, you know what you are trying to say, so you may not recognize when a section is confusing. Second, you may be too attached to what you have written to delete irrelevant sentences, phrases, and words.

You can overcome both of these self-imposed obstacles to revising an unclear section by using the following four tactics. First, put the draft aside for a few days. By the time you reread it, you may forget what you meant to say and be more able to focus on what you actually wrote. In addition, you may be less infatuated with passages that you should cut. Second, pretend that someone else has written the draft and that your task is to improve it. Third, read your paper aloud—or have the computer read it aloud to you. Fourth, have a friend read your paper and make comments. If you show your friend how to use the computer's voice annotation[7] feature, you can click on sections in the paper where your friend made a comment to hear what your friend had to say ("I'm confused about this point because . . .").

1.4.6 Address Readers' Objections

Some of your friend's comments may deal with objections to your argument. Even if your friend does not introduce objections, realize that other readers might. You want to address possible objections so that your reader does not say "But the writer did not consider . . ."

In addressing potential objections, be firm but fair. If you can successfully fend off an objection, explain why the objection is not serious. If the objection is serious, admit it. Modify your argument or qualify your conclusions to take the objection into account.

1.4.7 Polish Your Writing

Now that you have polished your ideas, you can start polishing your writing. One way to polish your writing is to vary the words you use. Here, a thesaurus can help. Use a thesaurus to find a synonym, then consult a dictionary to make sure that your synonym means what you want it to mean.[8] (Note that, because most word-processing software contains both a thesaurus and a dictionary, finding a synonym and then finding its definition often involves little more than a few clicks of a mouse.)

In addition to varying the words you use, vary your sentences. For example, if almost all of your sentences are short (fewer than 10 words), combine some of your sentences so that your professor does not label your writing style as "choppy."

Although we will discuss more tips on improving your writing in section 6.4, we will give you two tips now. First, you can usually improve your style by deleting words: When it comes to writing, less is more. To have a more compact and powerful style, go through your paper and see what words you can eliminate. Second, a powerful tool for helping you delete words is your computer's grammar checker. Your grammar checker can help you purge unnecessary words by pointing out phrases or sentences that are wordy. For example, your grammar checker might highlight

- a clumsy phrase ("at this point in time") that you could replace with a single word ("now"),
- a wordy, passive sentence ("It was written by me.") that you could replace with a shorter active sentence ("I wrote it."), and
- an unusually long sentence that you could split into two.

---

[7]For instruction on how to use this feature, go to our web site (http://www.writingforpsychology.com).

[8]If the synonym does not really reflect what the original word meant, you can have problems. One of the authors received a paper in which a student wrote, "we must defecate prejudice." Apparently, the student, tiring of using the word "eliminate," used the thesaurus to find an alternative.

1.4.8 Proof Language, Grammar, Spelling, Usage, and Punctuation

As we have pointed out, your grammar checker can be a powerful editing tool. How-ever, the strength of grammar checkers and related tools is that they alert you to some—but not all—of the following writing errors: improper language, improper grammar, improper usage, and improper punctuation.

Your grammar checker can be a valuable tool for catching inappropriate language that might creep into your paper. Your grammar checker can often alert you when inappropriately informal language slips into what is supposed to be a formal paper. For example, your grammar checker can alert you when you have used contractions, clichés, and slang terms. It can also help you when biased language sneaks into your writing. For instance, grammar checkers can often alert you when you have used a word that is either noninclusive ("chairman") or offensive. However, you cannot rely on a grammar checker to catch all your mistakes for at least two reasons. First, terms that were not offensive when the grammar-checking program was first released may now be considered offensive. Second, what is offensive may depend on context rather than on a specific word or phrase.

In addition to checking for inappropriate language, grammar checkers can, of course, help check your paper's grammar. However, do not delegate the entire job of grammar checking to software. If you do, you will run into two problems. First, the grammar checker will fail to tell you that some ungrammatical passages are ungram-matical. Second, the grammar checker will tell you that some grammatical passages are ungrammatical. Therefore, to check the grammar of your work, you need to have a clear understanding of grammar (see Chapter 6).

Although you may not be able to rid your paper of all grammatical errors, you should at least focus on the ones that are most likely to irritate your professor. Those errors probably include

- subject-verb disagreement (the subject of a sentence is plural, but the verb used is appropriate only for singular noun ["They is," "Data is"]—or vice versa ["It are," "Datum are"]);

- pronoun-noun disagreement (the noun is plural but the pronoun referring to it is singular ["The male experimenter received their training"]—or vice versa ["The male experimenters received his training"]);

- "paragraphs" that are only one sentence long;

- "sentences" that are really sentence fragments (they are incomplete sentences because they do not contain a complete thought ["To deal effectively."]); and

- any other grammatical error that your professor mentions.

Although you may be allowed a few minor grammatical errors, your paper should be completely free of spelling errors. As was the case with grammatical errors, software can help you, but it will not do all the work for you. Although your spell-checking soft-ware will correctly catch some errors, it will make mistakes. Spell-checking software will report many correctly spelled words as errors (e.g., names and psychological terms) and will not report cases in which you typed "there" for "their," "right" for "write," "filed" for "field," "casual" for "causal," or any other case in which you have "the wrong word spelled right" (Barkas, 1985, p. 75).

Using the wrong word is not always the result of a finger slipping on the keyboard. Sometimes, you may think you know what a word means, but you do not. By taking advantage of both our table of commonly misused words (see our "problem pairs" table in Chapter 6) and your computer's dictionary, you can avoid common but costly mistakes such as using "imply" when you mean "infer." If you learn that you have consistently misused a word, term, or phrase, use your word processor's "find and replace" feature to replace all instances of that wrong word with the correct word.

You have checked your paper for inappropriate language, grammar, spelling, and usage. Now, read your paper aloud to (a) recheck it for inappropriate language, grammar, spelling, and usage, and to (b) check punctuation. When you read aloud, check to make sure that there is appropriate punctuation at all the places you pause. If you are like most students, you will tend to have the most problems with the comma: omitting the comma, not knowing whether to use a comma or a semicolon, and not knowing whether to place the comma inside or outside of a quotation mark. If you need to learn or to review the basics of punctuation, see 6.2.

1.4.9 Final Formatting

Once you have proofed your paper for writing errors, you should proof it for formatting errors. For example, make sure that your entire paper is double-spaced. Fortunately, if you use word-processing software, you do not have to worry about memorizing many formatting rules because your word-processing software's normal formatting is usually the correct formatting. For example, APA has set the following formatting rules to be the same as most word-processing software's normal settings: how many spaces to indent a paragraph (five), how many spaces to leave after most punctuation marks (one), and what margins to leave (one inch). Whereas people using a typewriter might have to make sure they pressed the space bar five times to indent each paragraph and worry about whether their margins were correct, you have no such worries. Instead, for much of the paper, your main formatting worry may just be making sure that you turned on the "double- spacing" option.

You have even fewer worries if you use APA's *Style Helper* software (for ordering information (see http://www.writingforpsychology.com). *Style Helper* works with your word-processing software to make sure that headings, margins, and typefaces are consistent with APA style. If you do not have *Style Helper*, you can still set up your word-processing software to format your headings, margins, and typeface (to see how, consult http://www.writingforpsychology.com). Regardless of how you compose your paper, you should check your paper against our format checklist (see 7.4).

1.4.10 Five Final Checks

You are almost finished. Still, potential disasters lurk, so take five steps to avoid them. First, make sure that you have not plagiarized by checking your paper against your original sources and against the checklist at the end of this chapter (1.6). Second, make sure your citations follow APA format (see 4.3) and that they match your reference list. Third, make sure that your References section is in APA format (see 4.9). Fourth, make sure that your title page is in APA format (see 7.4.6). Fifth, make sure that your paper conforms to any additional requirements (e.g., word and page limits) that your professor has imposed.

Note that computer software can help you with the last four steps. The APA *Style Helper* program, for example, can work with your word-processing software to ensure that your citations follow APA format, to ensure that your citations match your reference list, to ensure that your individual references are in the proper format, to ensure that your reference list is in alphabetical order, and to ensure that your title page conforms to APA format. Even without *Style Helper*, your word-processing program can count the number of words in your paper to make sure you have not exceeded the word limit.

1.5 Submitting the Finished Product

Your paper is properly formatted. It looks good on your computer screen. To make sure it looks good when it reaches your professor's hands, you should (a) put plain, clean, white, sturdy (20-pound), bond paper into a printer that is producing dark, clear, clean print; and then (b) staple it together using one or two staples in the top left-hand corner.

1.6 Avoiding Common Problems: A Checklist

___ I started my paper early enough that I could find important sources, carefully read those sources, write a rough draft, and then revise, edit, proof, and polish subsequent drafts.

___ I did not plagiarize.

___ When I borrowed a person's words, it was clear that I was quoting that person.

___ I double-checked my sources to make sure that I had not either inadvertently quoted someone or paraphrased someone too closely.

___ When I borrowed someone's ideas without quoting them, it was clear that I was using their ideas.

___ I made an honest, original, fair, and evidence-based argument.

___ I supported my argument with logic (see Chapter 5) and with evidence from high quality sources (see 4.1).

___ I reported evidence that ran counter to my argument.

___ I quoted fewer than 50 words for every 1,000 of my own.

___ If I was unsure about my criticisms of the literature or the quality of the reasons for my position, I consulted Chapter 5.

___ My argument was easy to follow because my paper was well organized.

    ___ I wrote several drafts of my paper.

    ___ I outlined each draft and used that outline to improve the organization of subsequent drafts.

    ___ I revised any paragraphs longer than a page.

    ___ I made sure that every paragraph had a topic sentence that summarized my goal for that paragraph.

___ I proofed my paper so that it did not contain offensive language (see 1.3.4) or irritating grammatical errors (see Chapter 6).

    ___ I checked my paper against all examples, instructions, and warnings my professor gave the class.

    ___ I read my paper aloud.

    ___ I used computerized proofing tools, such as a spell checker and a grammar checker.

    ___ If I was unsure about the grammar or writing style of my paper, I consulted Chapter 6.

___ I checked to make sure that my sources were correctly cited in the Body of my paper.

    ___ Every reference in my References section is cited in the Body of my paper.

    ___ When I cited a source, I mentioned only the authors' last names and the year the source was published. I did not mention the authors' first names, university affiliations, degrees, or professional titles.

    ___ When I cited, I did not mention the title of the source—unless the source had no accredited author.

    ___ When I was unsure about how to cite a source in text, I consulted Chapter 4 or the *Publication Manual*.

___ I properly formatted quotes (see 4.7).

___ I made sure my reference section was properly formatted (see 4.9 and 4.10.3).

    ___ Except for any "personal communication" citations (see 4.3.3) and any citations to classical works (e.g., the Bible), every citation in text is cited in the reference page.

    ___ I started the first line of each reference flush against the left margin.

    ___ I indented subsequent lines of each reference five spaces.

___ If I was unsure about how to format a reference or how to format the reference section, I consulted Chapter 4.

___ I polished my paper so that the final copy looked professional and conformed to APA style.

    ___ I correctly formatted my title page (see model in 2.11, checklist in 7.4.6).

    ___ I double-spaced everything.

___ I used white, nonerasable, 8.5 × 11 in. (22 × 28 cm), 20-pound bond paper.

___ I used clear, dark, and black type.

___ I used an APA approved typeface such as 12-point Times Roman or 12-point Courier.

___ If I had any doubts about the format of my paper, I consulted Chapter 7 or the *Publication Manual*.

1.7 Summary

1. Writing well means knowing your audience. The audience for a scholarly paper will be members of the academic community. This audience shares certain values. For example, the academic community finds plagiarism and falsification of data completely unacceptable.

2. Plagiarism involves using other people's words or ideas without giving them credit.

3. The academic community values making a fair, logical argument based on careful consideration of the evidence.

4. American Psychological Association (APA) style refers to more than how to format references and citations. For example, to make your paper consistent with APA style, you should use simple, clear language; you should use respectful, inclusive language; and you should usually use the active voice.

5. In your first draft, the goal is to get your ideas on paper. Remember, your first draft is just a starting point.

6. In your second draft, revise the paper to make sure your ideas are well supported and well organized. Outlining your paper can help you revise it.

7. After you have revised the paper so that it makes sense to you, you need to start editing it so that it will make sense to other people. Rework your paper (a) to address objections that a skeptical reader might have and (b) to make it easier for the reader to follow your argument. To help readers follow your thinking, you may want to add subheadings, strengthen topic sentences, cut out unnecessary words, divide long paragraphs, and divide long sentences.

8. After you have edited your paper, you should proof it. Proof your paper to make sure that it is consistent with the APA style that your professor requires, as well as with any other requirements your professor has specified. In addition, proof your paper for inappropriate language, grammar, spelling, and usage.

9. Procrastination is one of the biggest obstacles to producing a good paper. Procrastination may prevent you from (a) obtaining valuable sources from interlibrary loan, (b) carefully evaluating your sources, (c) properly citing and referencing your sources, (d) revising, editing, and proofing your paper, and (e) turning in your paper on time.

C H A P T E R

2

Writing Term Papers

In the research proposals and research reports we discuss in Chapter 3, your task is to present at least one research question and to discuss a study that you either conducted or that you plan to conduct that addresses that question. In a term paper, on the other hand, your task is to discuss other people's studies and come to a conclusion. More specifically, you should collect information from multiple sources, summarize and evaluate that information, come to a conclusion, defend that conclusion, and present your conclusion in a professional and objective manner. Thus, writing a good term paper will help prepare you to write the professional reports that you will probably write as part of your postcollege job.

2.1 Thesis Statement

One key to a good term paper is choosing a manageable topic. Usually, the topic you start out with will be too broad and you will have to narrow it down to a subtopic that can be treated within the limits of a term paper. For example, suppose your initial topic was aggression. You could not possibly learn everything there is to know about aggression in the next few weeks, much less fit that information into a 15-page term paper. Therefore, you will need to choose a narrower topic.

One way to narrow your topic is to go to the library and look up "aggression" in the *Psychological Thesaurus* (see 4.1) to discover narrower terms for aggression. As a result of consulting the *Thesaurus*, you may decide that you want to look at a specific type of aggression, such as instrumental aggression. Even a casual literature search, however, will probably reveal that you need to narrow your topic further. To narrow your topic further, look at how another variable influences or is influenced by instrumental aggression. Thus, you might do a literature search on the effects of television violence on instrumental aggression. Based on your search, you may decide to limit your topic further by looking at a specific type of televised violence (e.g., cartoon) on a specific group (e.g., boys). After selecting a narrow topic, you are ready to write a *working thesis statement*.

Your working thesis statement should be a concise description of what you think your paper will show to be true. Rather than present a glib generalization, it should specify under what conditions a certain relationship will hold (see also 5.1). If your topic is aggression, your working thesis statement might be "Viewing cartoon violence on television leads to aggression in boys."

Although your working thesis statement may not be correct, it will still be useful. Without a working thesis statement, looking up references is fruitless. You would not know what types of articles to search for, what questions to ask if you ever found an appropriate article, and what notes to take on that article.

After you read a number of articles (if you are having trouble finding enough articles, consult 4.1.1 and 4.1.2), you may realize that your working thesis is wrong. If so, modify it into a thesis statement that is consistent with the literature. Depending on what you find out, your thesis statement might be

- viewing cartoon violence on television does not lead to aggression in boys;
- viewing cartoon violence on television leads to aggression in introverted boys;
- viewing cartoon violence on television leads to tolerance of aggression in boys; or
- it is unknown whether viewing cartoon violence on television leads to aggression in boys.

You would choose one of these arguments, or one that we did not list, after extensive reading on the topic convinced you of its truth.

Your thesis statement will guide you in writing three important parts of your term paper: Introduction, Body, and Conclusion. In the first section of your paper (Introduction), you will present your thesis statement and outline how you plan to defend it. In the second section (Body), you will review evidence and theories in favor of your thesis statement and show how evidence and theories that seem to conflict with your thesis statement can be made consistent with it (see 5.9). In the third section of your

FIGURE **2.1**   Headings (Centered) and Other Subdivisions (in Parenthesis) for a Term Paper

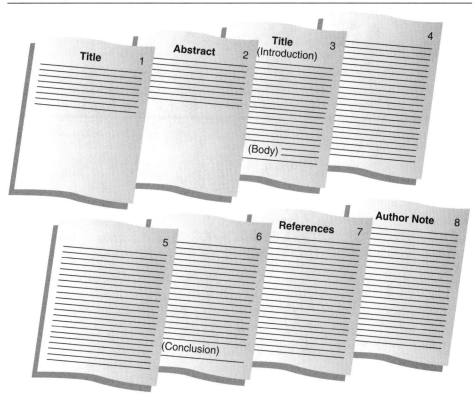

paper (Conclusion), you will summarize your defense of your thesis statement and then reiterate your thesis statement.

2.2 Basic Sections, Headings

Although it is useful to think about only three sections of your paper when making your argument, we will discuss seven parts of the term paper: Title, Abstract, Introduction, Body, Conclusion, References, and Author Note. As you can see from Figure 2.1, most of these parts begin on the top of a page with a centered heading.

2.3 Title Page

The heading for the first page, the title page, is the title. The title is your first chance to impress your professor. Write the title last to ensure that it reflects the main point of your paper. Keep the title focused on your topic: Its first two or three words will become the "short title," which will appear on the top of each page of your paper.[1] Keep the title short: It should never exceed 15 words. You should be able to generate a good title without using more than eight words. For example, if you have written a term paper about the influence of psychoanalysis on modern counseling practice, a catchy and informative eight-word title might be "Modern Counseling: Freudian Theory With a New Face."

Start your title page by putting the short title (in this case, "Modern Counseling"), followed by five spaces, and "1" (for page 1) in the top right-hand corner of the title page.[2] One double-spaced line below this line, starting in the left-hand margin, type the phrase: "Running head:" and a two- to six-word description of your paper. This short description

- should be in all capital letters;

- should be fewer than 51 characters;

- should, usually, state either the names of the two main variables you discussed (typically joined by the word "AND") or the name of your general topic area; and

- should, ideally, be either a shortened form of the title (in this case, "MODERN COUNSELING AND FREUDIAN THEORY") or, if the title is short enough, the title itself.

Near the middle of the page, centered, type your title, making sure to capitalize the first letter of each of its major words.[3] One double-spaced line below your title, type your first name, middle initial(s), and last name. One double-spaced line below that, type the name of your school. Be sure that your title, name, and school are centered (for an example, see 2.11).

2.4 Abstract

Some instructors do not require an Abstract: Check the written requirements for your term paper. If your professor requires an Abstract, you must write a one-paragraph summary of your paper. In this paragraph, devote a sentence each to (a) the general topic area, (b) your thesis statement, and (c) how you showed that your thesis statement is probably true. Do not exceed 120 words.

Wait to write the Abstract until after you have written everything except the title page. There are two reasons for waiting to write your Abstract, and both reasons make sense when you realize that the Abstract is a summary. First, you will find it easier to

---

[1]Use the short title if your professor wants you to use APA manuscript style. If, however, your professor wants you to use APA "final-form" style, do not use the short title. To make your paper conform to "final-form" style, see Appendix A and Chapter 7.

[2]If you are using a word-processor, type the short title and the page number into the header. If you do not know how to use the header, you can find instructions at (http://www.writingforpsychology.com).

[3]Major words are (a) all words longer than three letters and (b) all adjectives, adverbs, nouns, pronouns, and verbs. Thus, the articles "a," "an," and "the"; prepositions such as "on"; and conjunctions such as "and," "but," and "or" would not be capitalized.

write a summary once you have written what it is you are going to summarize. Second, you can use an outline of your final draft to guide you in writing your summary.

In terms of formatting, the Abstract

- begins on page 2;
- is announced by the centered title "Abstract";
- is one paragraph long;
- is free of personal pronouns such as "I," "we," and "mine";
- is, except for any cases in which a number begins a sentence, free of spelled-out numbers (all numbers, except those that begin a sentence, are expressed using numerals); and
- is not indented.

For an example, see 2.11.

2.5 Introduction

The Introduction should be the first paragraph of your paper following the Abstract. Its centered heading is not "Introduction." Instead, its centered heading is the title of your paper. Like the Abstract, the Introduction should be short. Like the Abstract, the Introduction should be self-contained: People reading your Introduction should understand it even if they have not read any other part of your paper. Despite the similarities between the Abstract and the Introduction, they have different goals: The goal of the Abstract is to summarize the paper; the goal of the Introduction is to foreshadow the rest of the paper.

2.5.1 Introduce Generally and Gently

Begin foreshadowing the rest of the paper by introducing your paper's general topic. Your first two sentences should engage the reader. You hope that the reader will be saying, "That is interesting," "That is an important topic," or "I know something about that, and I would like to know more."

After you make the reader receptive to your topic, your next step is to make the reader receptive to your argument. You hope the reader will be saying, "That sounds reasonable," or "I never thought about it like that, but that does make sense."

2.5.2 Introduce Key Issues

The way you get readers to be receptive to your argument is by briefly outlining the empirical and theoretical issues that set up your argument. A popular and efficient way of outlining those issues is to concisely trace the history of thought on the particular topic. Be sure to use citations to document this brief history.

Although you will have citations in the Introduction, do not use those citations to introduce specific findings. Instead, use citations to introduce issues, themes, and alternative approaches to a particular topic. At this point in your Introduction, do not go into specific details about a particular study.

2.5.3 Introduce Key Definitions

Although you should not go into detail about data, you should provide detailed and clear definitions of terms crucial to understanding your argument. However, do not define so many terms that your Introduction looks like a page from a dictionary. Instead, define a term only (a) if the definition of the term is an issue of debate, (b) if there are multiple accepted uses of the term, or (c) if your paper uses a specific definition of a more general term.

2.5.4 Introduce and Present Your Thesis Statement

Once you have defined key issues and key terms, introduce and present your thesis statement. Often, you can introduce and present your thesis statement by outlining the plan of your paper (e.g., " I will review [this side of the question], then I will review [the other side of the question], to show that [my way of reconciling or combining these two sides—my thesis statement—is the best answer to the question, given the available evidence]").

No matter how you introduce your thesis statement, make sure you put your thesis statement in your introduction. As a last resort, write, "In this paper, I will show that [my thesis statement] provides the best explanation of the available evidence" at the end of the last paragraph of your Introduction. If you include such a sentence, you will not get any style points for how smoothly you introduced your thesis statement, but at least you will not get points taken off for failing to put your thesis statement in your Introduction.

2.5.5 Invite Inquiry

State your thesis, but be sure to state your thesis in a way that arouses the reader's curiosity. To stimulate the reader to think about your thesis, avoid the common error of stating your thesis as an established fact. For example, in a paper on the origins of handedness, do not state, "It has been established that handedness is caused by genetic factors (Annett, 1972)." If the reader believes you, the reader should not be interested in reading the rest of your paper. Not only are you saying that the answer to your paper's question is not a subject for debate, but you are also saying that the answer to your paper's question is in Annett (1972). Therefore, if the reader wants to know more, rather than reading the rest of your paper, the reader should read the definitive source—Annett (1972). Thus, if you had drafted such a thesis statement, you should rewrite it. You might write, "Annett (1972) has argued that handedness is caused by genetic factors; others, however, have suggested the importance of the environment (e.g., Collins, 1975)." Alternatively, you might write, "In this paper, I will argue that handedness is caused by genetic factors." Notice the differences in the three versions of the thesis statement. In the first, the relationship between handedness and genes was described as "established." In the better versions, either the relationship was "argued" or other factors were "suggested." The more tentative forms allow further discussion; the definite form does not.

2.6 Body

In the Body of your paper, fulfill the promises you made in the Introduction. Introduce theories, data, procedures, and criticisms. However, your goal is not merely to introduce information. Instead, your goal is to develop your argument and work systematically toward a conclusion.

2.6.1 Integrate Material

Working systematically toward a conclusion means that you cannot merely summarize one study after another. It means that instead of transcribing your notes into a disorganized and purposeless set of article summaries, you must organize the body of your paper around ideas. If you are not sure how to organize your paper around ideas, use one of the five tried-and-true ways to integrate a term paper listed here:

1. Trace the development of ideas on the topic (i.e., an historical approach).
2. List the similarities and differences between two major theories (i.e., a comparative approach).
3. If the topic is posed as a problem, set out possible solutions, and then evaluate each (i.e., a problem-solution approach).
4. Present current opinions on a topic, then evaluate those opinions in light of scientific evidence and theory (i.e., an opinions-reasons approach).
5. Concentrate on the procedures of different studies to find out why seemingly similar ones produced conflicting results (i.e., a methodological approach).

Once you decide on an approach to organizing your paper, organize your notes so that they are consistent with that approach. For example, suppose you have decided to use the methodological approach. Put your notes on studies with results that support your thesis in one pile, put your notes on studies that neither support nor refute your thesis in another pile, and put your notes on studies that appear to refute your thesis in another pile. To help organize the studies, you might try constructing a table. Your first draft of the table might be little more than two lists: (a) a list of studies that obtained results consistent with your thesis, and (b) a list of studies that obtained results that are not consistent with your thesis. Your second draft will usually be a more complex table, in which you evaluate the studies according to common criteria and list the similarities and differences among them (to see an example, see Exhibit 4.2). Your table may enable you to see that the studies that support your thesis are more methodologically sound than those that do not support your thesis.

2.6.2 Be Both Concise and Precise

When you describe studies that support your thesis, you must be both concise and precise. You must be concise because you cannot describe every aspect of every study. Instead, most of the time, you can highlight only what happened in the study, what was found, and what was concluded. You must be precise because you need to show the reader how each study supports your point—and sometimes you can do that only by producing relevant details. Without those relevant details, you can tell the reader only that the study supports your point. Telling ("Trust me: I am right.") is not nearly as convincing as showing ("See for yourself that I am right.").

Showing, rather than telling, is especially important when describing a study that may, on the surface, appear to contradict your thesis. The results of such a study can usually be interpreted in many different ways, some of which will be consistent with your thesis. Therefore, you may choose to make the case that the study, if interpreted properly, does not contradict your thesis. To make that case, you need to present enough relevant details so that you can show your readers that your interpretation makes sense.

2.7 Conclusion

2.7.1 Conclude

The Conclusion is usually your last paragraph. In it, you summarize the main points you made ("tell them that you told them"), show how you have ruled out possible criticisms of your thesis, and restate your thesis. In your concluding paragraph, you should be able to make a statement that essentially says: "I have shown that (my thesis statement) is probably true."

2.7.2 Follow the Body's Logic to Your Conclusion

Anything you say in the Conclusion must follow logically from the Body of the term paper. Although you may state generalizations in the Conclusion that you did not state in the Body, you can do so only if you previously provided a firm rationale for those generalizations. If you need to introduce additional reasons or citations to defend those generalizations, those generalizations do not belong in your Conclusion.

If you come to new generalizations or insights in your ending paragraph, rewrite your paper. Move the citations and the arguments that set up your new insights out of the Conclusion and into the Body of your paper, thereby making sure that the reader is prepared for the Conclusion.

To reiterate, the concluding paragraph is not the place for introducing new data, introducing new interpretations of previously discussed data, or in any other way surprising your reader. Surprise endings are allowed in some mystery stories, but you should never introduce new material in the last paragraph of a term paper.

2.8 References

Start the reference list on a new page with the centered heading: References. All the sources cited in your term paper should appear on this list, with three exceptions. First, do not reference the source if it is a "personal communication" (see 4.3.3) because your reader will not be able to retrieve a conversation you had, a lecture you heard, a letter or e-mail you read, or an Internet site that no longer exists. Second, do not reference the original work if you know about the original work only through a secondary source. Instead, reference only the source you read. For example, suppose the citation in your paper was "Original's study (as cited in Interpreter, 2002)." In that case, you would not put "Original" in your reference list. Instead, you would provide a reference only to "Interpreter"—the source you did read (see 4.3.2). Third, do not reference classical works, such as the Bible.

Realize that, except for the three exceptions we just mentioned, the reference list is a "works cited" list. It is not a bibliography. It is not a list of suggested readings. Therefore, do not include books or articles you read but did not mention in your paper.

Formatting each reference is tricky. To see examples of acceptable formats for the major reference types and to learn the logic behind formatting references, see 4.9. For an example of how to format your references, see the sample term paper's references (2.11). Once you have each reference properly formatted, you need to make sure each reference is in the right place in your reference list. Looking only at the first author's last name, arrange your references in alphabetical order. Thus, "Alpha, R. T., & Omega, J. B. (2002)" would come before "Omega, J. B., & Alpha, R. T. (2002)." If you need more information on how to put your references in the right order, see 4.9.3.

2.9 Author Note

If your professor wants an Author Note (a note that contains your name and affiliation, acknowledgments, and information about how to contact you), start the Author Note on the last page of your paper using the centered heading: Author Note. For your paper, the most important aspects of the Author Note are making disclosures about (a) who, if anyone, helped you with your paper and (b) what part of your paper, if any, was used in another class. To write an Author Note, follow the example in the sample paper (2.11).

2.10 Tense

Most of the time, use the past tense (see 6.1.3 for more information on tense). Use the past tense for anything that has a definite date in the past, such as a citation (e.g., "In 2002, Sanders studied"). Use the present perfect tense (e.g., "For many years, researchers have studied") if the activity happened in the past but either (a) cannot be tied to a date or (b) is still ongoing. Use the present tense for (a) stating conclusions and for (b) anything current, including material in your paper, that you are inviting the reader to consider. Use the future tense when introducing your argument (e.g., "I will argue that").

2.11 Sample Term Paper

On the next few pages, you will find a sample term paper. There are only two aspects of the sample paper that you should not imitate. First, we have used footnotes to make comments so that you can appreciate particular points. In your own term paper, do not use footnotes. Second, we have used only old references so that no one could use this paper in a real class. In your own paper, do not use many old references. Instead, make sure that most of your citations are to articles published within the last three years.

To appreciate this particular term paper, imagine that you had been asked to write a term paper in an adult development and aging course. You narrowed your topic to "Intellectual Declines in Old Age." Your working thesis statement was that "Intellectual Abilities Declines in Old Age." You found sources by using *PsycINFO, Current Contents,* and *Social Science Citation Index* (see 4.1). After reading those sources, you decide your working thesis was wrong. Instead, you now believe that (a) methodological errors may have misled early researchers, and that (b) old age does not necessarily lead to declines in intellectual ability. You write the Body of your paper, then the Introduction and Conclusion, then the Abstract, title page, and reference page. You use a computer to write your first draft and then print out some copies, which you give to your friends to get their comments. You write the draft early, so you have some free time before you have to revise, rewrite, edit, polish, proof your rough drafts, and print out your final version. As a result, when you revisit the draft, you can take a fresh look at it and spot some of the problems a person reading it for the first time might have. You are not under extreme time pressure and so you are calm enough to take your friends' suggestions as helpful advice rather than as hurtful attacks. You use a spelling checker and a grammar checker before printing out the next-to-final version, which you read aloud and proof carefully. You then check your paper against our checklist (2.12), print out a final version, and hand it in on time. You are justifiably proud of your paper. When you get it back, you see that your professor is also happy with your paper.

Running[1] head: INTELLECTUAL DECLINES IN OLD AGE[2]

Intellectual Declines in Old Age: Fact or Artifact[3]

Ann A. Student[4]

Alpha University

---

[1]Ann is using APA manuscript format. If your instructor wants you to use published format, see Appendix A. If your instructor asks you to also add a cover sheet, do what your professor asks.

[2]Ann was able to verify that her running head was short enough (had fewer than 51 characters, including spacing) by using the "Word count" feature of her word-processing software.

[3]The first two words of the title became the short title, and the first five words became the running head. Also, note that prepositions such as "in" and conjunctions such as "or" that have fewer than four letters are not capitalized.

[4]Include your middle initial. Do not include the word "by."

Abstract[5]

Early[6] research using cross-sectional designs suggested that IQ scores decline with age.[7] Research using longitudinal designs, on the other hand, showed that IQ seems to be maintained as long as healthy participants take nonspeeded tests. It is argued that although both cross-sectional and longitudinal designs have methodological deficiencies, their good points can be combined in a cross-sequential design. An analysis of research using the cross-sequential design confirms that intelligence does not necessarily decline in old age.[8]

---

[5]The Abstract starts on page 2 and is announced by the centered heading "Abstract."

[6]The Abstract is not indented (2.4).

[7]The Abstract is double-spaced (7.1.1).

[8]In 76 words, Ann has introduced the topic, the argument, the evidence, and the conclusion.

Intellectual Declines in Old Age: Fact or Artifact[9]

Growing old involves a decrement in most biological processes (Botwinick, 1973). Some researchers have assumed that growing old also involves a decrement in intellectual function (e.g., Chown, 1972). Research using cross-sectional designs supports this assumption (e.g., Jones & Conrad, 1933). Specifically, Wechsler (1939) thought that intelligence "declines progressively after reaching a peak somewhere between the ages of 18 and 25" (p. 135).[10] Yet studies using longitudinal designs showed a less pronounced rate of decline (e.g., Owens, 1953). I will argue[11] that the two designs' different methodological weaknesses account for why the designs produce different results. Then, I will describe a way of combining the two designs into the cross-sequential design: a design that avoids the problems of both the longitudinal and cross-sectional designs (Schaie, 1974). Finally, I will argue that an examination of studies using the less-flawed, cross-sequential design reveals little or no decline of intelligence with age.[12]

Cross-Sectional Research

In the simplest case, cross-sectional researchers compare a group of people of one age (e.g., 45-year-olds) with a group of people of a different age (e.g., 75-year-olds). Researchers using cross-sectional designs have consistently found that the older adult groups scored lower on IQ tests than younger adult groups (e.g., Jones & Conrad, 1933).

Interpreting the older adult group's lower IQ scores, however, is difficult because of a serious weakness in cross-sectional designs. The weakness, as Botwinick (1967) pointed out[13], is that the older group is not merely older than the younger group, but also belongs to a different cohort[14] than the younger group. Consequently, with

---

[9]The Introduction begins on a new page. Its "heading" is the paper's title.

[10]Note the skilled use of quotation to summarize an idea that the writer is going to attack.

[11]Use future tense for introducing your argument (2.10).

[12]In the opening paragraph, the author has introduced the topic and described what the author plans to prove. The paragraph ends with the author's thesis statement.

[13]Note that Ann used the past tense because the activity can be tied to a date (1967).

[14]You might wonder why Ann did not use a nontechnical term such as "generation" instead of "cohort" (a term used by developmental psychologists to refer to a group born in a certain year). Ann used "cohort" to demonstrate that she knows an important technical term that her professor would expect her to know.

cross-sectional designs, it is hard to separate the effects of age from the effects of generation. In the case of cross-sectional research on IQ, the older group's lower IQ scores are not necessarily due to biological aging. Instead, the older group may score lower because their cohort was less prepared to take IQ tests than the younger cohort was. For example, Botwinick[15] pointed out that IQ scores are positively correlated with amount of education and that younger cohorts receive more education than older cohorts.

Longitudinal Research

Unlike cross-sectional researchers, longitudinal researchers study a single group as it ages. Researchers using longitudinal designs have found[16] little evidence of decline in IQ with age (Bayley & Oden, 1955; Owens, 1953).[17]

Although longitudinal designs avoid confounding age with cohort, they have two methodological problems. First, participants with the lowest scores may either die early or refuse to cooperate on subsequent retestings (Riegel, Riegel, & Meyer, 1967). As a result, longitudinal studies may fail to detect age-related declines in IQ. Second, changes that are observed during the study may be the result of environmental events rather than the result of aging. For example, if the same group of participants performs better on an IQ subtest at 70 years than at 65 years of age, this improvement[18] might be due to aging, but it might be due to new medications, improved nutrition, a new government program, or some other environmental change.

Cross-Sequential Designs[19]

To overcome the shortcomings of both cross-sectional and longitudinal designs, Baltes and Schaie (1974) advanced the cross-sequential design. The cross-sequential design

---

[15]Ann did not have to put the date here because she (a) cited the date earlier and (b) has only one Botwinick reference.

[16]Note use of present perfect tense ("have found") because the research referred to is continuing.

[17]When you have more than one citation within parentheses, the citations are in alphabetical order and are separated by semicolons.

[18]Ann added "improvement" after "this" so that readers would know that "this" referred to improvement.

[19]Note that (a) subheadings help readers see how the paper is organized and that (b) the heading "Cross-Sequential Designs" is a second level heading. You can tell it is a second level heading from its formatting: It is italicized, capitalized, and flush against the left margin. To learn more about how to format headings, see 7.2.3.

starts off as a cross-sectional design. Then, the groups are tested a few years later, adding a longitudinal aspect to the design. In some cross-sequential designs, new groups are added over time, thus replicating the original cross-sectional study.

Cross-sequential designs allow the researcher to avoid mistaking either environmental effects or cohort effects for age effects (Mitchell & Jolley, 1988). To illustrate, suppose that both the cross-sectional and the longitudinal parts of a cross-sequential design revealed consistent age-related differences. The longitudinal aspect of the design, in which the researcher compares the same cohort with itself over time, allows the researcher to rule out the possibility that the age-related difference is a cohort effect. The cross-sectional aspect of the design, by allowing the researcher to test the age groups at the same time, permits the researcher to rule out the possibility that the age-related difference is due to recent environmental events.

Using the cross-sequential method, Baltes and Schaie[20] (1974) and Schaie and Labouvie-Vief (1974) found virtually no decline in overall intellectual performance with age. Declines were usually limited to tests and subtests in which speed was important.

Reinterpreting Past Research

At first glance, the conclusion that intellectual performance does not decline with age seems to be at odds with previous research. However, one can reconcile this conclusion with past research by considering problems in the following three areas: (a) cross-sectional designs, (b) IQ measurement, and (c) speed tests.[21]

Problems with cross-sectional research.[22] Most evidence for the idea that IQ declines with age comes from the results of cross-sectional studies. However, the results of cross-sectional studies misrepresent the degree to which IQ

---

[20]Note that because the citation is not in parentheses, the two authors' names are joined by "and" rather than by "&."

[21]This paragraph previews and outlines the next sections. Using the term "speed tests" is an example of the appropriate use of terminology: By using that term, Ann is able to be both concise and precise.

[22]The heading "Problems with cross-sectional research." is a third level heading. As such, it is indented, ends with a period, and is not capitalized. To learn more about formatting headings, see 7.2.3.

declines with age because the results of cross-sectional studies are unduly influenced by (a) the low IQ scores of a few individuals suffering from chronic diseases and (b) cohort effects.[23]

Cross-sectional studies provide information about the average IQ of one age group relative to the average IQ of another age group. However, the average IQ of the older age group could be unduly influenced by a sharp decline in the performance of a few adults. Riegel and Riegel (1972) make the case that a few individuals in the older age group do suffer such sharp declines and that those individuals' scores mask the fact that most healthy adults do not suffer intellectual declines in old age. Specifically, Riegel and Riegel[24] found that people who die of old age exhibit a complex array of intellectual losses. They named this complex pattern of decline "terminal drop" (p. 306)[25] and detected it up to a year before death (Riegel et al., 1967).[26] They point out that if people with terminal drop are included within the older group in a cross-sectional study, those people's low scores will reduce the average IQ of the entire group.

Even if a cross-sectional study includes only individuals whose scores are not declining with age, the old age group may score lower than the younger group because their cohort is, relative to the younger cohort, at a disadvantage on IQ tests. For example, young people are more likely to have taken an IQ test than old people (Botwinick, 1967). Furthermore, as Schaie (1974)[27] noted, modern education relies more on problem-solving skills

---

[23]Note how the paragraph introduces the next two paragraphs (6.4.2).

[24]Ann could have followed this reference with the year. However, she did not have to because (a) she has already provided the year in the earlier reference and (b) she has only one Riegel and Riegel reference so the reader does not need the year to find the reference in her reference section.

[25]"Terminal drop" is a short quotation, so it is surrounded by quotation marks and followed by the page reference. If Ann had been using "terminal drop" as a technical term rather than as a quote, she should have italicized it.

[26]Note the use of "et al." Ann can use et al. because this is the second time she has mentioned this study and the study had three authors. Note how tricky the punctuation is (no comma between "Riegel" and "et," no period after "et, "but a period and a comma after "al").

[27]Note how each major statement of fact is defended with a parenthetical citation (4.3.1). The citations not only give credit where credit belongs (thus avoiding plagiarism), but also make Ann's case look stronger.

(a major component of intelligence tests) than memory skills, which characterized earlier educational methods.

Problems in measuring intelligence. Another problem that may lead both cross-sectional and longitudinal researchers to overestimate intellectual declines in old age is that IQ tests may not be appropriate for testing older adults. Historically, IQ tests were constructed to predict school performance (Binet & Simon, 1908, cited in Wechsler, 1939)[28] and not for testing older adults. Test items involve situations that have little meaning for older adults. According to Schaie (1974), younger people are less fearful of IQ tests and are more highly motivated to do well on IQ tests than older people. These differences in attitudes and motivation—differences that have nothing to do with intellectual ability—may cause older adults to score lower on IQ tests than younger adults (Schaie, 1974).

Problems with speed tests. Older adults are especially likely to score lower than younger adults on IQ tests and subtests in which speed is important. However, there are two problems with interpreting decreased performance on timed tests as declines in intelligence. First, as Botwinick (1971) pointed out, poor performance on a timed test by older people may represent slowed physical movements and greater susceptibility to fatigue rather than representing any intellectual decline. Second, mental speed may not be the same thing as intelligence.

Researchers have recognized the problem of what constitutes intelligence. Cattell (1963) differentiated two major kinds: crystallized abilities that are maintained with age and are culturally determined, and fluid abilities that are innate and subject to the same decrement as other biological processes.[29] Schaie and Labouvie-Vief (1974) showed that crystallized abilities, such as vocabulary and other abilities shaped largely by formal education, increase throughout adulthood, but that fluid abilities, such as speed and fluency, decline throughout adulthood.

---

[28]Note use of a secondary citation (4.3.2). Ann shows integrity by admitting she did not read Binet and Simon. Note that Binet and Simon will not appear in the reference list.

[29]Note how Ann shows that (a) she understands the field's terminology and that (b) she has used that understanding to make a critical distinction that qualifies her argument. This paragraph will impress her professor. In fact, this paragraph may boost her paper grade by an entire letter grade.

Conclusion

When researchers compare intellectual performance of widely different age groups, results from traditional cross-sectional studies show older adults to be intellectually inferior to younger adults. When researchers examine age-related changes using the more appropriate cross-sequential design, they find no decisive intellectual decrements over most of the adult life span (Schaie, 1974). I have shown that although older adults might have lower scores on IQ tests than younger adults, their lower scores are primarily due (a) to cohort effects rather than to the effects of age, (b) to attitudinal differences rather than to ability differences, and (c) to items reflecting fluid, rather than crystallized, intelligence.[30]

---

[30]The Conclusion restates the argument, making appropriate qualifications.

References[31]

Baltes,[32] P. B., & Schaie, K. W. (1974, July[33]). Aging and
    IQ: The myth of the twilight years. *Psychology Today,*[34]
    10, 35-40.

Bayley, N.,[35] & Oden, M. H. (1955).[36] The maintenance of
    intellectual ability in gifted adults. *Journal of
    Gerontology,* 10, 91-107.

Botwinick, J. (1967). *Cognitive process in maturity and old
    age.*[37] New York: Springer.

Botwinick, J. (1971).[38] Sensory-set factors in age
    differences in reaction time.[39] *Journal of Genetic
    Psychology,*[40] 119, 241-249.

Botwinick, J. (1973). *Aging and behavior.* New York:
    Springer.

Cattell, R. B. (1963). Theory of fluid and crystallized
    intelligence: A critical experiment.[41] *Journal of
    Educational Psychology, 54,* 1-22.

Chown, S. M. (1972). The effect of flexibility-rigidity and
    age on adaptability in job performance. *Industrial
    Gerontology,*[42] *13,* 105-121.

---

[31]Start the reference list on a new page (4.9.1) and center the heading ("References").

[32]In the reference section, the indenting style is the opposite of the indenting for the rest of your paper. Specifically, APA advocates "hanging indent style" in which the first line of a reference is not indented, but additional lines are indented five spaces. To see how to program your word-processor to make hanging indents, see our web site.

[33]For a magazine article, put the year, then a comma, and then either the month of publication (for magazines that are published once a month) or the month and day (for magazines that are published more than once a month).

[34]*Psychology Today* is a magazine, not a journal. Your professor will probably require that most of your articles be from journals rather than magazines (see 4.1.3).

[35]Always use a comma between authors' names—even when you have only two authors.

[36]You would not be able to use this term paper in any class because there are no recent references.

[37]Usually, only the first letter of the first word of a book title is capitalized. The entire title is always italicized.

[38]Although references are in alphabetical order, in the case of a tie, older references come first.

[39]Usually, only the first letter of the first word of the title of an article is capitalized.

[40]All major words in a journal name are capitalized.

[41]"A" is capitalized because it comes right after a colon.

[42]Note the difference in the rules in capitalization for titles of articles versus the titles of journals, books, or other publications.

Jones, H. E., & Conrad, H. S. (1933). The growth and decline of intelligence: A study of a homogeneous group between the ages of ten and sixty. *Genetic Psychology Monographs, 13,* 223-298.

Mitchell, M. L., & Jolley, J. M. (1988). *Research design explained* (1st ed.).[43] New York: Holt, Rinehart and Winston.

Owens, W. A., Jr. (1953). Age and mental abilities: A longitudinal study. *Genetic Psychology Monographs, 48,* 3-54.

Riegel, K. F., & Riegel, R. M. (1972). Development, drop, and death. *Developmental Psychology, 6,* 306-319.

Riegel, K. F., Riegel, R. M., & Meyer, G. (1967).[44] A study of the drop-out rates in longitudinal research on aging and the prediction of death. *Journal of Personality and Social Psychology, 5,* 342-348.

Schaie, K. W. (1974). Transitions in gerontology—from lab to life: Intellectual functioning. *American Psychologist,*[45] *29,* 802-807.

Schaie, K. W., & Labouvie-Vief, G. (1974). Generational versus ontogenetic components of change in adult cognitive behavior: A fourteen-year cross-sequential study. *Developmental Psychology, 10,* 305-320.

Wechsler, D. (1939). *The measurement of adult intelligence.* Baltimore:[46] Williams & Wilkins.

---

[43]The title is italicized, but not the edition.

[44]The fact that this reference occurs after the Riegel and Riegel reference illustrates one rule of alphabetizing: All other things being equal, the entry with fewer authors goes first.

[45]The *American Psychologist* is a fine journal meant for a broad audience. It summarizes current thinking and research on a topic. Reading an article from the *American Psychologist* can help you in at least two ways: (a) The article can help you understand a certain theory or issue, and (b) the article's reference list can help you identify important articles that you should read. However, your professor may not want you to use the *American Psychologist* because (a) using an article from it may prevent you from doing your own thinking on the topic and (b) reading an article from it, like reading a textbook account, does not allow you to develop skills in understanding and criticizing empirical research. In short, do not base your paper primarily on article(s) from the *American Psychologist* without checking with your professor.

[46]Baltimore is one of the few cities that can be listed without a state abbreviation. For a complete list of those selected cities, see page 217 of the *Publication Manual.*

Author Note[47]

Ann A. Student, an undergraduate student at the Alpha University.[48]

I[49] thank M. Y. Tutor for guiding my thinking on this topic and I. M. Good for commenting on previous drafts.

Correspondence concerning this article should be addressed to M. Y. Professor, Department of Psychology, Alpha University, Alpha, CA 97804. E-mail: myprof@alpha.edu

---

[47]The Author Note will usually be the last page of your paper.

[48]We know that this is not a grammatical sentence. However, we are following the format specified by the *Publication Manual.*

[49]Thank anyone who gives you general or editorial help (1.2.4).

2.12   Checklist for Evaluating Your Term Paper

___ My thesis statement is an argument about under what conditions a certain relationship holds (see 2.1 and 5.1).

___ My paper is well organized.
   ___ My paper focuses on the thesis statement.
   ___ My paper has a beginning, a middle, and an end.
      ___ The beginning includes my thesis statement and explains how I will make a case for my thesis statement.
      ___ The middle (Body) portion defends the thesis.
      ___ The end concludes by summarizing the case for the thesis statement.
   ___ I revised all three sections of my paper.
      ___ For the beginning section, I focused on cutting sentences and paragraphs that were not relevant to the main point of my paper.
      ___ For the middle, I emphasized organization: I outlined my paper, reorganized my paper, and re-outlined my paper until I was happy with how the paper was organized. Then, I added subheads and transitions to help readers see how the paper was organized.
      ___ For the end, I worked on (a) making sure that I had not added material that was not set up earlier (sometimes, I cut material from the ending; other times, I added material to the middle section) and (b) cutting material that was distracting, meandering, and rambling.
   ___ I reread my paper making sure that I could answer, for each paragraph, the question, "What is this paragraph doing?"
   ___ I made sure there were transitions between each paragraph so that my readers will not say "What is this paragraph doing here?" and that each paragraph has a clear topic sentence so my readers will not say, "What is the point of this paragraph?"

___ I found many recent journal articles that were (a) empirical (articles in which authors reported their own research) and (b) related to my topic.

___ I presented relevant evidence for my thesis statement by paraphrasing, summarizing, critiquing, and synthesizing journal articles (see Chapter 4).

___ I made a strong, fair, and thoughtful argument that included evidence and arguments that appear to oppose my position (see Chapter 5).

___ I proofed my paper for errors in grammar, spelling, punctuation, and usage (see Chapter 6) as well as for inappropriate and biased language (see Chapter 1).

___ I ensured that my paper adheres to APA format (see checklist in 7.4).
   ___ I cited and referenced my sources according to APA style (for citations, see 4.3–4.5; for references, see 4.9).
   ___ My title page adheres to APA format (see 2.11 for model and see 7.4 for checklist).

___ I adhered to the standards of academic honesty (see Chapter 1).

2.13 Summary

1. Usually, the first step in writing a term paper is to choose a narrow topic.

2. After selecting a narrow topic, you should write a *working thesis statement:* a brief, clear statement of what you think your paper will show to be true.

3. In the first section of your paper (Introduction), you will present your thesis statement and outline how you plan to defend it. In the second section of your paper (Body), you will defend your thesis statement. In the third section of your paper (Conclusion), you will summarize your defense of your thesis and then restate your thesis statement.

4. If your professor requires an Abstract, you must write a one-paragraph summary of your paper (see 2.4).

5. The Introduction should foreshadow the rest of the paper.

6. The main challenge many students face when writing the Body of the paper is organizing and integrating the material they have read. If you are having trouble organizing the Body of your paper, see 2.6.1.

7. Anything you say in the Conclusion must follow logically from the Body of the term paper.

8. All the sources in your reference list should be cited in your paper. To see an example of how to format your References, see the sample term paper's References (2.11). To learn more about formatting your reference page, see 4.9.

9. If your professor wants an Author Note, start the Author Note on the last page of your paper using the centered heading: Author Note.

C H A P T E R

3

Writing Research Reports and Proposals

3.1 Basic Sections, Headings

Research papers can be broken down into nine sections: Title, Abstract, Introduction, Method, Results, Discussion, References, Appendixes (optional), and Author Note. As you can see from Figure 3.1, (a) the Abstract, Introduction, References, Appendixes, and Author Note sections each begin on a new page, (b) every section begins with a centered heading, and (c) when a section is broken down into subsections (e.g., The Method section is usually broken down into at least two subsections: Participants and Procedure), these subsections have italicized subheadings that begin at the left margin.

FIGURE 3.1   Main Section Headings (Centered) and Subsection Headings (Left Flush, Italicized) for a Research Paper

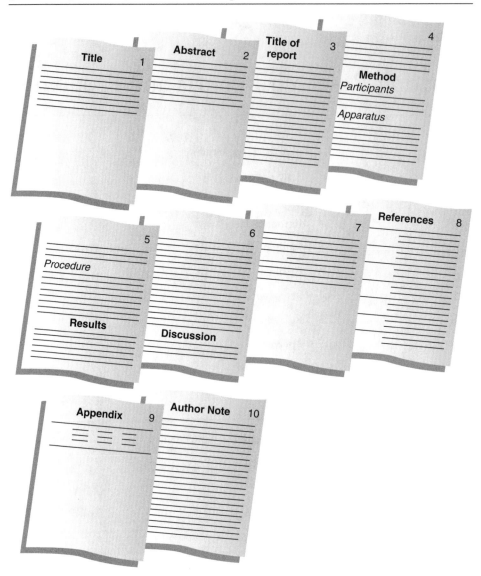

We will discuss each of these sections in the order that they should appear in your report. Although you should present the sections in this order in your report, you may find it useful to write the sections in a different order. For example, suppose you are writing a report on a study you did as part of an in-class exercise. In that case, you may find it easiest to start with the Method section because (a) all you have to do is describe what was done in the study, and (b) you can write it while the details of what you did are still fresh in your mind. Next, you may want to write the Introduction section, a section that should set up both the Method and Discussion sections. Then, you may want to write the Results section. In the Results, you should focus on reporting on whether the hypothesis was supported. Having written the Introduction and Results sections, you should have a relatively easy time writing the Discussion, in which you discuss implications of the results. Once you have written the Body of your paper, write the Abstract, which summarizes the paper. Then, write the title, which summarizes the Abstract. Add the References, Appendixes (if you have any), and the Author Note, and you have completed your rough draft.

If, on the other hand, you are writing a research proposal, you should write the paper in a different order than the one we just described. If you are writing a research proposal, write the Introduction first: Once you have described what you want to accomplish, the rest of the paper should be easier to write.

Regardless of the order in which you write the paper, you should understand the structure of a research paper (see Figure 3.2). The Introduction is designed like a funnel. The wide mouth of this funnel represents the beginning of the Introduction. In this beginning section, rather than introducing your narrow topic, you attract the reader by highlighting interesting aspects of a related but broader topic. You do little more than cite important research and theory related to that general topic so that you can narrow in on your specific topic. You quickly move from a general overview of a broader issue to an in-depth analysis of the particular, narrow aspect of theory that relates to your research study. This in-depth examination will usually include analysis of the strengths and weaknesses of research findings related to that particular aspect of theory. At the end of the Introduction, the bottom and narrowest part of the funnel, you state the specific hypothesis you will test.[1] In the Method and Results, you focus narrowly on the specifics of how you tested your hypothesis. The Discussion is like an inverted funnel: You start by considering what your results mean for your hypothesis but then broaden your scope by considering how the results of your study challenge, extend, or support both (a) published research and (b) published theory.

To see how you would write a research report, imagine that you and your classmates participate in a class exercise in which you are asked to rate how much you like a person described by a list of adjectives. You and your classmates are randomly assigned to one of two groups. One group of your classmates gets the list in this order: humorous, cold, intelligent, polite. The other group gets the list in a different order: cold, intelligent, polite, humorous. Both groups rate their liking of the person. After the students have completed their ratings, the professor leads a discussion about the study. As a result of this discussion, you realize that (a) the independent (manipulated) variable is the position of "humorous" in the list (first vs. last); (b) the dependent (measured) variable is the liking ratings of the person; and (c) the hypothesis is that a person will be liked more when a favorable adjective describing the person comes first in a list than when the same adjective comes last in a list. In the next few sections, we will look at how you would write a report on such a study.

---

[1]In some cases, rather than concluding your Introduction by stating your hypothesis, you might merely state a research question.

FIGURE **3.2**   The Basic Structure of a Research Paper

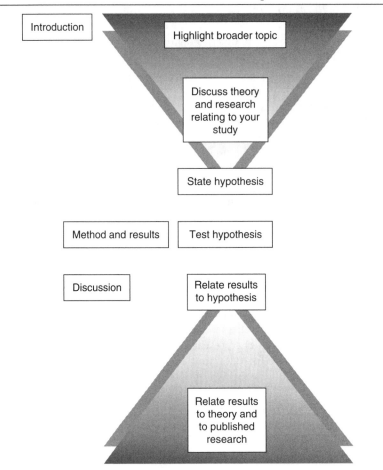

3.2 Title Page

The heading for the first page, the title page, is the title. The title is the first thing readers will see, so make the effort to make a good first impression. The title should be tantalizing enough to lead the reader on to the next, more substantial morsel: the Abstract. To keep the reader's attention, the title should be short—no longer than 15 words. It should also be direct and informative: In fewer than 16 words, it should summarize the main point of the report and identify the crucial variables or issues.

Identifying the crucial variables and issues is vital for three reasons. First, potential readers interested in certain variables or issues may search for articles by looking for titles of articles that contain those variables or issues. Second, the first two or three words of the title become the short title (which appears on the top of every page of your paper). Third, a shortened form of the title should become the two- to six-word phrase called the "Running head," which will appear on your title page. (If your manuscript becomes a published article, the running head will appear on the top of every other page of the published article.)

To practice judging titles, suppose you had written the following four titles for our example experiment:

✗ An Investigation of a Psychological Phenomenon
✗ Influences on Liking Ratings
✔ Effects of Descriptor Order on How Much a Person Is Liked
✔ Favorable First Descriptors Produce Favorable Impressions

Which title did you prefer? The last title is perhaps the best of the four because it communicates the most about the results of the experiment. The third title, however, is the most common sort of title, and its small mystery (what was the effect?) may make it more tantalizing.

There is more to the title page than the Title (for details, see 2.3). To see how to format your title page, see the sample paper's title page (3.12) and compare your title page to our title page checklist (7.4.6).

3.3 Abstract

As you can see from the sample paper, page one of your paper should be the title page. Page two of your paper should contain the Abstract. Begin the Abstract with the centered heading "Abstract" and follow that heading with an unindented paragraph. Without exceeding 120 words, and without using any first person pronouns (e.g., "I," "my," or "we"), provide a complete, self-contained summary of the report.

Start the Abstract by stating the research question. Then, describe the method, the nature of the participants tested, the results, and the main conclusion. To cover all this information in so few words, you have to make each word in the Abstract count. A possible Abstract for our example experiment follows:

Based on the primacy effect in serial recall, it was
hypothesized that a target person would be better liked when
positive information was presented first rather than last.
This hypothesis was tested in a simple experiment in which
half the participants were exposed to a description of a
person that began with an extremely positive adjective whereas
the other half received the identical description except that
the positive adjective ended the description. Consistent with
the hypothesis, participants whose descriptions began with a
highly favorable adjective rated the described person as more
likeable than participants who learned the favorable adjective
last. The results are discussed in terms of whether the
primacy effect reflects assumptions made by participants about
how people order descriptive information.

Although the previous example is consistent with what is found in journals as well as with the sample Abstract found in the *Publication Manual*, it is not consistent with the guidelines for abstracts set out on page 14 of the *Publication Manual*. Specifically, it does not contain detailed numerical information about the number, gender composition, and age of the sample, and it does not contain details about the results of statistical tests. The advantage of omitting specific numerical information from the Abstract is that it allows room for more general information about the study. However, as you can see from the 108-word sample Abstract that follows, if you are summarizing a single study, you can (a) meet the *Publication Manual*'s guidelines, (b) provide general information about the study, and (c) still stay within the word limit.

```
Does the order of adjectives describing a person affect how
much raters like that person? To answer this question,
24 introductory psychology students (14 women and 10 men,
mean age = 19.7 years) read a list of adjectives, and then
rated how much they liked the described person.
Participants were randomly assigned to two groups. Those
receiving "humorous" as the first adjective in the list
rated the person as more likeable than those receiving the
identical list except with "humorous" last, t(22) = 5.62,
p < .05. The results are discussed in terms of whether the
primacy effect reflects assumptions made by participants
about how people order descriptive information.
```

For more information about how to format the Abstract, see 2.4. In addition, consult the model in 3.12 and the checklist in 3.13.

3.4 Introduction

The Introduction begins the body of the paper. Its centered heading is the title of the paper, rather than the word "Introduction." In the Introduction, you must introduce the general area and your specific hypothesis. As readers scan the first paragraph, they should be saying, "Yes, that is an interesting and important research area." As they move through the rest of the Introduction, they should be saying, "That hypothesis makes sense. It really should be tested. I wish I had thought of that hypothesis." In addition, you are also setting up readers for the Method section, so that when they read the Method section, they say, "Yes, that is a good way to test the hypothesis."

3.4.1 Introduce the Broader Issue

Start the text of the Introduction with a sentence that introduces the major problem or issue of which a specific aspect is tested in your study (for more details, see 2.5.1). Follow with a brief summary of the major research bearing on the general issue. Use citations to introduce these data (for information on how to cite, see 4.3). State the relevant parts of theories thought to explain previous research data. Your summary should be logically interconnected, and it should go from general, theoretical considerations to the specific background of your hypothesis. As your professor reads your paper, you do not want your professor to be saying any of the following:

"This student has not read the recent research."

"This student is citing, but not critiquing, research studies."

"Does the research cited in this paragraph have anything to do with the student's hypothesis?"

"Why should anyone care about this hypothesis?"

"Why am I getting a detailed description of how the student will do the study? Such a description belongs in the method section."

3.4.2 Introduce the Hypothesis

End the Introduction with a simple, direct statement of your hypothesis. However, make sure that your statement of the hypothesis is not a surprise ending to the Introduction. That is, make sure that the rest of the Introduction clearly and logically leads up to the statement of the hypothesis. Thus, even before you state the hypothesis, the reader should not only know what the hypothesis is but also (a) how your hypothesis follows logically from theory and research, and (b) why it is important to test the hypothesis.

To introduce the hypothesis, use words such as, "In view of [the logic I spelled out earlier], I predicted that [my hypothesis]," or "If [the logic I spelled out earlier] is the case, then it should follow that [my hypothesis]." If the reader leaves your Introduction asking any of these questions, you are in trouble:

1. What was the hypothesis?
2. Why would anyone think that the hypothesis would be supported?
3. Does this study have anything to do with previous research or theory?
4. Why is this study being done?

3.5 Method

Whereas you use the Introduction to explain why your study was done, you use the Method section to describe how your study was done. In this "how to" section, do not describe everything you did. Instead, describe your procedures in just enough detail that an experienced researcher could replicate your study.

Start the Method section immediately after the Introduction. Label it with the centered heading: Method. Divide the Method section into its appropriate subsections, such as a subsection describing participants and a subsection describing procedures. Each subsection should start with a label (e.g., "*Participants*") that begins in the far left margin and is italicized. If these subsections are, in turn, subdivided into smaller subsections, label these subsections with italicized, indented paragraph headers (see 7.2.3).

All sentences within each section must be complete and intelligible. One mistake that beginning writers often make is treating a section's heading as if it were the beginning of the first sentence of that section. As a result, the first line of their "Participants" section might be the incomplete sentence "were 20 students." To avoid making that mistake, write complete and intelligible sentences that repeat the information contained in the headings. For example, follow the heading "*Participants*" with: "The participants were 20 students." rather than writing the incomplete sentence "were 20 students."

3.5.1 Participants or Subjects

Usually, you will devote the first subsection of your Method section to describing your sample. Specifically, you would describe (a) the general characteristics (how many women, how many men, average age, etc.) of the individuals you studied, (b) how you recruited and selected those individuals, and, if applicable, (c) how you assigned those individuals to different conditions. In this first subsection, you are providing information that will help (a) researchers who want to replicate your study, (b) reviewers who want to be sure your study was conducted ethically, and (c) readers who want to evaluate how representative your sample was. This section would be labeled and written differently if you had studied nonhuman animals rather than humans.

If you studied humans, label this section "Participants," and refer to the individuals you studied as "participants." Never refer to them as "subjects." Tell how many participants you studied, how many were women, and how many were men. State the average age of the participants, as well as either the age range or standard deviation. You may need to provide additional background information about the participants (e.g., race/ethnicity, religion, political affiliation, socioeconomic status, visual acuity) if (a) you are doing an analysis using one of those background variables or (b) that information is necessary for assessing the generalizability of your results.

To give the reader the ability to evaluate the representativeness of your sample and the ability to replicate your study with an equivalent sample, you must do more than describe the characteristics of your sample. You must tell how you selected your sample (e.g., "were a random sample of university students" or, more commonly, "were students in an introductory psychology class"), as well as what incentives you used to encourage those selected to participate (e.g., participants received money, received extra credit, received no compensation). In addition, you must state (a) the number of participants who dropped out, (b) the number of participants whose data were excluded from analysis, and (c) the reasons for these dropouts and exclusions.

Finally, if you arranged for different participants to receive different treatments, describe how you made these assignments. In an experiment, you would probably use random assignment. For correlational studies, you might assign participants to condition based on their scores on a certain test.

If, rather than studying humans, you studied nonhuman animals, do not label this section "Participants" because you did not have any participants: individuals who volunteered to participate in your study. Instead, use "Subjects" as the heading for this section. Provide the species name, strains and supplier, ages, sexes, and weights of your subjects. Describe how you treated these subjects: how much they were handled, their feeding schedules, the temperature they were kept at, and the lighting conditions. In addition, be sure to provide any other information about how your subjects were treated that would be necessary to replicate the study.

For both nonhuman and human animals, provide assurances that the study was conducted ethically. If the experiment involved individuals from whom informed consent is difficult or impossible to obtain (such as children or animals), you should state the ethical precepts under which the study was conducted. For example, if you had read APA's ethical principles, you might include the following statement: Animals were treated in accordance with the "Ethical Principles of Psychologists and Code of Conduct" (American Psychological Association, 2002). Often, authors provide some assurances in the report by stating that participants were volunteers. However, according to the *Publication Manual*, authors should explicitly state that participants were treated ethically. Thus, for our example study, a Participants section might look like the following:

> Participants
>
> Participants were 24 (14 women and 10 men) students enrolled in an introductory psychology class at University of Higher Education who volunteered as part of a class exercise. Their ages ranged from 18 to 25 with a mean of 19.25. All participants were treated in accordance with the "Ethical Principles of Psychologists and Code of Conduct" (American Psychological Association, 2002).[2]

3.5.2 Apparatus

If you used equipment to present or record information (e.g., computers, slide projectors, or stop watches), describe that equipment briefly in a subsection called "Apparatus." Provide brand names and numbers for complicated equipment (e.g., computers, skin-fold calipers), but not for simple, standard equipment (e.g., stopwatches, rulers). If pencil-and-paper tests were also used, describe them here (e.g., "Participants completed the WAIS."). Describe your materials well enough so that other researchers can obtain or replicate your stimuli (e.g., "Memory lists were printed on standard-sized (22 × 28 cm) sheets of white, bond paper in 12-point Times font. Distractor material was printed on every alternate line in a 10-point Times font.").

3.5.3 Materials

If you used only pencil-and-paper tests, instead of an Apparatus subsection, use a subsection entitled "Materials." If pencil-and-paper tests are well known, just name, abbreviate, and cite them (e.g., "Beck Depression Inventory (BDI; Beck, Ward, Mendelssohn, Mock, & Erlbaugh, 1961)"); if they are not well known, name, cite, and briefly describe the test(s). If you created a test for the research study, put a copy of

---

[2]Include this citation only if you read the *Principles*.

that test in an appendix (see 3.9). In our example study, a Materials section might look like the following:

> *Materials*
>
>   Each participant received a single sheet of white,
>   8.5 × 11 in. (22 × 28 cm) bond paper with these words
>   printed on it:
>
>   Imagine you are about to meet a person for the first
>   time. You know nothing about the person, except that
>   this person's friends describe her as humorous, cold,
>   intelligent, polite [or cold, intelligent, polite,
>   humorous]. How much do you think you would like this
>   person? Rate your answer on a 7-point scale where
>   1 means that you would dislike this person a lot,
>   4 means that you would neither dislike nor like this
>   person, and 7 means that you would like this person
>   a lot.

3.5.4 Design and Other Optional Subsections

If your design is too complicated to describe in a single paragraph, put information about the design in a separate subsection called "Design." Consider setting off any aspect of your Method section that requires more than a paragraph to describe (e.g., your manipulation checks, your coding scheme) in a separate subsection (e.g., "Coding," "Manipulation checks"). In addition, you may decide to start your Method section with an "Overview" subsection.

3.5.5 Procedure

Whereas the decision to use an Overview or Design subsection is usually optional, the decision to use a Procedure subsection is not. The Procedure is a step-by-step account of what happened to the participants during the study. The section should so clearly focus on participants that readers should be able to imagine themselves as participants in your study. To focus on participants, consider making participants the subject of most sentences. For instance, rather than writing, "I read the stimulus words," you might write, "Participants heard the stimulus words." The following example illustrates how to keep the focus on the participants:

> *Procedure*
>
>   Participants received a randomly distributed response
>   sheet. They had 2 min to read it and write their responses
>   on it.

In addition to helping readers visualize what it would be like to be a participant in your study, you need to include information that will help readers replicate your study. Specifically, you need to include information about instructions and methodological wrinkles.

Include information about instructions, especially about how these instructions are different for your different groups. However, rather than stating your instructions word-for-word, you can usually summarize them (e.g., "Participants read standard instructions that can be found in Appendix B.").

Include any methodological wrinkles that boost the study's validity. Thus, if you used a double-blind procedure, be sure to mention that you did. If you used a sophisticated procedure to control for order effects, describe that procedure (e.g., "Order and serial position of the six conditions were counterbalanced using Latin squares."). If you have not already described the design (e.g., in a separate "Design" subsection or in a "Participants and Design subsection"), describe the design of the study, including the manipulated and measured variables. For our example experiment, you might write the following:

```
The study was a two-level, between-participant experiment
with sequence of information ("humorous" first vs. last) as
the independent variable. The dependent variable was the
liking ratings.
```

3.6 Results

The Results section starts one double-spaced line after the end of the Method section with the centered heading: Results. Start the text of this section by telling the reader exactly which data you analyzed—if those data differ from the measured variable you described in the Method section. For example, you would need to say whether you had transformed data in any way (e.g., percentage correct in a memory test rather than number of items recalled), and if any data were omitted (e.g., data from practice trials).

Once the reader knows what data you are analyzing, you can describe how you analyzed those data. If you did any significance tests, tell the reader

- why you did the test (e.g., "To test the hypothesis that the sequence of presenting the information had an effect on likeability, I . . .").
- what the test was (e.g., "performed an independent-groups t test . . .").
- what your two-tailed significance (alpha) level was (e.g., "using an alpha level of .05" or "The probability of a Type I error was .05 [or whatever level you used] for all analyses.")—unless you are using a one-tailed test. If you are using a one-tailed test, tell the reader (e.g., "Using a one-tailed test and an alpha level of .05").
- what the result of the test was in terms of both the significance test and in terms of the reason you performed the test. Often, the reason will be to test a hypothesis (e.g., "As hypothesized, participants who received 'humorous' first rated the person as significantly more likeable than those who received 'humorous' last, $t(22) = 3.46, p < .01$.").
- what the relevant summary statistics (averages and measures of spread) are for the important conditions. These descriptive statistics may help readers see the pattern in your data. For example, you might write, "Specifically, the mean rating from those receiving 'humorous' first was 5.75 ($SD = 1.06$), whereas the mean rating from those receiving 'humorous' last was 4.5 ($SD = 0.67$)."

What we want to emphasize is that you should include, at the very least, the previous information. That information, skillfully presented (a) gives the casual reader a clear understanding of whether the results support the hypothesis; (b) gives a skeptical reader evidence that your results support your claims; and (c) gives a reader doing a meta-analysis the information necessary to combine your results with those of related studies. We do not mean that you must include the information in the order in which we presented it. The key is to organize the information so it tells a story. For example, you might organize the information as follows:

> To test the hypothesis that participants receiving "humorous" first would rate the person as more likeable than participants receiving "humorous" last, I used a between-subjects t test on the likeability ratings. As hypothesized, participants who received "humorous" first rated the person as more likeable ($M = 5.75$, $SD = 1.06$) than those who received "humorous" last ($M = 4.5$, $SD = 0.67$), $t(22) = 3.46$, $p < .05$.

Alternatively, you might find it useful, at least in your first draft, to state the conclusion (the implication of the results for your hypothesis) first. Then, you can use the rest of the paragraph to provide support for that conclusion, as we did here:

> As hypothesized, participants who received "humorous" first rated the person as more likeable than those who received "humorous" last. The mean rating from those receiving "humorous" first was 5.75 ($SD = 1.06$), whereas the mean rating from those receiving "humorous" last was 4.5 ($SD = 0.67$). Using a between-subjects t test, this difference was significant, $t(22) = 3.46$, $p < .05$.

3.6.1 Statistical Significance

If, as in the previous case, your results are statistically significant, the *Publication Manual* encourages that significant results also be accompanied by (a) effect size estimates and (b) confidence intervals. Check to see if your professor wants you to include any of those statistics.

If, on the other hand, your results are not statistically significant, the *Publication Manual* encourages that you report your study's power. That is, tell the reader that if the variable had an effect of a certain size, what the chances of your study finding that effect statistically significant would be. Check to see if your professor wants you to do a power analysis and, if so, what form that power analysis should take.

Note that results are either statistically significant or not. Do not treat results that are not significant as significant. For example, do not use terms like "marginally significant."

Note also that you are allowed to use the adjective "significant" only as a statistical term. More specifically, you can use "significant" only when you mean that the null hypothesis has been rejected. You are not allowed to use "significant" as a synonym for "important." Therefore, do not use the phrase "significant result" when you mean "important result."

Finally, note that you can use "insignificant" only when you mean unimportant. You cannot use "insignificant" as a synonym for the statistical term "not significant." Therefore, if you mean that the results fail to disprove the null hypothesis, do not refer to the results as "insignificant results." Instead, refer to results either as "not significant" or as "nonsignificant."

3.6.2 Formatting Statistical Information

As you saw from the examples of result sections in 3.6, formatting statistical information is different from formatting regular text. Some numbers are italicized, some numbers below one are expressed with a leading zero in front of the decimal point (e.g., 0.20), some numbers below one are expressed without a leading zero (e.g., .20), some material is in parentheses, and some commas are used in unusual ways. Fortunately, there are rules:

- Italicize all statistical symbols that are standard alphabetic letters (e.g., t, p, F, df, M, SD).
- Do not italicize any Greek letters (e.g., Σ, μ).
- For any inferential statistical test, give its name, the degrees of freedom in parentheses, an equals sign, the statistic's value, and the probability level. For chi-square, give the sample size as well (use N for the whole sample, n for a subsample).
- Separate inferential statistical information from the sentence with a comma.
- State percentage and integer data as whole numbers. For any other numbers, go to two decimal places, except for probability values. With probability values, you can go to as many decimal places as necessary.
- Do not put zeros in front of the decimal point for either (a) probabilities ("p" values) or (b) correlation coefficients.

Three examples follow:

```
The increase in mean confidence ratings was significantly
greater in the experimental condition (M = 5.01, SD = 3.52)
than in the control condition (M = 3.84, SD = 3.02),
t(26) = 2.66, p < .01.

    There was a significant interaction, F(1, 34) = 123.07,
p < .001, plotted in Figure 4.

    The distribution of preferences shown in Table 6 was
not significantly different among the four categories,
χ² (3, N = 300) = 6.00, ns.
```

3.6.3 Deciding Whether You Need Either a Figure or a Table

If you are going to compare only two means, you do not need either a figure or a table—unless your professor requires one. (Your professor may require figures or tables so you can learn how to format them.) If your table or figure is merely going to duplicate what you have already said in text, you should not use a figure or a table.

3.6.4 Best Times for Tables

Sometimes, you must include many numbers in your Results section. However, if you include all those numbers in text, you may overwhelm and confuse your reader. In such a case, you should use either a table or a figure. If your goal is to show that the data fit a pattern (e.g., to show that performance increases over time, to illustrate that there is a linear relationship between two variables, or to show that an interaction is X-shaped), then you may wish to use a figure to paint that general picture. If, on the other hand, the exact numbers are important, you will probably want to use a table. As a general rule, use a table if you are presenting:

- between 4 and 10 means (and their standard deviations),
- more than four correlation coefficients,
- the results of an analysis of variance (ANOVA),
- a list of factor loadings, or
- the results of a multi-stage regression analysis.

3.6.5 Making Tables

Your goal in using a table should be to summarize information for your reader. For your table to accomplish that goal, your reader should be able to understand your table without reading the accompanying text. However, the table is not supposed to simply stand by itself, waiting for the interested reader to absorb it. Instead, in your Results section, you must refer to the table by its number and highlight the table's most relevant numbers or patterns of numbers (e.g., "As can be seen in Table 2, the treatment group scored higher than the control group on every dependent measure."). If you cannot refer to the table, then it is unnecessary. Delete it.

One reason it is important to refer to the table by number is that the tables in a manuscript submitted for publication do not appear right next to the text that refers to them. Instead, tables must be placed, one per page, after the References. (You may wish to ask your professor if you can deviate from APA manuscript style and put the table in the text near where it is discussed.)

All tables consist of three parts: (a) a caption appearing above the rest of the table, which includes a table number and title; (b) headings for the table's columns and headings for the table's rows; and (c) the table's data. In addition, some tables contain a fourth part: explanatory notes. We will now discuss each of these four parts. To follow our discussion, you may find it useful to refer to Exhibit 3.1.

EXHIBIT **3.1** An Example of a Table

Table 2
Mean Differences in Reaction Time (in ms) Between No-Noise and Noise Conditions

Noise level (dB)	Mean difference[a]	t
	Simple RTs	
60	-7.21_z (9)[b]	2.62*
70	-7.45_z (8)	3.55**
80	-9.15_z (10)	4.49**
90	-9.72_z (9)	3.85**
	Choice RTs	
60	-11.05_y (5)	2.82*
70	-11.92_y (9)	9.90****
80	-4.91_x (10)	3.61**
90	0.33_w (10)	1.41

Note. This table is made up. If it had been previously published, we would have cited the study here. Numbers having different subscripts differ significantly at $p < .01$ by t test.
[a]Negative numbers indicate noise RT was slower than no-noise RT.
[b]Number in parentheses is number of participants in each condition.
* $p < .05$. ** $p < .01$. **** $p < .0001$.

The first part of the table caption is the table number. Use Arabic numbers (e.g. "2") and number the tables according to the order in which you refer to them in text. Thus, the second table you refer to will be "Table 2."

The second part of the table caption is the table title. It should be a brief, telegraphic, but meaningful description of the relationship between (a) the data in the table and (b) the variables or statistics identified by the column and row headers. If your data can be expressed in units (milliseconds, liters), put the unit of measurement in parentheses. Italicize the table title and capitalize the first letter of each major word. Place the table caption above the table.

The column and row headings tell the reader what the data in the table represent. The left-most column heading identifies the major manipulated variable (i.e., noise level). Under that column header are the row headings. The row headings label the levels (amounts) of the major manipulated variable (i.e., 10 dB). Other column headings specify levels of other manipulated variables, or different measured variables (e.g., "Mean difference").

Often, your tables will have three horizontal lines. Near the top of the table, put a horizontal line right below the table caption to separate it from the column headings. Next, put a line right below the column headings to separate them from the body of the table. Finally, put a line at the bottom of the body of the table to separate the body of the table from the explanatory notes. Use other horizontal lines sparingly. Do not use vertical lines.

T A B L E **3.1**   Superscripts for Probabilities of Two- and One-tailed Statistical Tests

$p <$	Two-tailed	One-tailed
.05	*	†
.01	**	††
.001	***	†††
.0001	****	††††

If there are decimal points, the decimal points of the numbers in a column should line up with each other. Write out numbers to two decimal places, except when the data are integers or percentages (see 7.2.6).

Set any notes that you have at the bottom of the table in unindented paragraphs. The first paragraph would be *general notes* relating to the entire table (e.g., "Numbers having different subscripts differ significantly at $p < .01$ by t test."). Start this general notes section with the italicized word *Note* followed by a period. Make each note a complete sentence, and end each note with a period (see Exhibit 3.1).

Your second paragraph would start on a new line, and would be *specific notes* applying to particular entries, columns, or rows (e.g., "[a]Negative indicates noise RT was slower than control RT."). Identify those notes, both in the table in the notes, with superscript letters (e.g.,[a]).

The third paragraph would start on a new line and would be *probability notes*. You use probability notes when you use symbols, such as asterisks (*) and daggers (†) to indicate that a result is statistically significant. Probability notes spell out the connection between your symbols (e.g.,*) and the significance level (e.g., $p < .05$) they represent. Table 3.1 shows a common way of using superscripts to express probability levels. Exhibit 3.1 provides an example of probability notes in action.

3.6.6 Best Times for Figures

A figure is a picture you use to help your reader see the point you are trying to make. In the Results section, figures can be very useful for helping your reader see the shape of a relationship between two variables, for helping your reader understand an interaction among variables, and for presenting a very large number of data points. You might also use a figure in the Method section to illustrate anything that would otherwise be hard to describe, such as the appearance of stimuli or the layout of apparatus.

3.6.7 Making Figures

As was the case with tables,

- your reader should be able to understand your figures without reading the accompanying text;

■   figures should do more than duplicate information already in text;

■   the text should draw the reader's attention to the important aspects of your figure; and

■   the text should refer to the figure by number (e.g., "As can be see in Figure 1").

In referring to figures, note three points. First, regardless of whether your "figure" is a graph, a photo, or a diagram, always refer to it by the word "Figure" followed by the figure number. Second, as was the case with tables, it is important to refer to the correct figure number because the figure is not next to the text to which it refers. Instead, the figures are put, one per page, on the pages after the figure captions—and the figure captions are put on the page after the tables (which, in turn, are put after the References). Third, software packages, such as *Excel, SPSS,* and *DeltaGraph* can help you construct graphs (consult http://www.writingforpsychology.com for tips on how to use these programs). However, when using such programs, realize that (a) using them may be extremely time-consuming, (b) using them may result in figures that violate APA standards, and (c) using them to construct appropriate graphs is easier if you know the terminology associated with the four parts of a graph:

1.   the axes of the graph—the "x" (horizontal axis) and the "y"(vertical) axis;

2.   the representation of the data—the data points and lines joining them or the bars representing them;

3.   the figure legend—a box within the figure that describes what the bar shadings, symbols, or lines represent; and

4.   the figure caption—a heading that includes the figure's number, the figure's title, and explanations of what lines, symbols, and abbreviations represent—if those explanations are necessary for understanding the figure and those explanations could not fit in the legend.

We will now discuss each of these four components. To follow this discussion, you may find it helpful to refer to Exhibit 3.2.

Axes. Choose scale values for each axis that spread out the data and allow the figure to fit comfortably on one page. Your figure should be wider than it is tall: Ideally, it would be only about two-thirds as tall as it is wide.

Make the horizontal axis by drawing a line that starts near the left-hand, bottom side of the page and goes straight across toward the right-hand, bottom side. If you conducted an experiment, this horizontal axis will represent your independent variable. If you conducted a nonexperimental study, this horizontal axis will represent your predictor variable. Starting at the far left end of that line, draw a straight line up toward the top of the page. Make this vertical line about two-thirds as long as your horizontal axis. This vertical line, your vertical axis, will represent your dependent (measured) variable. Thus far, your graph has two lines for the two axes. The two axes are two sides of an incomplete rectangle. Complete the rectangle (add the top and the right side)—

EXHIBIT **3.2**   An Example of a Line Graph

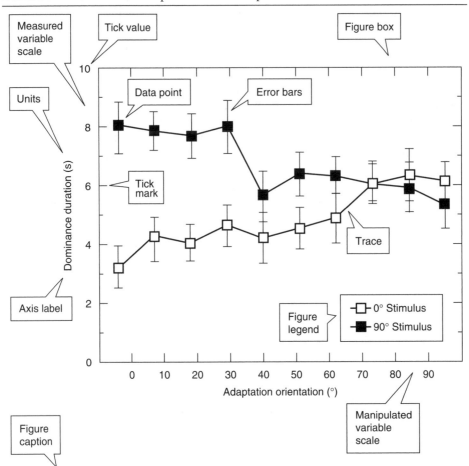

Figure 2. Mean duration of binocular-rivalry dominance of vertical (0°) and horizontal (90°) stimuli following adaptation to a monocular grating of various orientations. Vertical lines show ±1 standard error of the mean.

at least for this first draft.[3] This rectangular box will separate any points, lines, or bars that represent your data from (a) the axis labels and (b) the scale values of the axes.

Inside that box, place *tick marks:* small marks that will be used to indicate values of the variables on your axes (see Exhibit 3.2). Then, place the numbers corresponding to the tick marks on the outside of the box. Print those numbers in their normal orientation.

---

[3]If you are making a scatterplot or a bar graph, you will remove both the line that forms the top of the rectangle and the line that forms the right side of the rectangle from the final draft of your figure. If you are making a line graph and the final graph looks better without those two lines, remove them.

You now need axis labels to help the reader understand what those numbers represent. The two axis labels should be meaningful but brief. To make the labels meaningful, let the reader know the units to which the numbers are referring (e.g., meters, milligrams, decibels) by including that information in the axis labels. To help make the axis labels brief, try to abbreviate the name of the units (to see a list of abbreviations for common units, see 3.6.8). Put the unit abbreviation—or, if you were unable to use an abbreviation, the unit—in parentheses. Once you have your axis labels, center them and print each one parallel to its axis.

Data. For your purposes, there are three main types of graphs: line graphs, bar graphs, and scattergrams. We have purposely omitted the pie graph because people often use a pie graph when their point would be clearer had they used either a bar graph or a table.

The three types of graphs are not interchangeable. The type of graph you should use depends on the type of data you have. In the next section, we will show you how to choose the type of graph that matches the type of data you have.

Line graphs. Use a line graph when you have conducted an experiment and at least one manipulated variable has numerical values (e.g., drug dosage, number of onlookers, or, as in Exhibit 3.2, orientation in degrees). Your first manipulated variable should be represented on your horizontal axis. Put your measured variable on the vertical axis. Plot your data as points and join the points with lines. If you have a second manipulated variable, distinguish the levels (amounts) of this variable by (a) using differently shaped points (e.g., circles for one level, squares for the second level) and (b) join points with different kinds of lines (e.g., solid lines for one level, dotted lines for the other level). Each set of points and joining lines is called a *trace*.

If your data are means, you can also give your reader some idea of the variability of scores around each mean by engaging in a three-step process. First, compute the standard error of the mean *(SE)* for your first mean.[4] Second, draw a line that starts one SE directly above the point representing your first mean, continues down through that point, and stops one standard error below that point. (You should now have a line that is 2 *SE*s in length and has the mean as its midpoint.) This line is an error bar. Third, draw error bars for each of your means. To see what these standard error lines look like, see Exhibit 3.2.

Bar graphs. Use a bar graph when you have conducted a study and all your predictor variables are non-numerical (e.g., different kinds—rather than amounts—of treatments, or, as in Exhibit 3.3, experimental vs. control). The measured (dependent variable) will be on the vertical axis. If you have one manipulated (independent) variable, that variable will be on the horizontal axis. If you have two manipulated variables, only one can be on the horizontal axis. The levels of the other one will have to be expressed by differently shaded bars (e.g., black, white, gray). To determine which manipulated variable you should express with bars, make one graph putting one manipulated variable on the horizontal axis and make another graph putting the other

---

[4]The standard error is the standard deviation of the scores making up the mean divided by the square root of the number of scores making up the mean.

EXHIBIT 3.3 An Example of a Bar Graph Showing an Interaction

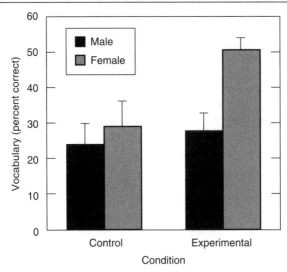

Figure 3. Mean percent-correct words in experimental and control groups as a function of sex. Vertical lines show 1 standard error of the mean.

manipulated variable on the horizontal axis. Then, compare the graphs to see which graph makes your conclusions clearer.[5]

In working with your bars, there are three rules you should obey. First, do not distinguish the levels of the other manipulated variables by using differently colored (e.g., red, purple, green) bars. Instead, use differently shaded bars (e.g., black, white, gray). Second, do not use diagonal lines to shade the bars; diagonal lines will create the illusion that your bars are tilted. Third, do not add 3-D effects: Those effects make it more difficult for readers to understand your graph. Instead, add standard error lines above the bars to show the variability in your data (see Exhibit 3.3).

Scattergrams. If you have a numerical manipulated variable, use a line graph. If you have a non-numerical manipulated variable, use a bar graph. If you do not have a manipulated variable, you may want to use a scattergram. A scattergram is especially useful when you have given two tests to your participants. Put the variable you consider the predictor variable on the horizontal axis and the criterion variable on the vertical axis. Then use dots to plot your data on the graph. If you want to provide more information than what a bunch of dots can convey, add a regression line to your scattergram (see Exhibit 3.4).

Legend. In the figure's legend (the box inside the figure, see Exhibit 3.2), provide explanatory information to help the reader understand any abbreviations, bar shad-

---

[5]Sometimes, changing which variable you put on the horizontal axis will make no difference in how easy your graph is to read; other times, changing which variable you put on the horizontal axis can make your graph much easier to grasp. To see examples of both cases, go to our web site (http://www.writingforpsychology.com).

EXHIBIT **3.4** An Example of a Scattergram

Figure 4. Scattergram of grades in MATH 140 and average of the PSYC-311 tests. The line is the best-fitting regression line. Its equation is: Y = 23.59 + 1.63X; R^2 = .22.

ings, symbols, and lines that you are using. The legend should be contained within the borders of the graph (see the legend in Exhibit 3.2). If there is not enough room within the borders of the graph to write out all the necessary explanatory information, place the explanatory information in the figure caption instead (e.g., if, for Exhibit 3.2, we had been unable to fit "unfilled squares designate the 0° stimulus; filled squares designate the 90° stimulus" in the legend, we would put that information in the figure caption [the figure's heading]).

Figure caption. APA manuscript style requires that manuscript figure captions all appear together on a new page following the tables. This new page must have the centered label: Figure Captions. However, your professor may allow you to deviate from APA manuscript style and put each figure caption under its figure, as we have done in Exhibit 3.2.

Regardless of whether you put the caption under the figure or on a separate "Figure Captions" page, start the caption on the far left margin and treat the caption like an unindented paragraph. Realize that there are two parts to every figure caption.

The first part of the caption is the figure number ending with a period (e.g., "*Figure 1.*" Note that this first part is italicized.

The second part of the caption is the figure title. In the title, describe the figure in a brief sentence or phrase, capitalizing only the first letter. Note that the figure title is not italicized.

Right after this second part, some figure captions contain a third part. This third part consists of information that the reader needs to understand the figure, such as what the different lines, symbols, and abbreviations represent. Often, you will not need to include that information in your caption because that information is already presented in your legend. Sometimes, however, information vital to understanding your figure will not fit in the legend. For example, in Exhibit 3.2, because the explanation of the vertical lines would not fit in the legend, that explanation was added to the caption.

3.6.8 Units

You may not be comfortable with the metric system. However, both the American Psychological Association and the international scientific community use the metric system. Specifically, they conform to a set of metric system standards called the International System of Units (SI). Units of measurement in any part of your report should almost always be expressed using SI. If you originally took your measurements in non-SI units (e.g., inches), you can report those measurements in non-SI units—but you must also report the measurements in SI units (e.g., centimeters). To be more precise, you "must report the SI equivalents in parentheses immediately after the nonmetric units" (APA, 2001, p. 130). In the rare instances in which non-SI units of measurement are universally used (e. g., decibels), you can use the non-SI unit.

Regardless of whether you use an SI or non-SI unit, abbreviate the unit (to see how to abbreviate some common units, see Table 3.2). When abbreviating the units, omit periods from the abbreviation—unless you need the period to make it clear that you are abbreviating a unit rather than writing out a word. For example, if you did not put a period after "in," readers might think you were typing the preposition "in" rather than abbreviating "inches."

You may find that some SI units are too big or too small for your purposes. For example, suppose that you were trying to report the smallest bump that participants could reliably detect in an otherwise flat surface. Putting the size of this bump in meters (e.g., ".0005 m") would be awkward and hard to understand. Put the size of the bump in millimeters instead (e.g., .5 mm). Table 3.3 can help you find a unit that best allows you to express your measurements.

3.7 Discussion

The Discussion follows immediately after the Results and starts with the centered heading: Discussion. In the Discussion, you review your findings and show how they relate to the literature. The Discussion provides you with the opportunity to interpret, reinterpret, qualify, and explore the theoretical importance of your results. If your Discussion makes up less than one fourth of the body of your paper, be concerned: You may not have thought enough about your results. However, do not ramble on merely to lengthen this section: Ultimately, your discussion section will not be judged on how long it is but on how well organized and on how meaningful it is. Remember that you have taken your reader on a journey though the Introduction, Method, and Results. In the Discussion, you should convince your reader that the journey was worthwhile because you have arrived somewhere interesting.

TABLE **3.2**   Some Common SI and Non-SI Units and Their Abbreviations[6]

Quantity	Unit	Abbreviation	SI Unit
Acceleration	meter per second squared	m/s^2	same
Angle	radian	rad	same
Area	square meter	m^2	same
Concentration	molecules per cubic meter	mol/m^3	same
Density	kilogram per cubic meter	kg/m^3	same
Electric current	ampere	A	same
Electric potential	volt	V	same
Electric resistance	ohm	Ω	same
Force	newton	N	same
Frequency	hertz	Hz	same
Length	meter	m	same
Luminance	candela per square meter	cd/m^2	same
Mass	kilogram	kg	same
Power	watt	W	same
Pressure	pascal	Pa	same
Sound pressure level	decibel	dB	N/m^2
Temperature	degree Celsius	°C	°Kelvin
Time	second	s	same
Velocity	meter per second	m/s	same
Visual angle	degree	°	radian
Volume	cubic meter	m^3	same
Weight	see Mass		

TABLE **3.3**   Common SI Prefixes

Factor	1 ×	Prefix	Symbol	Example	
billion times	10^9	giga	G	Gb	gigabyte
million times	10^6	mega	M	MV	megavolt
thousand times	10^3	kilo	k	kHz	kilohertz
one tenth	10^{-1}	deci	d	dB	decibel
one hundredth	10^{-2}	centi	c	cm	centimeter
one thousandth	10^{-3}	milli	m	mA	milliamp
one millionth	10^{-6}	micro	μ	μs	micrometer
one billionth	10^{-9}	nano	n	nm	nanometer

---

[6]If you need help making these abbreviations in your word processor, see our web site (http://www.writingforpsychology.com).

3.7.1 Briefly Restate the Results

In the first lines of the Discussion, let the reader know whether your results are consistent with your original hypothesis. Briefly inform the reader whether the obtained results are (a) statistically significant and consistent with your hypothesis, (b) statistically significant but inconsistent with your hypothesis, or (c) not statistically significant.

To keep your description of the results brief, (a) leave out means, probability values, and other numbers, and (b) focus solely on whether the results support the hypothesis. However, do not be so brief that you fail to remind the reader what it was you set out to test. Do not make a vague statement like, "The results of this study confirm the hypothesis." Instead, say something specific like

```
As predicted, students who rated the likeability of a
person described by a list of adjectives are favorably
impressed by a positive adjective that comes first in the
list.
```

After relating the results to the hypothesis, you should relate the results to the work of other researchers. If other researchers have found similar results, explain how your work supports and extends their findings. If other researchers obtained different results, explain why your findings are different from theirs.

3.7.2 State Qualifications and Reservations

If the results of your study were significant, at least three major questions arise (see 5.9). First, can the results be generalized to a broader population? For example, if your results were based on a sample of students, those results might not generalize to all adults. Second, are the methods you used to measure and manipulate variables valid? For example, if you timed your participants with a stopwatch to induce stress, is this time pressure a valid manipulation of stress? Third, can you legitimately make a cause-effect statement from your results? You probably cannot if there are any other variables that vary along with the manipulated variables (see 5.9.1).

Although you should mention limits on the generalizability and validity of your results, try to be positive. Otherwise, your readers (including the professor grading your report) will feel that they have been taken for a ride rather than taken on a useful journey. Therefore, instead of downplaying your research because you studied only students, for example, you could suggest that students are more suspicious of psychological testing than other people, so any effect that students show is likely to be even stronger in other people. Similarly, rather than deriding your study because you used a weak stressor, you could say that the effects of stress on performance must be quite strong if a weak stressor managed to produce a significant effect.

You should mention any defects in the method or design of the study (e.g., some participants did not follow instructions, the measuring device was difficult to use, the apparatus was unreliable). Do not dwell on these defects, however, unless they were systematic. If the defects were unsystematic, they reduced the chances of obtaining significant results. Consequently, the fact that you obtained significant results in spite of these unsystematic defects is a tribute to the strength of the hypothesis.

If the method or design defects were systematic (e.g., only participants in the experimental group misinterpreted the instructions, the difficulty in using the measuring device led to more errors in one condition than in the others, the apparatus was unreliable for only one of the conditions), then you should admit that those errors were systematic and make it impossible for you to come to a firm conclusion about the effect of your treatment. For example, if you found that students using mnemonic techniques (your manipulated variable) recalled more words (your measured variable) than students who did not use such techniques, yet you tested the mnemonic group in a quiet room and the control group in a noisy room, then you should admit that your experiment is flawed. Point out that the mnemonic technique may not have increased learning in the experimental group; instead, the noise may have decreased learning in the control group. In short, if there are alternative explanations for your results, you should tell the reader about these alternative explanations.

If your results were not significant, there are going to be a variety of possible explanations for your results. Spend part of your Discussion considering why you obtained nonsignificant results. You can guard against making the reader feel that your study has been a dead end if you write about the validity and potency of your manipulations and measures and how they could be improved in future studies.

3.7.3 State the Theoretical Importance

Once you have satisfied the reader that your results should be taken seriously, you can go on to discuss the implications your results have for theory. When discussing these implications, some speculation is allowed. However, such speculation should be (a) closely related to your results, rather than wild speculation; (b) brief, rather than long-winded; and (c) clearly indicated as speculation, rather than being pawned off as fact.

3.7.4 Conclude

Sometimes, your last paragraph will be a brief mention of the practical implications of your results or some suggestions for future research. You should always end by stating a conclusion that will make readers believe that your report has important implications for theory, research, or practice. The following are examples of how you might begin your concluding paragraph:

- The present findings suggest a _____ explanation for _____.
- The present findings lend new support for a _____ explanation of_____.
- The present findings go beyond previous explanations of _____.
- The effects reported in this article have two important practical implications.
- Practitioners should be aware of (these findings) when they _____.
- There are two important findings from this study.
- Results from the current study suggest several promising directions for future research.

- The results raise serious questions about _____ (explanation/theory).
- This study is an important step in understanding_____.
- The results presented here should lead psychologists to take a serious look at _____ and its potential impact on_____.
- Future research should (be like my study, but make the following changes).

The conclusion can be longer than a paragraph. In journal articles, the conclusion is often several paragraphs long and labeled with a subheading titled "Conclusions." If you are writing a long report, you will probably have more than a one-paragraph conclusion. However, if your report is as short as the typical student research report, you can probably conclude with a single paragraph.

3.8 References

Every journal article you cite in your paper should appear in the Reference section. The citations should be in alphabetical order according to the last name of the work's primary author. The Reference section should start on a new page with the centered heading: References. The format is demonstrated in both the Reference section of the sample term paper (2.11) and the sample research report (3.12). The rules for the Reference page are set out in 4.9, and a checklist for the Reference section is provided in 4.10.4.

3.9 Appendixes

In published articles, appendixes are rare. When an appendix appears in a published article, the appendix is used to present important material, such as unpublished test materials and details of especially constructed equipment that, if presented in the paper's method section, would interrupt the paper's flow. In student reports, on the other hand, appendixes are much more common. Students are often required to prepare appendixes that contain exhibits documenting what either the students or the participants did: raw data, stimulus materials, questionnaires, consent forms, data summary sheets, and statistical calculations. Raw data should be presented in a table, using the same directions as for tables in the text (see 3.6.5). The only difference is that, rather than being labeled with a number (e.g., "Table 1"), each data table will be labeled with a capital letter (e. g., "A" if the table is in Appendix A, "B" if it is in Appendix B), followed by a hyphen, followed by a number (e.g., "Table A-1" for the first table in Appendix A, "Table A-2" for the second table in Appendix A).

Your appendix will begin on a new page after the references. If you have only one appendix, it will have the centered heading "Appendix." If you have more than one, the heading for the first one will be "Appendix A"; the heading for the second one will be "Appendix B." Unless your professor states otherwise, appendixes must be referred to in the Body of your paper. For example, suppose you had appendixes that contained (a) data about your three participants' vision from their eye doctors, (b) your three participants' scores on the task ("raw data") that you later analyzed, and (c) analysis of variance summaries on four measured variables. You would need to refer to all three appendixes. You might refer to them as follows:

> The participants were three men with normal visual acuity and stereoacuity. Details of their optometric characteristics are presented in Appendix A.
>
> Results
>
> Raw data for the three participants are presented in Tables B-1, B-2, and B-3 . . . Analysis of variance summary tables for reaction times to hits, misses, false alarms, and correct rejections are shown in Tables C1-C4 respectively. Consistent with the hypothesis . . .

3.10 Author Note

If your professor wants an Author Note (a note that contains your name and affiliation, acknowledgments, and information about how to contact you), start the Author Note on the page following the appendixes (if you do not have appendixes, start the Author Note on the page following the references) using the centered heading: Author Note. For your paper, the most important aspects of the Author Note are disclosures about (a) who, if anyone, helped you on the paper and (b) what part, if any, of the paper has been used in another class. To write an Author Note, follow the example in the sample paper (3.12).

3.11 Tense

If you are writing a report on a study you performed, most of your report involves describing what you did or reporting on what others did. Therefore, for most of the report, use the past tense. Use the present tense only when you are (a) referring to an existing, permanent condition, (b) referring to conclusions, or (c) referring to other parts of your report (e.g., a figure).

- ■ Jones (1994) *found* [past tense] . . .
- ■ Smith (1990) *argued* that attribution *is* [present tense for a situation that exists and will continue to exist] internal . . .
- ■ As can be seen in Figure 3 [present tense for part of a report], the means *differ* [present tense for an existing and continuing condition] . . .
- ■ In conclusion, X *appears* [present tense for conclusion] to affect Y.

If you are writing a proposal, you are proposing what you will do, so you will use the future tense much more than in a report. For example, whereas the Method section of your report will be in the past tense (e.g., "Participants read a list of 10 traits."), the Method section of your proposal will be in the future tense (e. g., "Participants will read a list of 10 traits."). For more information about tense, see 6.1.3.

3.12 Sample Research Report

Imagine that you are sitting quietly in class one day, waiting for the lecture to begin. However, instead of announcing the day's lecture topic, the professor announces that the day will be devoted to conducting an experiment. Then, your professor asks you to take out pens and paper. The professor tells you that a list of 12 digits will be read aloud, and after 30 seconds, you are to write down as many as you can remember in order. After that is done, the instructor repeats the procedure with a list of 12 letters. The professor then hands out the lists and asks you to count how many entries you matched on each list. Next, the numbers of digits and letters that each student recalled are collated and a statistical test is performed. Finally, the instructor tells the class that a report, in APA style, on the experiment just conducted is worth 20% of the course grade and is due in a week.

At first, such a writing assignment might seem overwhelming. Eventually, however, you might come up with something resembling the following report. Your report should differ from our report in only two significant respects. First, we have annotated our report with footnotes so you can appreciate particular points about the example report. In your own reports, do not use footnotes. Second, we have used only old references. In your own reports, cite current research.

Running[1] head: DIGITS VS. LETTERS IN SERIAL RECALL[2]

Memory for Digits and Letters in a Serial Recall Task[3]

Ann A. Student[4]

Alpha University

---

[1]Ann is using APA manuscript format. If your instructor wants you to use published format, see Appendix A. If your instructor asks you to also add a cover sheet, do what your professor asks.

[2]Ann was able to verify that her running head was short enough (had fewer than 51 characters, including spacing) by using the "Word count" feature of her word-processing software.

[3]The first three words of the title became the short title. Also, note that, for the title, if a word has fewer than four letters and is (a) a preposition (e.g., "of" and "in"), (b) an article (e.g., "a"), or (c) a conjunction (e.g., "and"), then that word is not capitalized.

[4]Include your middle initial. Do not include the word "by."

Abstract[5]

[6]The experimenter read a 12-digit list and then a 12-letter list to a class of 72 students (50 women and 22 men, mean age = 20.4 years) to test the hypothesis that letters are more easily recalled than digits. The results did not support the hypothesis: Letters were not recalled significantly more than digits, $t(71)= -1.21$, $p = .60$.[7] Either letter stimuli have no memory advantage, or design problems in the experiment obscured the effect.[8]

---

[5]The Abstract starts on page 2 and is announced by the centered heading "Abstract."

[6]The Abstract, unlike every other paragraph in your paper, is not indented.

[7]Everything is double-spaced (7.1).

[8]In only 67 words, Ann has stated her hypothesis, described her method, described her participants, described her findings (including significance levels), and described her conclusions.

Memory for Digits and Letters in a Serial Recall Task[9]

Ebbinghaus (1855/1913,[10] cited in Woodworth & Schlossberg, 1954)[11] considered memory[12] to consist of the formation of associations between stimuli. In attempting to test the capacity of memory, researchers should therefore control prior associations between stimuli.[13]

Ebbinghaus controlled for prior associations by inventing nonsense syllables and discarding any that reminded him of real words, were well-known initials, or had any emotional tone. When Ebbinghaus memorized a list of nonsense syllables, he seemed to be tapping pure memory, uncontaminated by any prior associations. However, prior associations may contaminate current memory tests.[14, 15]

One current memory test[16] is rote memory for digits. Rote memory for digits is sometimes treated as a test of pure memory and is incorporated into IQ tests (Wechsler, 1939). The usual method is to present a few digits on the first trial and then to increase the number until learners reach their limit and cannot repeat all of the digits (Woodworth & Schlossburg, 1954).[17]

Rote memory for words or letters is less commonly tested. The reasons for not using such stimuli follow from the work of Hilgard and Bower (1966), who established that (a) individuals have prior associations to words and letters and that (b) one individual may have a stronger prior association to a particular word or letter than another individual. The problem of individuals having prior associations to word and letter stimuli cannot be solved by using nonsense syllables. Glaze (1928)[18]

---

[9]The introduction begins on a new page. Its "heading" is the paper's title.

[10]1855 is when Ebbinghaus published the work; 1913 refers to when the English translation (which Woodworth & Schlossberg consulted) was published.

[11]Note the use of a secondary citation. Ann will not put Ebbinghaus in her reference list because she did not read Ebbinghaus's work.

[12]The first sentence introduces the general area of investigation (3.4.1).

[13]This sentence sets up the next paragraph.

[14]The first two paragraphs briefly set the theoretical scene (3.4.1).

[15]The last sentence of this paragraph introduces the next paragraph.

[16]Repeating a phrase from the previous paragraph helps the reader make a connection to the previous paragraph.

[17]Note that "&" instead of "and" is used to join authors' names inside parentheses.

[18]Whenever possible, you should use recent citations. This paper's sources would have been recent enough about 40 years ago.

found[19] that using nonsense syllables did not entirely eliminate prior associations and thus associative value.[20]

   Even though the associative strength of letter stimuli is weaker for some individuals than for others, the average associative strength of letter stimuli should be stronger than the average associative strength of digits. Letters can be formed into words, rich with associative strength, whereas[21] digits can be formed only into numbers, poor in associative strength.[22] Consequently, if no other variable is operating to favor the retention of digits,[23] people should have better recall for letters than for digits. Therefore, I[24] predicted that when a set of digits and a set of letters are presented to a group of learners for rote memorization, the learners will[25] remember more letters than digits.[26]

Method[27]

Participants[28]

   Seventy-two[29] members of an introductory psychology class (50 women and 22 men,[30] mean age = 20.4 years[31] *SD* = 2.1)

---

[19]Ann used the past tense because Glaze's study was performed in the past and it can be tied to a specific date (1928). In most of your paper, you will use the past tense.

[20]This paragraph and the previous one provide a brief review of the relevant literature.

[21]Ann wisely used "whereas" instead of "while" so that readers would know she meant "but" rather than "during."

[22]Ann used parallel structure to help the reader note and remember the difference between the rich associative strength of words and the poor associative strength of numbers.

[23]Admit flaws in your argument, questionable assumptions you are making, and qualifications to your argument before your readers think they have discovered a problem that you overlooked.

[24]The use of "I" is proper. The experiment did not make the prediction. "We" did not make the prediction. Ann made the prediction—and said so.

[25]One of the few times to use the future tense in a research report is when stating your prediction about what will happen. Note, however, that because Ann made the prediction in the past, Ann wrote, "I predicted."

[26]The last paragraph of the Introduction develops the logic of the study and ends by stating the hypothesis (3.4.2).

[27]Note that the Method section does not start on a new page. Note also that the heading is centered.

[28]When studying humans, use the term "participants" to acknowledge participation rather than the term "subjects." Note that major sections, such as Method, Results, and Discussion, are headed with centered headings. Subdivisions within these sections are indicated by italicized headings that start on the left margin. The text they head begins on a new line as a paragraph.

[29]The general rule is that numbers 10 and above are not spelled out, but are instead expressed in digits. However, one exception to the general rule is that all numbers starting a sentence are spelled out rather than expressed in numerals.

[30]Do not use the term "females." Furthermore, do not use one term (e.g., "girls") to describe female participants while using a non-equivalent term (e.g., "men") to describe male participants (1.3.4).

[31]According to the *Publication Manual*, you must be specific about the age of your participants.

participated voluntarily as part of a class exercise. All participants were treated in accordance with the "Ethical Principles of Psychologists and Code of Conduct" (American Psychological Association, 2002).[32]

[33]*Materials*

The list of letters was[34] *G, U, X, K, P, M, B, T, C, S, L, F.* The list of digits was 3, 5, 9, 4, 1, 0, 5, 3, 6, 2, 5, 0.[35] Both lists were selected to exclude any meaningful combinations.[36]

Procedure

The experimenter read out the set of 12 digits at 1 digit per s. After another 30 s,[37] the class was asked to write down as many as they could remember, in order. The set of 12 letters was then read out and treated in a similar manner.[38] Finally, learners scored their own lists, giving themselves one point for each item that they had recalled in the correct position. They summed the number correct for each list to get a total for each list.[39]

Thus, the design was within-subjects with two levels (letters vs. digits). The dependent measure was how many items were correctly remembered from each list.[40]

---

[32]According to the *Publication Manual*, you must state that participants were treated ethically.

[33]If the experiment had used any specialized equipment (not standard laboratory equipment such as stopwatches), Ann might have added an Apparatus section. The Apparatus section, like the Materials section, would probably have come before the Procedure section.

[34]Note that "list" is the subject of the sentence. It is singular and requires a singular verb. Therefore, Ann wrote that the list "was" rather than that the list "were." In other words, "of letters" is a prepositional phrase, not the subject of the sentence.

[35]If including the materials had taken up much more space, Ann would have probably put them in an appendix.

[36]Always mention any steps you took to improve the validity of your study. These steps not only boost your credibility, but also help others replicate your study.

[37]Abbreviate standard units and do not put a period after the abbreviation (3.6.8).

[38]Note that the Procedure section is organized around time—what happened first, what happened second, etc.

[39]Ann needed to provide this information so that (a) readers could understand how Ann obtained the scores that were entered into the analysis, (b) other researchers could replicate the study, and (c) readers could evaluate the possibility that the results would have been different if someone other than the learner had scored the recall. Sometimes, an author will put this information in a separate section called "Data scoring."

[40]The last two sentences could have been put in a separate Design section or could have been put into the Participants section.

Results

The number of items correctly remembered from each list was analyzed using a within-subjects t test and an alpha level of .05.[41] The hypothesis was not supported: Participants did not recall letters ($M = 6.22$, $SD = 7.92$) significantly better than digits ($M = 6.44$, $SD = 8.04$),[42] $t(71) = -1.21$.[43, 44]

Discussion

The results failed to confirm the hypothesis that letters would be easier to remember than digits.[45, 46] There are at least four explanations for the failure to confirm the hypothesis.

First, perhaps the hypothesis that letters are better recalled than digits is wrong. Letters may not be better recalled than digits because any associative advantages letter stimuli might enjoy are offset by other advantages of digit stimuli. For example, digits may be easier to recall because (a) there are fewer digits than letters (10 as opposed to 26) and (b) digits are more commonly used in isolation than letters.

Second, although letters, as a rule, have more associative strength than digits, perhaps this general rule might not have held for the carefully selected list used in this experiment. It seems likely that a set of letters such

---

[41]State the significance (alpha) level of your statistical test(s) (see 3.6.1).

[42]Note the use of summary statistics describing the typical score (usually using means) and the spread of the distribution (often using standard deviations). These descriptive statistics are included to (a) help the reader understand the pattern of the results and to (b) help investigators who might want to include your study in their meta-analysis of related studies.

[43]Confine your evaluation of the results to a statistical evaluation; do not discuss methodological problems that may account for the results. Such discussions belong in the Discussion.

[44]There is no need for either a table or figure of these results because Ann has only two means to discuss. With such simple results, the reader does not need a table or figure to understand the results (3.6.3). However, your professor may still require you to make a table or figure to give you practice in making tables or graphs.

[45]The first sentence summarizes the results (3.7.1).

[46]Note that participants actually recalled more digits than letters. However, because the difference was not significant, Ann wisely does not discuss the difference as though it were significant (3.6.1).

as *U N I V X Y Z B S* would be relatively easy for some people to remember. Future research should take into account a wider range of possible association values in the letters (cf. Glaze, 1928).[47]

Third, even if most people show a memory advantage for letters over numbers, this advantage might not have held for the particular participants in this study. University students may be more experienced than the general population at remembering numbers.[48]

Fourth, procedural problems in this study could have obscured the advantage of memory for letters. For example, the experimenter always presented letters second. Consequently, participants could have experienced fatigue that reduced their recall for letters (see Woodworth & Schlosberg, 1954, for a review of fatigue effects). In addition, the sample size of 72 may have been insufficient to detect the superior recall for letters, especially if the effect is small.[49, 50]

The question about the advantage of letter stimuli in memory is still open. Further research could use larger and more varied samples of both learners and of stimuli. It could also balance order of presentation of letter and digit stimuli. This experiment, however, suggests that any effect of letters being better recalled than digits is not extremely robust.[51]

---

[47]"cf." is an abbreviation for "compare." The abbreviation is used because the comment is inside parentheses (7.2.5).

[48]Point out weaknesses and limitations of your study.

[49]Usually, numbers above 10 are expressed using digits.

[50]With nonsignificant results, power should be discussed. However, Ann did not have the statistical background to present detailed information about power.

[51]Note use of present tense for conclusions (3.11).

References[52]

[53]American Psychological Association.[54] (2002). Ethical principles of psychologists and code of conduct. *American Psychologist,*[55] *57,*[56] 1060-1073.

Glaze, J. A. (1928). The association value of nonsense syllables.[57] *Journal of Genetic Psychology, 35,* 225-269.

[58]Hilgard, E.,[59] & Bower, G. H. (1966). *Theories of learning.* New York: Appleton-Century-Crofts.

Wechsler, D. (1939). *The measurement of adult intelligence.* [60]Baltimore: Williams & Wilkins.

Woodworth, R. S., & Schlossberg, H. (1954). *Experimental psychology* (rev. ed.).[61] London: Methuen.[62]

---

[52]Start the reference list on a new page (4.9.1) and center the heading ("References").

[53]In the Reference section, the indenting style is the opposite of the indenting for the rest of your paper. Specifically, APA advocates "hanging indent style" in which the first line of a reference is not indented, but additional lines are indented five spaces. To see how to program your word-processor to make hanging indents, see our web site.

[54]This is an example of a case where the author is an organization.

[55]All major words in a journal name are capitalized; the entire journal name is italicized.

[56]Volume number and journal title are italicized.

[57]Usually, only the first letter of the first word of the title of an article is capitalized. The article title is not italicized.

[58]References are listed on the page in alphabetical order according to the last name of the first author. Thus, this reference comes after, rather than before, Glaze.

[59]Always use a comma between authors' names—even when you have only two authors.

[60]Usually, only the first letter of the first word of a book title is capitalized. However, the entire title is always italicized.

[61]The title of the book is italicized, but not the information in parentheses informing the reader that it is a revised edition.

[62]The reference list for this paper is weak: The references are out of date and only one is a journal article reporting on an empirical study.

Author Note[63]

Ann A. Student, an undergraduate student at Alpha University.[64]

I thank[65] M. I. Tuder for guiding my thinking on this topic and I. M. Goode for commenting on previous drafts.

Correspondence concerning this article should be addressed to I. B. Professor, Department of Psychology, Alpha University, Alpha, CA 97804. E-mail: myprof@alpha.edu.

---

[63]The author note will usually be the last page of your paper.

[64]We realize that this is not a sentence. It is, however, in the form prescribed by the *Publication Manual*.

[65]Thank anyone who gives you general or editorial help (1.2.4).

3.13   Report and Proposal Content Checklist

___ My title is simple and to the point. It contains the names of the relevant variables (in an experiment, the independent and dependent variables; in a correlational study, the predictor and criterion variables).

___ My Abstract is a brief summary of the following sections of my paper:
  ___ the Introduction—what I studied and why,
  ___ the Participants section—who the participants were,
  ___ the Procedure section—what the participants did,
  ___ the Results section—whether the data supported the hypothesis, and
  ___ the Discussion section—the meaning of the results.

___ I cited any source from which I got ideas—even if I did not directly quote that source.

___ My citations are free of common content errors.
  ___ When citing authors, I limited myself to stating authors' last names. I did not mention authors' first names, professional titles (e.g., "Dr."), or professional affiliations.
  ___ When citing sources, I used parentheses. I did not use footnotes to cite sources.
  ___ I did not mention any article titles in the text of my paper.

___ Most of my citations are from recent journal articles describing actual research studies rather than from secondhand sources (textbooks, magazines, etc.).

Introduction

___ The beginning of my introduction illustrates why my topic area is important.

___ I explained why testing my hypothesis is important: I showed how my study builds on previous work or fills a gap in previous work.

___ I explained why I believe that the hypothesis might be true. To make the logic behind my hypothesis clear, I explained relevant concepts and theories.

___ My hypothesis is clearly stated.

___ My Introduction foreshadows the rest of the paper (especially the essence of the Method section).

Method Section

___ I divided the Method section into at least two subsections (Participants and Procedure).

___ I have been specific about
    ___ how I selected or recruited my sample.
    ___ how participants were compensated (if they were compensated).
    ___ major demographic characteristics
        ___ number of participants of each gender,
        ___ age of participants (average age and either standard deviation or range of ages), and
        ___ other demographic characteristics, if appropriate.
    ___ the number of participants who dropped out of the study or whose data was not analyzed and the reasons for not having data from all my participants.
    ___ how participants were assigned to condition.

___ I made it clear that participants were treated ethically.

___ If I used standard laboratory equipment, I identified the manufacturer and model number.

___ I focused on what happened to participants and what participants did— and presented the information in order from the first thing that happened to the last thing that happened.

___ Someone reading my report could replicate (repeat) my study.
    ___ It is clear how (under what conditions) I tested each participant.
    ___ It is clear how I turned each participant's response into a score.

___ I made a case for the study's validity.
    ___ It is clear what I did to reduce researcher bias.
    ___ It is clear how a control or comparison group ruled out an alternative explanation for a difference between groups.
    ___ It is clear that the measure being used is reliable and valid.
        ___ If I used a published measure, I cited evidence of the measure's reliability and validity.
        ___ If I collected data related to the measure's reliability or validity, I reported those data. For example, if I had data related to the extent to which two different observers' scores agreed when scoring the same response, I reported those data.
    ___ It is clear from my paper that my study is a good way to test my hypothesis.

Results

___ I included enough information about descriptive statistics to help readers know more than just the outcome of the statistical significance test. For example, if I used a t test, I presented means and standard deviations for the two conditions.

___ I determined my professor's views about reporting analyses beyond that of significance tests. Thus, I know whether my professor required me to follow the *Publication Manual*'s suggestions that I

   ___ include a confidence interval, or

   ___ report an estimate of effect size, such as Cohen's *d* (e.g., "$F(2,46) = 3.85, p < .05, d = .27$")

___ I made it clear to the reader

   ___ what data I used in the analyses (how behaviors were turned into scores), if it was not obvious or if I did not include this information in the Method section;

   ___ what analyses I used on those data;

   ___ what significance level I used (if I used a significance test);

   ___ why I did that analysis;

   ___ which groups scored significantly higher (I usually did this by including, in the text, average scores for my different groups. The summary statistics I included in text (averages) were usually sufficient to help the reader see the pattern in my data. However, I used a table or a graph if (a) I had more than four conditions, or (b) my professor required one.); and

   ___ whether the results support my hypothesis.

___ If I used tables, I made sure that

   ___ each table added meaningful information beyond that which was presented in the text of my Results section.

   ___ each table was referred to in the text of my paper (e.g., "As Table 1 indicates,").

Discussion

___ My first sentence summarizes the results as they relate to my hypothesis.

___ I compared my Discussion against the citation checklist.

___ I interpreted my results in the context of the theory, past research, and practical issues that I noted in my Introduction. For example, I compared my results to what other researchers found.

___ I tried to explain results that were not predicted.

___ I addressed alternative explanations for my results. I tried to rule out these alternative explanations, but when I could not, I admitted that I could not.

___ I pointed out the weaknesses and limitations of my study. I even sketched out future research that could be done to correct these weaknesses or overcome these limitations.

___ If I believed I could make a case for generalizing my results (I had a representative sample, the results were similar to what others had found, etc.), I made such a case.

___ I treated nonsignificant results as inconclusive.

___ I did not use nonsignificant results as proof that a treatment had no effect.

___ I did not use nonsignificant results that were almost significant as evidence that the treatment had an effect.

References

___ All the references in this section are also cited in my paper. If a reference was not cited, I either added that citation to the Body of my paper or I deleted the reference.

___ All the sources cited in my paper are also listed in this section except for
___ "personal communication" citations (see 4.3.3),
___ original works that I did not read, but which I learned about through a secondary source (see 4.3.2), and
___ classical works, such as the Bible

3.14 Summary

1. A research report or proposal can be broken down into nine main sections. The nine sections should appear in this order: Title, Abstract, Introduction, Method, Results, Discussion, References, Appendixes (optional), and Author Note.

2. The title should be short. For an experiment, it should usually include the independent variable(s) and the dependent variable.

3. The Abstract is a short, unindented paragraph that summarizes the paper.

4. In the Introduction (the "why section" of the paper), you should introduce and state the hypothesis.

5. The Method section (the "how section" of the paper) usually has at least two subsections: a "Participants" section (called a "Subjects" section if you studied nonhuman animals), and a "Procedure" section.

6. In the Results section, for each analysis, tell the reader what the analysis was, why you did it, and whether the results of that analysis support your hypothesis.

7. You may be able to present your results without a figure or a table. If you have a table or a figure, refer to it in text.

8. Line graphs are usually best when you are summarizing the results of an experiment in which you manipulated the amount of a variable. Bar graphs are usually best when you are summarizing the results of an experiment and the manipulated variable is non-numerical (you are manipulating kinds of treatments rather than amounts of a treatment) or if you are comparing a treatment group with a control group. Scattergrams are often most appropriate when your study did not involve manipulating a variable (e.g., you correlated scores on two tests).

9. Usually, units of measurement in any part of your report must be expressed in metric units.

10. Begin the Discussion by relating the results to the hypothesis. Next, relate your results to previous research. Then, discuss limitations of your study that may qualify your conclusions. Finally, discuss the implications of your study for future research.

11. All the sources in your reference list should be cited in your paper. To see an example of how to format your references, see either the term paper's references (2.11) or the sample research report's references (3.12). To learn more about formatting your reference page, see 4.9.

12. If your professor wants an Author Note, start the Author Note on the page following the appendixes using the centered heading: Author Note. (If you do not have appendixes, start the Author Note on the page following the references.)

C H A P T E R

4

Finding, Reading, Citing, and Referencing Sources

Sources are the raw material from which you build your paper. Professors expect that you will find, extract, and refine that raw material. Unfortunately, many students lose at least one letter grade on their papers because they do not live up to their professors' expectations about reading, citing, and referencing. Some students are penalized for failing to find enough high-quality sources. Even more students lose points for not showing that they have thought about what they read. Still more students lose points for incorrectly citing and referencing sources. In addition to the many who lose points for improper citing, a few lose much more: They are expelled for plagiarism. In this chapter, we will show you how to avoid problems in reading, citing, and referencing.

4.1 Finding Information

4.1.1 Starting Your Search

Your professor will expect you to read current journal articles related to your paper's topic. There are two strategies you can use to find current articles.

The first strategy is to use a database designed to help researchers find recent articles on a topic. Commonly used databases are *Psychological Abstracts, PsycINFO, Social Science Index, Current Contents, Educational Resources Information Center (ERIC)*, and *Social Science Citation Index*. The key to using these systems is to know what search terms you should use. You can find the right search terms by using the *Psychological Thesaurus*.

Many of these databases come in either a printed version (e.g., *Psychological Abstracts*) or a computerized version (e.g., *PsycINFO*). If you have the choice, try to use the computerized version. The computerized databases can get you information faster. For example, if you are using the computerized version of *Psychological Abstracts (PsycINFO)* and want to look up a term in the *Thesaurus*, you just click on that term and press the "F9" key. If you are not using the computerized version, you need to find your library's copy of the *Thesaurus* (it will usually be near the *Abstracts*) and then look up the term. The biggest advantage of computer searches, however, is when you want to search for more than one term at a time. For example, on a computer, you can find—in less than a minute—all the review papers on recovered memory of sexual abuse among males that were published in APA journals between 1993 and 2003.

Four problems sometimes crop up in computerized searches. First, you may actually get too many references. In that case, see Table 4.1.

Second, you may have too few references. If that is the case, see Table 4.2. If, after consulting Table 4.2, you still have too few references, consult a reference librarian.

Third, your library will probably not have all the references you have found. Fortunately, you can probably obtain most of those articles through interlibrary loan. Unfortunately, interlibrary loan takes time—so if you put off your library search you may be in trouble: Searches delayed are often searches denied.

Fourth, you may be tempted to read the abstracts of articles you cite rather than the articles themselves. Although reading abstracts can help you separate out the articles that are relevant to your paper from the articles that are irrelevant, you will not get enough detail from the abstract to allow you to analyze the article. You will learn far more if you read the papers themselves. Therefore, when the on-line abstract of an article suggests that the article is relevant to your paper, take the time to find and read the entire article.

In addition to using databases, there is a second strategy for finding journal articles—consulting secondhand sources. As we will discuss in the next section, consulting a textbook, a chapter in the *Annual Review of Psychology*, or a review article in the *American Psychologist* might provide you with a lead to a relevant article.

T A B L E **4.1**   What to Do If a *PsycINFO* Search Produces Too Many Sources[1]

Use an "and" search rather than an "or" search to limit your search to articles that include all your search terms.

Use the language (LA) field to limit your search to articles that are in English (e.g., "and LA = English").

Use the publication year (PY) field to limit your search to works that have been published recently (e.g., "and PY > 2002").

Use the journal (JN) field to limit your search to certain journals, such as journals your library has, or journals your professor recommends (e.g., "and JN = *Journal of Personality and Social Psychology*").

Use the title (TI) field and the "NOT" command to eliminate articles that are clearly not what you want. For example, if you were interested in human memory, but were getting many articles that had "computer memory" in the title, you could add "and not computer in TI" to your search criteria.

Use the descriptor (DE) field together with the "NOT" command to limit your search to empirical articles. That is, you can avoid getting review articles by adding "and NOT review in DE" to your search criteria.

Use the population (PO) and age (AG) fields to limit your search to studies that examined the participant population that is most relevant to your purposes. If you wanted studies done only on humans, you would put "and PO = human." If you wanted studies done only on adult humans, you would add "and AG = Adult."

Use the thesaurus to find a narrower search term. In the *Thesaurus* entry for your term, the narrower term will be to the right of a capital "N"("N" stands for "narrow").

[1]Most of this advice is also relevant for computer searches in *ERIC* and other databases.

4.1.2 Using One Reference to Find More References

Once you find one relevant article, you can use that article to find other relevant articles. Imagine that you have only found one reference for your assignment: Researcher (2003). When you read Researcher's paper, you may discover that the topic was first identified by Originator (1986), that much of the important work was conducted by Refiner (1999), and that some current work is also being done by Current (in press). You can find these sources from Researcher's reference list. Originator (1986), Refiner (2003), and Current (in press) may have other useful sources in their reference lists.

Although looking at reference lists can educate you about the history of the topic, it will not get you the recent references you need. Fortunately, there are three ways that an older reference can lead to newer references.

First, you may be able to use the older article to make your electronic search more productive. If your electronic search has been unproductive, you may not have the right search terms. To obtain more appropriate search terms, do a title search ("[the

TABLE **4.2**   What to Do If a PsycINFO Search Retrieves an Insufficient Number of Sources[2]

Go back to the *Thesaurus* and be sure you have the right search term. Double-check that you have spelled the term correctly.

Replace the last few letters of your search term with an asterisk (*). Thus, your search for "adolescen* in AB" would find Abstracts that contained the words "adolescent," "adolescents," and "adolescence."

If you have the right search term, consider using a broader term. In the *Thesaurus* entry for your term, the broader term would be to the right of a capital "B" (the "B" stands for broader term).

Realize that you can search for your keywords in the following fields:

TI: title of the article,
AB: abstract of the article,
DE: descriptor field (the key terms that, according to the person indexing the article, relate to the article), and
KP: key phrases.
If you did not find enough articles when you searched one field, you may want to search in another field.

Do a search looking for your key terms in the Abstracts of articles (e.g., look for "deception in AB").

Do a search for key terms in the descriptor (DE) field and key phrases in the key phrases (KP) field. One way to find relevant key terms and key phrases is from a promising entry you already found. If you find an entry that contains a promising Abstract, search the rest of the entry for the DE and KP fields. The key terms and phrases used to describe your promising article may also have been used to describe related articles. Therefore, use the key terms and phrases you found to conduct new "DE" and "KP" searches.

Do an "OR" search rather than an "AND" search. A search for "adolescents" AND "drugs" in DE would turn up only articles that included both of those terms in the descriptor field. A search for "adolescents" OR "drugs," on the other hand, would include articles that had either of those terms in the descriptor field.

If you are using a CD-ROM, make sure that you are using the one that covers the years you are trying to search.

[2]Most of this advice is also relevant for computer searches in *ERIC* and other databases.

older article's name] in TI") to retrieve the entry (often called a "record") for the older article. That entry will tell you what search terms would retrieve the older article. For example, in the descriptor ("DE") field, it will list the descriptors used in indexing the older article and, in the key phrases ("KP") field, it will list the key phrases used in indexing the older article. Articles similar to your older article should be indexed by these same descriptors and key phrases. Therefore, you should do a search using these descriptors and key phrases (e.g., "[descriptor used to describe original article] in DE" or "[key phrase used to describe original article] in KP").

Second, you can search for more recent work by the researcher who wrote the original article. A search for other articles written by the same researcher (e.g., "[name of author of original article] in AU") will probably lead you to other relevant articles because the researcher probably did not immediately abandon a line of fruitful research. In addition to tracking down that researcher's published papers, you may want to track down that researcher's web site. The author's web site may provide links to relevant unpublished work (e.g., papers written by the author or by the author's graduate students) and to the Web sites of other researchers doing work relevant to the topic.

Third, you can use an older article to get leads to more recent articles by using *Social Science Citation Index.* For example, if Refiner (1999) is a particularly important paper for your assignment, go to the 2003 volume of *Social Science Citation Index* and look up Refiner (1999). The index will give you a list of papers written in 2003 whose authors cited Refiner (1999). If Innovator (2003) and Novel (2003) are on that list, those papers are probably relevant to your assignment. If they are, their reference lists (and their authors' web sites) may lead you to still more references.

4.1.3 Reading the Right Stuff

An important part of understanding your assignment is understanding what sources your professor will accept. Most professors, as well as the editors of the *Publication Manual,* expect that you will read, cite, and reference *empirical articles* (articles in which authors report their own research) from high-quality journals. Unfortunately, students often violate this expectation. These violations come in three forms.

The most serious violation is reading an article in a magazine (e.g., *Psychology Today, Time, Newsweek*) rather than a journal article. (If you are unsure of the difference between magazines and journals, see Table 4.3.) At worst, magazine articles may misrepresent and misinterpret research findings. At best, magazine articles provide few details about how the research was conducted. In any case, reading secondhand accounts of research in magazine articles does not help you develop the ability to read and critique the firsthand accounts of research that you find in empirical journal articles.

The second most serious violation is reading review articles (in which authors discuss other people's research) instead of reading empirical articles (in which researchers provide firsthand reports of their own research).[3] Although review articles integrate many research studies, they are still secondhand accounts of research. These secondhand accounts may be slanted by their authors' theoretical positions. Furthermore, reading secondhand accounts of research does not give you practice in critiquing firsthand accounts of research studies. (To learn about a few of the journals that specialize in firsthand accounts of research, see Table 4.4.)

---

[3]Your professor may want you to read review articles in addition to—but not instead of—empirical articles. Note also that because a review article will cite and reference empirical articles, a recent review article may help you find relevant empirical articles.

TABLE **4.3**   How Psychological Journals Differ from Magazines

Journal Articles	Magazines
Follow APA format. For example, they have an Abstract and a Reference list.	Do not follow APA format.
Usually list reviewers or consulting editors—and their professional (usually university) affiliation inside the front or back cover. Most of these individuals will have Ph.D.s.	List the magazine staff (but no affiliations) somewhere in the first few pages of the publication. It is likely that none of these individuals will have Ph.D.s.
Usually have instructions for how to submit papers for publication.	Usually do not provide instructions on how to submit articles.
The title of the journal often includes the word "Journal," "Research," or "Bulletin."	The title usually does not include the word "Journal."
If the publisher is not the American Psychological Association, the American Psychological Society, or another scientific organization, the journal describes itself (usually on the cover, inside the cover, or on a page before the articles start) as the journal of a certain scientific society or organization.	The magazine is rarely affiliated with a professional organization. For example, *Psychology Today* is not affiliated with any group of professional psychologists.
In journals, there are no discontinuous pages for an article: Once a reader starts an article, the reader does not have to skip any page to continue reading the article.	Articles in magazines often have discontinuous pages: To continue reading an article, the reader may have to skip over pages of ads, or the reader may have to follow instructions such as "continued on page 121."
Journals have a more serious look: They usually do not have color pictures. Ads are usually for professional books and other products of interest only to professionals in the field. There are no ads for consumer products.	Most magazines are designed to attract a popular audience. The overall impression is less serious than a professional journal. The magazine contains many color pictures and ads for commercial products.

T A B L E   **4.4**   A Sample of Journals That Publish Research Articles

Journal	Brief Description
American Education Research Journal	Reports research in education.
Behavioral Neuroscience	Emphasizes biological basis of behavior. Some of the articles are difficult to understand if you do not have a background in chemistry and endocrinology.
Developmental Psychology	Primarily reports research relating to child and adolescent development.
Journal of Abnormal Psychology	Articles focus on the treatment and diagnosis of psychopathology. Occasionally reports experimental studies on humans or animals related to emotion or pathology. Sometimes reports studies that test hypotheses derived from psychological theories.
Journal of Applied Behavior Analysis	Articles report a sizable effect on an important behavior, usually employing a single-participant design.
Journal of Applied Psychology	Reports research relating to industry, government, health, education, consumer affairs, and other applied areas.
Journal of Comparative Psychology	Articles may include both laboratory and field observation of species. Emphasis is on relating findings to the theory of evolution.
Journal of Counseling Psychology	Publishes research articles evaluating the effectiveness of (a) counseling and (b) techniques for selecting and training counselors.
Journals of Experimental Psychology	Publishes research on fundamental mechanisms and processes. There are four different journals: *Journal of Experimental Psychology: General* *Journal of Experimental Psychology: Animal Behavior Processes* *Journal of Experimental Psychology: Learning, Memory, and Cognition* *Journal of Experimental Psychology: Human Perception and Performance*
Journal of Experimental Social Psychology	Almost all articles report the results of social psychological experiments.

TABLE **4.4**   A Sample of Journals That Publish Research Articles—*continued*

Journal	Brief Description
Journal of Personality and Social Psychology	Contains three sections: (a) attitudes and social cognition, (b) interpersonal relations and group processes, and (c) personality and individual differences.
Journal of Social Psychology	Source of relatively short articles.
Memory and Cognition	A good source of articles in human experimental psychology. See also *Journal of Experimental Psychology: Learning, Memory, and Cognition.*
Personality and Social Psychology Bulletin	Contains short articles that are often easy to understand.
Psychological Assessment: A Journal of Consulting and Clinical Psychology	Publishes research that assesses the validity of a variety of tests and measures.
Psychological Record	Source of short articles.
Psychology and Aging	Source of easy-to-read articles on physiological and behavioral aspects of aging during older adulthood.

The third most serious violation is failing to use articles from high-quality journals. There are three main reasons that students fail to use articles from elite journals.

First, students may not appreciate that journals vary in quality. They do not know that most professors see journals as varying from high quality (typically sponsored by APA or American Psychological Society [APS] and publishing only a small percentage of the manuscripts submitted to it) to low quality (journals not sponsored by a professional psychological organization and publishing the majority of the manuscripts submitted to it).[4]

Second, students may fail to use articles from a high-quality journal because they are using Internet sources instead. Unfortunately, the Internet is often a questionable source. Some of the information presented as fact on the Internet has little research support. Much of the research reported on the Internet is not of sufficient quality to make it into a reputable academic journal. Although there is some trustworthy information on the Internet, that information is usually trustworthy because it already appeared in a reputable, reviewed, printed journal.

Third, students may fail to use articles from a high-quality journal because students fail to see that those articles are relevant to their paper. Many students believe that the only way an article can be relevant is if that article focuses on the specific, narrow topic that the student is investigating (e.g., discrimination against students who

---

[4]Usually, the organization sponsoring the journal will be prominently mentioned on either the front or the back of the journal's cover.

smoke). However, elite journals are unlikely to publish articles that are limited to such a narrow topic. They might publish an article that examined that topic, but only if the article had implications beyond that specific instance of discrimination. That is, elite journals publish articles that shed insight into a general area, such as discrimination. Often, less highly regarded journals publish articles that follow up on findings published in the elite journal to verify that the general principle holds in a specific situation. For example, a lower-quality journal might show that the principles of discrimination discovered in a journal article published in an elite journal also apply to discrimination against students who smoke.

In short, your sources should include articles from elite journals. Three tips for including such articles follow.

1. Realize that the particular phenomenon you are investigating probably represents a particular example of a more general phenomenon. Consequently, principles that affect other attitudes also affect the attitude you are studying; principles that affect other behaviors probably also affect the behavior you are investigating. Therefore, do not exclude an article from your paper merely because it does not study exactly the same behavior or attitude that you are investigating.

2. If you find an article that does examine the behavior or attitude you are focusing on, check its reference list for articles from elite journals that investigated a more general topic.

3. Make sure that at least some of your sources come from journals sponsored by APA or APS.

4.2 Reading

4.2.1 Read Purposefully

As we have discussed, you should find recent journal articles that contain firsthand research. Before you start reading those articles, be sure you are clear about the questions you are trying to answer. Your questions should relate to your thesis statement (if you are writing a term paper) or to your hypothesis (if you are writing a research report). Focusing on the questions you are trying to answer will help you decide which articles to read: You will know, after reading only an article's Abstract, whether you should read the rest of that article. As you read the article, continue to focus on the question you want to answer. Focusing on the questions you are trying to answer will help you take useful notes on the article.

4.2.2 Take Notes

Before you start taking notes on the article, record the full reference (see 4.9.11). Recording the full reference will allow you to return to the source if you need to and prevent you from needing to return to the source (often the night before the paper is due) merely to complete your reference page.

EXHIBIT **4.1**   Note-Taking System to Encourage Critical Thinking

1. APA style reference
2. Short description of study
   a. Type of study (correlational/experimental)
   b. The results support (do not support) my hypothesis/thesis because
   c. This study is related to the following other studies
   d. I will use this study in my paper to
   e. The study's main strength is
   f. The study's main weakness is
3. In-depth analysis
   Measure
     Consistency with definition
       Evidence of validity
       Potential for bias
     Manipulation
       Strength
       Potential for bias
         Standardization
         Blind/masked
     Sample
       Size
       Age
       Gender composition
       Diversity
Were the author's cause-effect statements justifiable (5.9.1)?
Were the author's generalizations justified (5.9.5)?
Were null results properly interpreted (5.9.2)?
What other explanations are there for the results?
4. Notes taken from individual pages of the source

Source page number	Note from that page	Type of note (Q = quote, P = paraphrase, SU = summary, MR = my reaction)	Reason for note I took that note because _____ (e.g., the passage supports [contradicts] my thesis).

Before you take notes, you may also want to spend some time deciding how you are going to take notes. For example, you might decide to use a note-taking system like the one in Exhibit 4.1.

Before you take notes, read through the article at least once, understand the article, and reflect on how it relates to your paper. Taking many notes while you are reading an article for the first time is often just a substitute for thinking about what you are reading. At best, you have merely copied material. At worst, you may be setting yourself up to plagiarize.

To avoid plagiarizing, be sure (a) to place quotation marks around any paragraphs, sentences, or even phrases of three or more words that you copy and (b) to note the page number. To prevent yourself from merely copying information, use a system of note taking that encourages you to think. The following system might work for you: Precede each "fact" you note with an *S* if it is the author's own idea, conclusion, theory, or opinion (S because the author Stated it); a *C* if it is another's fact the author has Cited; or an *R* if it is a Result of the author's research. Alternatively, you might try using Exhibit 4.1 as a guide for note taking. Using a system like the one described in Exhibit 4.1 will help you spot common flaws in research (for more help on spotting flaws in research, see Chapter 5).

4.2.3 Reread

You will have to read articles more than once. Your job is not to scan them, but to dissect them. Many professors spend hours studying a single article. Do not expect that you can gain an in-depth understanding faster than professors can. To help you understand what you will get by reading an article more than once, study Table 4.5. As you can see from studying Table 4.5, the first time through the article, your focus is on understanding what the author is saying. The second time through, your focus is on questioning what the author is saying.

4.2.4 Revise Your Notes

Revising your notes before you start writing can help you in at least three ways. First, revising your notes will help you understand the material better. Whereas your original notes will probably consist largely of copied phrases, your rewritten notes should consist of paraphrases, summaries, and critiques. Second, organizing your notes will help you organize your paper. Third, rewriting your notes will help you see relationships among studies. For example, reorganizing your original notes using the scheme presented in Exhibit 4.2 should help you organize your paper and help you get insights into how studies fit together.

4.3 Citing

Whenever you put information from your notes on a source into the text of your paper, you must accompany that information with a *citation* to that source. Usually, your citation will consist of the last names of the source's authors and the source's year of publication. Usually, the last names of the source's authors and the source's publication date will be enough to achieve the main goal of most citations: to provide the reader with enough information about the source that the reader can use your citation to find the complete *reference* to the source in your reference list (see 4.9).

You must take thorough notes so that you can back up the claims you will make in your paper. Whenever you make a claim, you should provide evidence (e.g., a study,

TABLE **4.5**   What to Look for in a Journal Article

	First Time Through	**Second Time Through**
Introduction	Why do we care about this area of research? Do I understand the theory or the studies that set up this research? If not, what references do I need to read? What are the hypotheses? Why do the authors expect their hypotheses to be supported? If this study cures a weakness in previous research, what was wrong with previous research? If this study fills a gap in previous research, what was that gap?	Do I agree with their arguments? Does the hypothesis really follow from theory or previous research? If they had obtained different results, what would they have changed in their introduction?
Method	How were participants selected? What was the age and gender composition of the sample? What population did the sample represent? What was done to the participants? If there were manipulated variables, how were those variables manipulated? What did participants do? What was the measured variable? What was the design? Do I understand how the study's method allowed the researcher to test the hypothesis?	Are there any reasons to expect that the researchers might have obtained different results with a different population of participants? Were groups equivalent before study began? Were there enough participants? Was there a problem with participants dropping out of the study? Are there any variables that the researchers should have controlled or manipulated? If I had been a participant, would I have guessed the hypothesis? Would I have taken the task seriously? Were the control groups adequate? Would it have been better to use a different measure?
Results	How were participants' responses turned into the scores used in the analyses? What are the average scores for the different groups? Do the results support the hypothesis?	Do the statistics directly test the predictions made in the introduction? Do the statistical tests match up with the verbal descriptions? That is, if the authors say that Group 1 scored better than Group 2, do they have an analysis that directly compares Group 1 against Group 2? Are the statistics appropriate? Did they correctly report their null (nonsignificant) results as failing to reject the null hypothesis?

T A B L E **4.5** What to Look for in a Journal Article—*continued*

	First Time Through	**Second Time Through**
Discussion	Do they think the results matched their predictions? How do they explain any discrepancies? What additional studies do they recommend?	What are other explanations for the results? The other explanation could come from (a) a problem with their study that the authors did not mention or from (b) a theory or hypothesis that the author did not mention. Are there additional studies I would recommend? Did the authors make cause-effect statements on the basis of correlational evidence? Did the authors state something that was not supported by the results? For example, did they treat a nonsignificant result as significant or talk about a comparison that they did not statistically test?

E X H I B I T **4.2** A System to Help See Connections among Studies

	Research Study	
	Study 1	Study 2
APA style reference Type of study (Experimental vs. Correlational) Measures used Sample (number and type of participants) Precautions used to prevent bias Results of study (supported hypothesis, null results, contradicted hypothesis)		

a statistic) to support your claim. When you provide evidence, you must cite the source of that evidence, unless (a) your evidence is a well-known fact or (b) your paper is the source of that evidence (e.g., it was reported in your Results section).

You must also use citations whenever you present someone else's ideas (e.g., words, concepts, criticisms, theories, methods). If you fail to give a source's authors credit for their ideas, you are guilty of plagiarism. To avoid plagiarism, (a) if you borrowed ideas from a source, cite that source—even if you did not quote that source; and (b) if you are in doubt about whether to cite a source, cite it.

4.3.1 Choosing a Citation Type

In psychology papers, you do not use footnotes to cite your sources. Instead, you have a choice between two citation types: *name* citations and *parenthetical* citations.

If you use a name citation, you will probably make the author's(s') last name(s) the subject of the sentence. Right after the names, put the year of publication. Enclose that year, but not the name(s), in parentheses. Thus, you might write, "Jones (2000) noted that the studies failing to find a significant effect had insufficient power." If you wanted to use a name citation without making the author's(s') the subject of the sentence, you might write, "According to Jones (2000), the studies failing to find a significant effect had insufficient power."

In a parenthetical citation, you provide the same information, but both the author's(s') last name(s) and the year of publication are in parentheses. Thus, you might write, "The studies failing to find a significant effect had insufficient power (Jones, 2000)."

In your paper, you should use both name and parenthetical citations. Varying your citation type creates variety in your sentence structure, thereby making your paper more interesting to read. More important, the two citation types accomplish different goals. Consequently, as you will see in the next section, a citation type that works well with one citation may be awkward with another citation.

Use a name citation when you are going to paraphrase extensively, such as when you are introducing a study that is important to your paper. A sentence such as "Smith (2003) conducted an experiment on the problem of response bias in psychological tests" lets the reader know that the rest of what follows is Smith's experiment (e.g., "She tested 20 people . . ."). You may also want to use a name citation when introducing a well-known work by a well-known author. In such a case, a name citation would assist readers who are already familiar with the work of the person you are citing by providing them with a clue about what they are about to read. For example, if you write, "Piaget (1953) stated," psychologically sophisticated readers will anticipate the particular points of Piaget's theory that you are going to outline.

When using name citations, the authors' names must fit into the grammar of the sentence. Thus, if you have more than one author, verbs relating to what the authors did must be plural rather than singular. Examples of common errors are "Smith and Brown (1967) *states*," or "Brown et al. (1978) *states*." The correct forms are "Smith and Brown (1967) state," and "Brown et al. (1978) state" (et al. means "and others"; see 4.4.4).

Unlike name citations, parenthetical citations come after the information to which they refer. A parenthetical citation is particularly useful when you want the reader to focus on the results of a study rather than on who performed the study. By putting the author's name last, you imply that the same results would have been obtained were anyone to have done the study; for example, "IQ and socioeconomic class are correlated (Wiseman, 1969)."

Parenthetical citations also make it easy to cite related studies. To see the superiority of parenthetical citations over name citations for describing related studies, suppose you had used name citations to describe the following studies:

✔ Wiseman (1969) did a study in which he found IQ and
    socioeconomic class to be correlated. Harris (1975) confirmed

> this in another study. Finally, Jones and Smith (1977)
> uncovered the same relationship in a more recent study.

Using parenthetical citations allows you to convey the same information much more efficiently, as you can see from the following example:

 Many studies have found that IQ and socioeconomic class are correlated (e.g., Harris, 1975; Jones & Smith, 1977; Wiseman, 1969).[5]

Using parenthetical citations also allows you to show the reader how related studies fit together. In the next example, note how using parenthetical citations summarizes the common information, yet preserves the detail that the studies were conducted in different countries:

 Researchers have found that the relationship between IQ and socioeconomic status exists in American (Wiseman, 1969), Australian (Jones & Smith, 1977), and British (Harris, 1975) samples.

4.3.2 Citing from Secondary Sources

Citation from secondary sources refers to citing what one person has done or said after reading a second person's account of what the first person did or said. As a student, you may be tempted to use secondary citations for two reasons. First, after reading a secondhand account of an article and therefore believing you already know what the article is about, it may be hard to motivate yourself to track down the article. Second, reading about an article in a magazine, newspaper, or textbook is easier than reading the original article.

Although you might be tempted to use a secondary source, resist that temptation. Instead, read, study, understand, and cite the original source. The only times APA journal editors will allow you to cite secondhand, hearsay evidence are when the primary source is in a foreign language or when the primary source is unavailable. The rationale for editors' distrust of secondhand sources is clear: A secondhand account is an incomplete account—and it may also be an inaccurate account.

Your teacher may be more lenient than a journal editor. You might ask your teacher if you can use one or two secondary sources. If you are allowed to use secondary sources, name the original source and then cite the secondary source. For example, if you read about Original's work in Interpreter's article, then your citation would be

> Original (as cited in Interpreter, 1970) found . . .

In your reference section, you would not mention "Original." Instead, you would provide a reference only to the article you read (i.e., Interpreter, 1970).

---

[5]Note that the citations are not in order by date. Instead, they are in alphabetical order according to the last name of each article's first author. To learn more about how to sequence a series of citations, see 4.5.1.

To reiterate a point that is very important if you are to benefit from (and do well on) your assignment, do not substitute secondary sources for primary sources. Take the time to find the original article, even if you have to get it from interlibrary loan.

4.3.3 Citing Personal Communications

From a lecture, a conversation, an e-mail, an on-line news group, or an on-line bulletin board, you may get an idea from someone and put it in your paper. If so, give that person credit by using a *personal communication* citation. For such a citation, write the person's initials, last name, the words "personal communication," and the date the communication occurred:

- ✔ I.B. Hepfl (personal communication, May 13, 2003) [name citation] told me
- ✔ . . . is an alternative explanation (I.B. Hepfl, personal communication, May 13, 2003) [parenthetical citation].

Note that personal communication citations will not be listed in your references because the reader will be unable to access that lecture, conversation, or electronic communication. Note also that most of your citations should usually be from sources that could be accessed by either visiting a major university library or by logging on to a reputable electronic database such as *PsycINFO*.

4.3.4 Citing Information Obtained from the Internet

Although you can use the Internet to retrieve articles that appear in paper journals (by using *PsycINFO, Proquest, Infotrac*, and other full text article retrieval services), you can also use the Internet to retrieve information that has never appeared in a paper journal. For example, you may find information on an individual's or an organization's web site. Be very skeptical about information from such a source. That source may put information on the web site that has not been evaluated by outside experts. Even if an Internet source does report original research, a paper journal's description of the same research may provide a more complete and more permanently retrievable source.

If the Internet source you located is already no longer available on the Internet, do not put that source in the reference section. If you cannot find it, readers probably will not be able to find it. Instead, if you must cite that source, cite it as a personal communication (see 4.3.3).

4.4 Formatting Individual Citations

Citations point readers to the sources of your ideas. Usually, your sources will be research articles. The value of the source is based on the quality of the research, not the personality, fame, or status of the person doing the research. Therefore, the citation will not include the author's title (e.g., Dr., Professor), the author's first name, the author's affiliation (e.g., Harvard), or any other author information that is irrelevant to evaluating the research (e.g., the author's hometown). Instead, citations usually include only two things: (a) the year the source was published and (b) the author's(s') last name(s).

Usually, providing the year of publication is straightforward. There are probably only five situations in which you will not just put down the year. First, as previously discussed, you put the precise date for personal communication citations. Second, if the original source is dated differently from the translation, you separate the original year from the translation year with a slash (e.g., Kant, 1781/1965). Third, if the article has not yet been published, you put "in press" (e.g., Jones, in press) rather than the date. Fourth, if the worth has no documented publication date, you put "n.d." (no date) for the date (e.g., Smith, n.d.). Fifth, if you are using a name citation for an article more than once in the same paragraph, you can omit the year the second time you mention the article—unless leaving off the date would prevent readers from knowing which article you meant (e.g., if your reference list contains three articles by Jones, the citation "Jones" would not tell the reader which article you meant).

Usually, providing the author's last name is straightforward, especially when the work has one author. When the work has two to five authors, providing the authors' last names is still straightforward. The only added difficulty is that you have to make sure that you put the authors in the correct order (on the first page of a published article, the authors will be listed in order below the title). We will illustrate what to do in more complicated cases (e.g., no author, six or more authors) in the next section. However, before you try to absorb all the specific rules of citations, realize that most of those rules boil down to one general rule: A citation must be complete enough to allow the reader to find the reference in your reference list.

4.4.1 Work by One Author

```
Crovitz (1964) found . . .
. . . was found (Crovitz, 1964).[6]
. . . was found (Anonymous, 2002).[7]
. . . was found (Clarion University, 2002).[8]
```

4.4.2 Work by Two Authors

Always include the first author's last name, the second author's last name, and the year the work was published—and include them in that order. To join the authors' names, use the word "and" when you are using a name citation, but use an ampersand ("&")

---

[6]It does not matter whether the person's full name is Danny Crovitz, Danny Crovitz, Jr., or Daniel Crovitz III: The last name is Crovitz, and the last name is the only name you put in the citation.

[7]If the author is officially listed as "Anonymous," then "Anonymous" takes the place of the author's last name.

[8]If the author is an organization, the organization's name takes the place of the author's last name.

when the authors' names are in parentheses. Note that neither the "and" nor the "&"
are preceded by a comma.

```
Spear and Ganz (1975) found . . .
. . . . was found (Spear & Ganz, 1975).
```

4.4.3 Work by Three, Four, or Five Authors

The first time you cite such a source, list all of the authors' last names. Separate the
authors' names with commas. Thus, there will be a comma between the first and second authors' names, a comma between the second and third authors' names, and a
comma before the final "and" (for a name citation) or "&" (for a parenthetical citation). After the names, put the year the work was published. The publication year will
be in parentheses (for a name citation) or preceded by a comma (for a parenthetical
citation). If you cite that source again, do not mention all the authors' names. Instead,
state only the primary (first) author's last name followed by "et al." and then the year.

```
Spear, Chow, Masland, and Murphy (1972) discovered
that . . . confirmed the well-established effect (Spear et al.,
1972). Also, Spear et al. (1972) commented that . . . have
been found (Burton, Nagshineh, & Ruddock, 1977).
```

Do not replace the authors' names with only the first author's name and "et al." if
doing so would make it unclear which reference you were citing. For example, citing
"(Wenderoth et al., 1989)" at the end of the following paragraph was a mistake
because readers cannot know which of the three Wenderoth references the writer
intended to cite.

```
✗  Wenderoth, Johnstone, and van der Zwan (1989) initiated the
   study of the phenomenon when they found. . . . In a related
   study, Wenderoth, van der Zwan, and Johnstone (1989)
   showed. . . . In addition, Wenderoth, Apple, and Johnstone
   (1989) found that. . . . To reconcile these disparate
   findings, one could reinterpret the results of Wenderoth
   et al. (1989).
```

In such cases, the general rule is that you should include the minimum number of
authors' names that avoids confusion, then "et al." followed by the publication year.
However, note that "et al." means "and others." Therefore, if, after listing the minimum number of authors' names, only one other author is left, do not use "et al."
Instead, list all the authors. Thus, in the previous example, the last citation should
read, "Wenderoth, van der Zwan, and Johnstone (1989)."

4.4.4 Work by Six or More Authors

Provide the first author's last name followed by "et al." and the date (e.g., Smith
et al., 2002), unless that citation could lead readers to more than one reference in
your reference list. To illustrate how an "et al." citation could lead to confusion, sup-

pose you referenced 10 seven-author sources that all (a) had Smith as the lead author and (b) were published in 2002. In that case, "Smith et al., 2002" would not tell readers which of the 10 you meant. In such a case, provide the second author's last name as well (Smith, Thomas, et al., 2002). If that citation would still not point to one—and only one—source in your reference list, add the third author's last name (Smith, Thomas, Schadle, et al., 2002). In short, provide the minimum number of authors' names that avoids confusion.

4.4.5 Work by Author Sharing Same Last Name as Another Cited Author

If two different first authors have the same last name, use their first and second initials when you cite their work.

```
G. J. Burton, Nagshineh, and Ruddock (1977) found. . . . H. E.
Burton (1945) set out. . . . R. F. Burton (2003) stated . . .
```

4.4.6 Work With No Author

If the source has no identified author, use the source's title in place of the author's last name (e.g., "Keep the small fish," 2002). To inform the reader that you are referring to the title of a source, you should differentiate the title from the rest of the text of the sentence. Specifically, if it is the title of an article or the title of a book chapter, enclose the title in quotation marks; if it is the title of any other work (e.g., a title of a book), italicize it.

```
The chapter "Social psychology" (2002) gave . . .
. . . the common definition ("Social psychology," 2002).
The book General psychology (2003) . . .
. . . the common definition (General psychology, 2003).
```

4.5. Formatting Multiple Citations

Sometimes you will have more than one citation for a statement. In this section, we will show you how to format such citations.

4.5.1 More than Two Works by Different Authors

Within parentheses, list multiple citations of different authors in alphabetical order according to the primary author's last name. Thus, just as is the case with the reference list, "Alpha & Omega, 2001" would come before "Omega & Alpha, 2001" (for more about ordering citations and references, see 4.9.3). Separate the citations with semicolons.

```
Several studies (Burton et al., 1977; Crovitz, 1964, 1972;
Spear & Ganz, 1975) have found . . .
```

4.5.2 More Than Two Works by the Same Author

Order multiple citations of the same author(s) from oldest to most recent.

```
Crovitz (1964, 1972) found . . .
 . . . was found (Crovitz, 1964, 1972).
```

If you refer to works by the same author(s) published in the same year, alphabetize the references on the first word of the title (e.g., if you cited several articles that Kakizaki published in 1950, the one titled "Androgens in action" would come before the one titled "Zebras in zoos"). Once you have ordered those references, put an "a" after the year for the first reference (e.g., Kakizaki, 1950a), a "b" after the year for the second (e.g., Kakizaki, 1950b), and so on until each citation is distinct.

```
Kakizaki (1950a) found that. . . . Kakizaki (1950b)
confirmed his finding. . . . a well-established finding
(Kakizaki, 1950a, 1950b).
```

4.6 Paraphrasing

When you paraphrase properly, you take ideas from a source and restate those ideas in your own words. Although you are not using the source's words, you are using the source's ideas. Therefore, when you paraphrase, just as when you quote, you must cite your source. Despite the similarities between paraphrasing and quoting, you should usually try to paraphrase rather than quote because paraphrasing shows that you understand what you have read.

Unfortunately, many students who intend to paraphrase unintentionally plagiarize because they make one of the following three errors. First, some students mistakenly believe that they do not have to cite a source that they do not quote. Do not risk your academic career by making that mistake. Second, sometimes students cannot tell, from their notes, whether they copied or paraphrased material—and they incorrectly assume that they paraphrased the material. Third, some students mistakenly believe that anything other than an exact quote is a paraphrase. They believe that replacing a few words with synonyms counts as a paraphrase or that deleting or moving a few words around counts as a paraphrase. They are wrong: A paraphrase must be in your own words.

To put a passage in your own words, you must first understand the passage. Therefore, before paraphrasing a sentence or passage, read it carefully. Then put away the passage and try writing a paraphrase in your own words. Then go back and compare what you have written with the original. If your paraphrase is too close to the original, try again. Otherwise, you will be guilty of plagiarism (see 1.2.4). To be more successful on your second attempt, study the passage again to be sure you understand it. Then, wait until the next day to write your paraphrase. Waiting gives you a chance to forget the original passage's wording (Clarion University of Pennsylvania, n.d.).[9] If your paraphrase still closely resembles the original, consider quoting the original.

4.7 Quoting

There are two main forms of quotation: *embedded quotations* and *block quotations.* Use embedded quotations for short quotations of fewer than 40 words. As we mentioned in Chapter 1, for every 1,000 words in your paper, you should have no more than 50 quoted words. Therefore, if you do quote, try to use embedded quotations.

4.7.1 Embedded Quotations

If you use embedded quotations, the following advice will help you format them correctly.

- Provide a normal citation in the appropriate place and enclose the quotation in double quotation marks.

  ```
  Example.
  Jones (1984) argued that both "may follow Morgan's canons"
  ```

- Provide the original page number(s) from which the quotation comes. Those page numbers should be put at the end of the quotation and should be enclosed in parentheses.

  ```
  Example.
  Jones (1984) argued that both "may follow Morgan's canons"
  (p. 232).
  ```

  If you have an Internet source for which you cannot identify the page numbers, count how many paragraphs it comes after a major heading. Then, to help the reader locate the quote, give the heading and the number of paragraphs (abbreviated "para.") that the quote follows the heading. Thus, if you were quoting from the third paragraph of the results section, your citation might be as follows:

  ```
  (Merton, 2003, Results section, para. 3)
  ```

- The original spelling, punctuation, and wording of the quotation must be maintained even if incorrect. Any error should be followed by "[sic]" to emphasize that the error is not yours, but instead was present in the original.

  ```
  Example.
  Jones (1984) argued that both "may follow Morgans [sic]
  canons" (p. 232).
  ```

---

[9]This citation is unusual because the author is an organization (Clarion University) and the publication does not have a date ("n. d." means "no date").

■ Use ellipses (three dots) to indicate omission of material from within the original quotation. Add the usual end-of-sentence mark (e.g., period, question mark) to the end of an ellipsis if the quotation resumes on the following sentence.

> Example.
>
> Jones (1984) argued that "lower-level judgments, . . . may follow Morgans [sic] canons" (p. 232).

■ Use brackets [thus] to indicate any material you have inserted into the quotation to make it fit into the sense of your text.

> Example.
>
> Jones (1984) argued that "lower-level judgments, . . . [arguing that both] may follow Morgans [sic] canons" (p. 232).

■ Use single quotation marks to indicate quotation marks within the quotation.

> Example.
>
> Jones (1984) applied "the term 'perception,' . . . to [both] aesthetic judgments, . . . [and] to lower-level judgments, . . . [arguing that both] may follow Morgans [sic] canons" (p. 232).

■ The first letter of a quotation may be capitalized if what follows forms a complete sentence of its own.

■ To highlight particular words in a quotation that are important for your argument, place them in italics. Follow the italicized words with [italics added].

■ If a period is next to the closing (right) quotation mark, the period should be inside the quotation mark—even if the period has nothing to do with the quote.

■ If a comma is next to the right (closing) quotation mark, the comma should be inside the quotation mark—even if the comma has nothing to do with the quote.

■ If the quotation itself ends with a question mark or exclamation mark, enclose the question mark or exclamation point within the quotation marks. If, on the other hand, the sentence, rather than the quotation, contains the question mark or exclamation point, then put the question mark or exclamation point outside of the quotation marks.

To understand these rules, study the following examples:

> ✔ He argued, "The term 'perception,' *when applied to aesthetic judgments* [italics added], must be distinguished from the term applied to lower-level judgments" (Jones, 1984, p. 232), but he went on to . . .
>
> ✔ Jones (1984) applied "the term 'perception,' . . . to [both] aesthetic judgments, . . . [and] to lower-level judgments, . . . [arguing that both] may follow Morgans [sic] canons" (p. 232).

4.7.2 Block Quotations

If your quotation is 40 words or more, use a block quotation. To format block quotations, use most of the same principles you would use if you had an embedded quotation. The difference is that instead of using quotation marks to identify the material you are quoting, you will use indentation. Specifically, indent all lines of the first paragraph of the quotation by about five characters from the left margin so that the first paragraph of the quote forms a block of text.

If your quote is longer than a paragraph, signal the start of each subsequent paragraph by indenting the first line of that paragraph by five more spaces than the lines immediately above and below it. Thus, if you were quoting three consecutive paragraphs, you should start every line of the quote five spaces from the left margin except for the first line of the second paragraph and the first line of the third paragraph, both of which you should start 10 spaces from the left margin.

End block quotations by citing the quotation's source. Specifically, after the final period of a blocked quotation, enclose the last name(s) of the author(s), the publication year, and page number(s) of the quote in parentheses, as we have done in Exhibit 4.3.

4.8 Deciding What to Reference

Your references should be a list of all the sources (except for major classical works such as the Bible) that (a) you studied and then cited in text and that (b) your reader has a reasonable chance of retrieving. This statement has important implications for what to include and exclude from your reference list. You must include every article that you both read and cited in text. You must exclude any source that you did not cite in text—even if you read that source. In addition, as you will see in the next sections, you must exclude two types of cited sources from your reference list: (a) sources that readers cannot retrieve and (b) sources that you, rather than actually reading, read about in a textbook or other secondary source.

EXHIBIT **4.3**   An Example of a Section of a Paper that Contains a
Block Quotation

```
    When astronomers try to explain visual perception, their explana-
tions can be confusing, as the following quote illustrates.

    Mach bands are present because cones do not operate independently.
    One cone "knows" what its neighbor is seeing [italics added] and
    responds both to the amount of light falling on it and the adja-
    cent receptors. At the high contrast bright boundary . . . a bright
    stripe [is visible] where the image becomes dark [and vice versa].
    (Lynch & Livingston, 1995, p. 225)

    This explanation is confusing because cones neither see nor know
what other cones are doing . . .
```

4.8.1 Referencing Nonstandard Sources

Personal communications, such as conversations, letters, and e-mails, do not appear in the reference list because there is no easy way to allow a reader to obtain a copy. Messages posted to newsgroups, discussion groups, and electronic mailing lists are also usually considered personal communications. Thus, such messages usually would not appear in your reference list. However, you may put such a message in your reference list if you are reasonably confident that the reader will be able to access that message.

4.8.2 Referencing Secondary Sources

You reference only sources you actually read. Therefore, if, rather than reading the original work, you read about the work only in a secondary source, you would reference only the secondary source. The only mention of the original work will be in the text's citation (see 4.3.2). As we mentioned earlier, you should try to read the original work whenever possible. Usually, your professor will expect your paper to be based on journal articles you read—not on journal articles you read about in secondary sources such as magazines, newspapers, encyclopedias, or textbooks. If you are citing secondary sources, most of these citations should usually be limited to the first paragraph of your Introduction.

4.9 Formatting References

In the next few sections, you will learn how to format the major types of references. We did not provide you with every type of reference for two reasons. First, because at least 75% of your references should be journal articles, we focused on teaching you how to format journal articles. Second, we could not provide an example of every type of reference: The *Publication Manual* lists 95 different reference types—and warns that it has not included every reference type. Therefore, you may run into a reference that is outside the guidelines we list. In that case, do not panic. Your professor will probably not penalize you for mistakes in referencing some obscure reference type. Most teachers are delighted when students can reference journal articles correctly. We would be shocked if your professor penalized you for having a comma out of place in a reference to an anonymous, reprinted article in a United Nations technical report. However, if you are extremely concerned about perfectly formatting the reference for an unconventional source, see the *Publication Manual* or use APA's *Style Helper 3.0.*[10]

4.9.1 Starting the Reference Page

Begin your list of references on a new page with a centered heading: References. Realize that you will probably not be able to complete your references unless you have the following four pieces of information for each reference:

---

[10]Both the *Manual* and *Style Helper* can be ordered from APA's web site (http://www.apastyle.org).

1. who the author(s) is (are),
2. what the title of the work is,
3. when the work was published or presented, and
4. where the work was published or presented (for a conference presentation, the name of the conference and the name of the city in which the conference was held; for a book, the name of the publisher and the name of the city in which the publisher is located; for a journal article, the name of the journal, the volume number of that journal, and the page numbers).

4.9.2 Form of Each Reference

Do not indent the first line of each reference. Instead, start the first line of each reference at the left margin. Subsequent lines for that reference should be indented five spaces. This indentation style is called "hanging indent." If you are having trouble indenting references in this way, go to the "help" menu of your word-processing program and look up "hanging indent."

If your reference has a single author, the beginning of your reference will probably adhere to the following format:

1. Author's last name, comma, first initial, period, second initial, period

   Example: `Fehr, B. F.`

2. Date in parentheses followed by a period

   Example: `(1999).`

3. Title of the source followed by a period.

   Example: `Laypeople's conceptions of commitment.`

If the source is a book, the source's title is italicized. The source above is not italicized. Therefore, you know that "Laypeople's conceptions of commitment" does not refer to a book title.

After providing the author's name ("who"), the publication date ("when"), and work's title ("what"), you need to provide the publication data ("where"). For a book (see 4.9.8), stating the "where" may be as simple as stating the name of the city where the publisher is located followed by a colon, the publisher's name, and a period (e.g., "New York: Wiley."). For a book chapter (see 4.9.9), stating the publication data is more involved because you must specify in what book the chapter is in, on what pages in that book the chapter is in, as well as providing the publisher's name and address (e.g., "In *Applied multiple regression/correlation analysis for the behavioral sciences* (pp. 73–122). New York: Wiley."). For a journal article (see 4.9.10), stating the publication data involves stating the title of the journal [italicized] followed by a comma, the volume number [italicized] followed by a comma, and the first page of the article followed by a hyphen followed by the last page of the article followed by a period (e.g., "*Journal of Personality and Social Psychology, 76*, 90–103."). If you accessed your source from the Internet (see 4.9.12), you will probably end your reference with a statement of when you retrieved the source and where in cyberspace (the database or the URL) you retrieved it (e.g., "Retrieved June 15, 2002, from PsycARTICLES database." or "Retrieved June 15, 2002, from http://faculty.washington.edu/agg/bytopic.htm").

4.9.3 Order

References must be in alphabetical order according to the primary (first) author's last name. Thus, Alpha, Z. Z. would come before Beta, A. A. If different authors have the same last name, then break the tie by looking at initials. Thus, Burton, H. E. (1945) would come before Burton, R. F. (2003). For references with the same first author, alphabetize on the second author. Thus, Wenderoth, P., Johnstone, S., & van der Zwan, R. (1989) comes before Wenderoth, P., & van der Zwan, R. (1989). For references with the same author(s), put the oldest references first. Thus, Lehmkuhle, R. T., & Fox, S. L. (1962) comes before Lehmkuhle, R. T., & Fox, S. L. (1994). For references with the same author(s) and year, alphabetize on the first word of the title (ignoring "a" and "the"), and distinguish references by single, lowercase letters immediately after the year. Thus, to distinguish the two articles that Kakizaki published in 1950, the one coming first in the reference list would be Kakizaki, S. (1950a), whereas the one coming second would be Kakizaki, S. (1950b).

With compound names (such as von Helmholtz, van der Zwan), check the author's own reference list to see where the author's name appears (in van der Zwan's case, it is with the Vs). If you cannot find the author's name in the author's own reference list, alphabetize on the first capitalized part of the name. Put the uncapitalized parts of the name after the initials (e.g., Helmholtz, H. L. von).

> *Examples.*
>
> Burton, G. J., Nagshineh, S., & Ruddock, K. H. (1977). Processing by the human visual system of the light and dark components of the retinal image. *Biological Cybernetics, 27,* 189-197.
>
> Burton, H. E. (1945). The optics of Euclid. *Journal of the Optical Society of America, 35,* 357-372.
>
> Burton, R. F. (1884). *The book of the sword.* London: Chatto & Windus.
>
> Crovitz, H. F. (1972). Transient binasal hemianopia in a pair of plastic soupspoons. *Psychonomic Science, 28,* 234.
>
> Helmholtz, H. L. von (1962). *Handbook of physiological optics* (3rd ed.) (J. P. C. Southall, Trans.). New York: Dover. (Original work published 1910)
>
> Kakizaki, S. (1950a). The effects of preceding conditions upon binocular rivalry (I.). *Japanese Journal of Psychology, 20*(2), 24-32.
>
> Kakizaki, S. (1950b). The effects of preceding conditions upon binocular rivalry (II.). *Japanese Journal of Psychology, 20*(4), 11-17.

Spear, P. D., Chow, K. L., Masland, R. H., & Murphy, E. H. (1972). Ontogenesis of receptive field characteristics of superior colliculus neurones in the rabbit. *Brain Research, 45,* 67-86.

Spear, P. D., & Ganz, L. (1975). Effects of visual cortical lesions following recovery from monocular deprivation in the cat. *Experimental Brain Research, 23,* 181-201.

van der Zwan, R., Wenderoth, P., & Alais, D. (1993). Reduction of a pattern-induced motion aftereffect by binocular rivalry suggests the involvement of extrastriate mechanisms. *Visual Neuroscience, 10,* 703-709.

Wenderoth, P., Johnstone, S., & van der Zwan, R. (1989). Two dimensional tilt illusions induced by orthogonal plaid patterns: Effects of plaid motion, orientation, spatial separation, and spatial frequency. *Perception, 18,* 25-38.

Wenderoth, P., & van der Zwan, R. (1989). The effects of exposure duration and surrounding frames on direct and indirect tilt aftereffects and illusions. *Perception and Psychophysics, 46,* 338-344.

Wenderoth, P., van der Zwan, R., & Johnstone, S. (1989). Orientation illusions induced by briefly flashed plaids. *Perception, 18,* 715-728.

4.9.4 Author Names

Invert authors' names (i.e., put the last name first, then the initials). Separate last names from initials with a comma. Separate initials with a space. Separate different authors' names with a comma. For two or more authors, separate the final name from the rest with a comma then an ampersand (e.g., Burton, G. J., Nagshineh, S., & Ruddock, K. H.; see 4.4.2). Do not use "et al." in the reference list unless you have more than six authors. If there is no identifiable author, put the title of the work in the author position.

Examples.

Benjamin, L. T., Jr. (1988). A history of teaching machines. *American Psychologist, 43,* 703-712.

Crovitz, H. F. (1972). Transient binasal hemianopia in a pair of plastic soupspoons. *Psychonomic Science, 28,* 234.

Helmholtz, H. L. von (1962). *Handbook of physiological optics* (3rd ed.) (J. P. C. Southall, Trans.). New York: Dover. (Original work published 1910)

High-handed professor's comments called hot error.
      (1985, August 16). *USA Today*, p. 2c.

Social Psychology (1995). (17 paragraphs) [CD-ROM] In
      Britannica CD 2.0. Chicago: Encyclopaedia Britannica.

Social Psychology (1999). In *The new encyclopaedia
      Britannica* (Vol. 27, pp. 802-803). Chicago: Encyclopaedia
      Britannica.

4.9.5 Date of Publication

For most sources, put the year of publication of the reference in parentheses followed by a period. For books, this is the most recent copyright year and is usually found on the page after the title page. For journals, the year is the publication date of the journal. For a book that has been translated into English, put the year of the translation (e.g., Kant, 1965), and then add "(original work published in [date])" at the end of the reference.

For some sources, you will provide information other than the year of publication. For example, with a daily newspaper article, knowing what year it was published would not be nearly as helpful as providing the date it was published. Therefore, for daily and weekly publications, enclose the year of publication, a comma, and the month and day of publication in parentheses, followed by a period. Thus, a reference for a newspaper article might start as follows: Homichl, J. (2003, July 16). You may use the same procedure for an Internet journal, if the date is provided. Similarly, you may provide the month or season (Winter) of the publication of a newsletter. Finally, if your source is a paper or poster presented at a conference, always follow the year of the conference with a comma and the month the conference was held (e.g., "2003, August").

Thus far, we have discussed cases in which you have access to more information than just the publication year. However, sometimes, you will not even know what year the source will be published. If the source has been published but there is no date, put "n.d." in place of the date. If the source has been accepted for publication, but is not yet published (the delay between article acceptance and publication is often more than a year), use "in press" in place of the date.

Examples.

Honomichl, J. (1990, August 6). Answering machines threaten
      survey research. *Marketing News*, 11.

Kant, I. (1965). *Critique of pure reason.* N. K. Smith
      (Trans.). New York: St. Martin's. (Original work
      published 1781)

Neisser, U. (1984, August). *Ecological movement in
      cognitive psychology.* Invited address at the annual
      meeting of the American Psychological Association,
      Toronto, Canada.

TABLE **4.6**   Abbreviations Used in References

Abbreviation	Translation	Usage
2nd	second	No period; same for all numbers
c.	about	When a publication year is uncertain
chap.	chapter	
Ed(s).	Editor(s)	
ed.	edition	
n.d.	no date	
p.	page	For one-page newspaper or magazine articles
pp.	pages	For book chapters
Rev.	revised	
Trans.	Translator(s)	
Vol.	Volume	When part of a title
vols.	volumes	When part of publication data
–	to	As in "pp. 22–33"

4.9.6 Title

Type the title of the reference exactly as it appears in the original, including the original spelling. Capitalize only the first letter of book, journal article, and book chapter titles. Capitalize only the first letter of book and book chapter subtitles. Italicize book titles and subtitles. End the title section of each reference with a period.

4.9.7 Abbreviations

As you will see in 4.9.8, for books published in the United States, use the U.S. postal service's abbreviation for that state instead of spelling out the entire state name. In addition to using U.S. postal service abbreviations for states' names, there are other abbreviations you should use in the reference section. The most common of these are listed in Table 4.6.

4.9.8 Book Reference

Usually, fewer than one fourth of your references should be books. Usually, books will be the shortest and easiest sources to reference. Like most references, book references start with the author's name (inverted), followed by parentheses enclosing the year the work was published, and a period.

Next comes the book title. Note that the book title is italicized. As a general rule, the first letter of the first word of the book title is the only letter capitalized. The exceptions to this general rule are that you capitalize (a) the first word after a colon and (b) proper nouns (see 6.1.1).

Usually, the book title is immediately followed by a period. If it is not followed immediately by a period, then the book has probably either been through several editions or has been translated. For such a book, there is a parenthesized, nonitalicized phrase telling the reader which edition of the book you are using or who translated the book. Thus, if the title alone would not necessarily lead the reader to the right source (e.g., the book is a revised edition, a third edition, a translation, the second volume, etc.), you need to add information after the title that will help the reader locate the right source. Abbreviate that information and put it in parentheses, in normal, nonitalicized font (rev. ed., 3rd ed., Trans., Vol. 2).

Next comes the place of publication. If the place is a famous city (e.g., New York, London), the city name is sufficient. If the city is not famous and is in the United States, follow the city name with the U.S. postal service's abbreviation for the state rather than typing out the entire state name (e.g., "PA" instead of "Pennsylvania"). Note that the postal abbreviation is capitalized and does not contain any periods. If the city is not famous and not in the United States, you will usually follow the city name with the country name.

After the publishing location, put a colon and the name of the publisher (e.g., "Pacific Grove, CA: Wadsworth."). In listing the publisher's name, keep it short by not including the words or abbreviations for "Company" or "Incorporated." Put a period after the publisher's name.

Normally, your reference will end at that period. However, there may be cases in which the year you are citing for the book is quite a bit later than the year the book was originally published. For example, a book may be reprinted over a hundred years after it was first published or it may be translated into English decades after it was first published. Consequently, your citation date may make it seem like a person who has been dead for years has just published a book. Without an explanation, such a citation date might confuse the reader. Therefore, after the ending period, add a parenthetical explanation such as "(Original work published in 1871)."

General form.

Author, I. N. (year). *Book title italicized* (information about specific
    edition—if needed). Place of publication: Publisher. (Explanatory
    material—if needed)

Examples.

Alhazen, I. (1989). *The optics of Ibn Al-Haytham: Books
    I–III: On direct vision* (A. I. Sabra, Trans.). London:
    The Warburg Institute. (Original work published c. 1024)

Burton, R. F. (1884). *The book of the sword.* London: Chatto
    & Windus.

Helmholtz, H. L. von (1962). *Handbook of physiological
    optics* (3rd ed.) (J. P. C. Southall, Trans.). New York:
    Dover. (Original work published 1910)

Strunk, W., Jr., & White, E. B. (1972). *The elements of style* (2nd ed.). New York: Macmillan.

4.9.9 Book-Chapter Reference

Referencing a specific book chapter involves a few more steps than referencing a book. As with a book reference, provide the author's name (inverted) followed by the year of publication, in parentheses, followed by a period. After that, provide the chapter title—but do not italicize it.

Then, if there is an editor, provide the name of the editor. Three common mistakes students make in formatting the editor information are (a) putting the editor's name where the author's name should be, (b) inverting the editor's name, and (c) not putting "(Ed.)," after the editor's name.

Next, put the book title in italics, just as you would if you referenced an entire book. After the book title, put "pp." followed by the number of the first page of the chapter, a hyphen, the number of the last page of the chapter, followed by a left parentheses and a period (e.g., "pp. 56–92."). Finally, add the publication information using the same format you would if you were referencing an entire book. Specifically, you put the place of publication followed by a colon, followed by the name of the publisher, followed by a period (e.g., "Belmont, CA: Wadsworth.").

General form.

Author, I. N. (year). Chapter title. In A. N. Editor (Ed.), *Book title italicized* (information about specific edition) (pp. start page-finish page). Place of publication: Publisher.

Examples.

Leibowitz, H. W., Post, R. B., Brandt, T., & Dichgans, J. (1982). Implications of recent developments in dynamic spatial orientation and visual resolution for vehicle guidance. In A. Wertheim, W. Wagenaar, & H. L. Leibowitz (Eds.), *Tutorials in motion perception* (pp. 231-260). New York: Plenum Press.

Westheimer, G. (1981). Visual hyperacuity. In *Progress in sensory physiology* (Vol. 1) (pp. 1-30). Berlin: Springer.

4.9.10 Journal-Article Reference

As we mentioned earlier, most of your references should be to journal articles. Fortunately, the general form is not difficult and applies to most journal articles.

General form.

Author, I. N. (year). Article title. *Journal Title Italicized and Capitalized, volume number italicized* (issue number if each issue begins with page 1), start page-finish page.

Examples.

Aitken, J. (1878). On a new variety of ocular spectrum. *Proceedings of the Royal Society of Edinburgh, 10,* 40-44.

Spear, P.D., & Ganz, L. (1975). Effects of visual cortical lesions following recovery from monocular deprivation in the cat. *Experimental Brain Research, 23,* 181-201.

van der Zwan, R., Wenderoth, P., & Alais, D. (1993). Reduction of a pattern-induced motion aftereffect by binocular rivalry suggests the involvement of extrastriate mechanisms. *Visual Neuroscience, 10,* 703-709.

Wenderoth, P., Johnstone, S., & van der Zwan, R. (1989). Two dimensional tilt illusions induced by orthogonal plaid patterns: Effects of plaid motion, orientation, spatial separation, and spatial frequency. *Perception, 18,* 25-38.

As you can see, most articles adhere to the following format:

1. Author's last name, comma, first initial, period, second initial, period
   Example: Fehr, B. F.
2. Date in parentheses followed by a period
   Example: (1999).
3. Title of article followed by a period
   Example: Laypeople's conceptions of commitment.
4. Title of journal (italicized) followed by a comma
   Example: *Journal of Personality and Social Psychology,*
5. Volume number (italicized) followed by a comma
   Example: *76,*
6. First page of article followed by a hyphen followed by the last page of the article followed by a period.
   Example: 90-103.

Variations in author's last name come from four cases. First, when there is more than one author, a comma is used to separate one author's name from the next author's name. In addition to a comma, an ampersand (&) is used to join the last author's name to the list. Second, if the original source does not provide an author's middle initial, you will not include that author's middle initial. Third, if the article has more than six authors, only the first six are listed. After the sixth author, place a comma and "et al." Fourth, sometimes the author is not known. In that case, use the title of the article as the author.

Variations in the date come from three cases. First, magazines, newsletters, and newspapers often provide more detail than the year of publication. For example, Internet journals and newsletters may note the season (2003, Winter) or months (2003, September/October) that they come out, whereas newspapers and magazines may produce the exact date (2003, August 26). Second, if the article is not yet published, the phrase "in press" is put in parentheses. Third, if the article has no date, such as some Internet sources, put "n.d." in parentheses rather than the date.

Variations in the rest of the reference are rare. There are, however, four variations you might encounter. First, if you read only the electronic version of a printed article, put "[Electronic version]" after the journal title. Second, if each issue in a journal begins on page 1, then, after the volume number, put the issue number in parentheses. Third, if you are referring to newspapers, use "p." before the page number of an article that appears on a single page (e.g., "p. D4," "p. 5") and use "pp." before the page numbers of an article that appears on multiple pages (e.g., "pp. D4–D6," "pp. 1, 5"). Fourth, if you are referring to an Internet source, you may not have page numbers or volume numbers.

4.9.11 Journal-Article-Abstract Reference

If you have searched sources such as *Psychological Abstracts*, you have access to journal articles' abstracts. If you want to cite one of these articles, you should find and read it. If, however, an abstract is all that is available (e.g., your library does not subscribe to the journal and you cannot obtain it from interlibrary loan), cite the Abstract using the following format:

General form.

Author, I. N. (year). Article title. *Journal Title Italicized and Capitalized, volume number italicized* (issue number if each issue begins with page 1), start page-finish page. Abstract obtained from name of source, year of source, publication year of source, volume number, "Abstract No.", abstract number, and period.

Example.

Lo, T.Y. (1925). Correlation of name and fame. *Chinese Journal of Psychology, 3,* 701. Abstract obtained from *Psychological Abstracts, 1927, 1,* Abstract No. 319.

Usually, if you have access to the entire article, you should read the entire article. You should not merely skim the Abstract. However, if, for some reason, you access the source, but read only the Abstract (e.g., your professor specifically stated that for a particular writing assignment reading Abstracts was all that was required), cite the abstract using the following format:

General form.

Author, I. N. (year). Article title [Abstract]. *Journal Title Italicized and Capitalized, volume number italicized* (issue number if each issue begins with page 1), start page-finish page.

Example.

Spear, P.D., & Ganz, L. (1975). Effects of visual cortical lesions following recovery from monocular deprivation in the cat [Abstract]. *Experimental Brain Research, 23,* 181-201.

4.9.12 Referencing Internet Sources

We have saved Internet referencing for last because referencing Internet sources is not much different from referencing any other source. In fact, if you are accessing an electronic version of a published source, often the only difference is that you add "[Electronic version]" after the title. For example, suppose an exact copy of a published article was put on the primary author's web site, a journal's web site, the APA web site, the APS web site, or on the electronic library reserve web site your professor set up for your class. By including the same reference information as you would for the printed source, the reader can obtain the information you saw by going to the printed source. By adding "[Electronic version]," you admit that you saw an electronic version rather than a printed one: You do not have to pretend that you saw the printed source.

For other Internet sources, usually the main differences are that (a) you need to put the phrase "Retrieved" followed by the date you retrieved the information (e.g., January 14, 2004), followed by a comma and the Uniform Resource Locator (URL) (e.g., http://www.writingforpsychology.com),[11] and (b) you do not end your reference with a period. You need to include the date that you retrieved the source because web sites change. You need to include the URL so readers can access the source. You do not end a URL reference with a period because the reader might think the period was part of the URL.

Electronic version of a printed book

General form.

Author, I. N. (year). *Book title italicized* (information about specific edition—if needed) [Electronic version]. Place of publication: Publisher. (Explanatory material—if needed)

Example.

Strunk, W., Jr., & White, E. B. (1972). *The elements of style* [Electronic version]. New York: Macmillan.

Book existing only as an Internet document

General form.

Author, I. N. (year). *E-title italicized.* Retrieved date (e.g., March 13, 2003), comma, and URL (the URL should be on a new line if there would otherwise be a line break in the pathname)

Example.

Li, X., & Crane, N. (1996). *Electronic sources: APA style of citation.* Retrieved October 12, 2001, from http://www.uvm.edu/~xli/reference/apa.html

---

[11]Note that the URL should not be underlined. Unfortunately, your word-processing software may automatically underline it. To learn how to turn off that feature, see our web site (http://www.writingforpsychology.com).

Electronic version of a book chapter from a printed book

General form.

Author, I. N. (year). Chapter title. In A. N. Editor (Ed.), *Book title italicized* (information about specific edition) (pp. start page-finish page) [Electronic version]. Place of publication: Publisher.

Example.

Strunk, W., Jr., & White, E. B. (1972). Elementary principles of composition. In *The elements of style* (pp. 15-33)[Electronic version]. New York: Macmillan.

Book chapters from a document existing only on the Internet

General form.

Author, I. N. (year). Title of e-chapter. In A. N. Editor (Ed.) *E-title italicized.* Retrieved date, comma, from URL

Example.

Dennett, D. C. (1994). Consciousness in human and robot minds. In S. Harnad (Ed.), *CogPrint: Cognitive sciences eprint archive.* Retrieved July 15, 2002, from http://cogprints.soton.ac.uk/archives/comp/papers/199803/199803001/doc.html/concrobt.htm

Journal articles

There are two main types of electronic journal articles: (a) articles from journals that exist only electronically (e.g., *Psycoloquy*), and (b) articles from conventional paper journals that are reproduced electronically (e.g., the electronic version of *American Psychologist*). For an Internet-only journal, use the following format.

General form.

Author, I. N. (year). Article title. *Electronic Journal Title Italicized and Capitalized, volume number italicized,* article number (if available). Retrieved date, from URL

Examples.

Forgie, M. L. (1995). Are ovarian secretions all that females "need"? Commentary on Fitch & Denenberg on sex-brain. *Psycoloquy, 6,* Retrieved June 27, 2001, from ftp://ftp.princeton.edu/pub/harnad/Psycoloquy/1995.volume.6/psyc.95.6.22.sex-brain.3.forgie

Hoffman. W. C. (1998). The topology of wholes, parts and their perception-cognition: Commentary on Latimer & Stevens on Part-Whole-Perception. *Psycoloquy, 9.* Retrieved September 10, 2001, from http://www.ai.univie.ac.at/archives/Psycoloquy/1998.V9/0003.html

If you saw the electronic version of a printed journal article from any source other than a database, then you reference it as a conventional journal article. The only difference is that you put "[Electronic version]" after the title.

Example.

Greenwald, A.G., & Farnham, S.D. (2000). Using the Implicit Association Test to measure self-esteem and self-concept [Electronic version]. *Journal of Personality and Social Psychology, 79,* 1022-1038.

If you retrieved the article from a database, your citation would reflect that fact. Note that you do not put "[Electronic version]" in such a citation.

Example.

Greenwald, A.G., & Farnham, S.D. (2000). Using the Implicit Association Test to measure self-esteem and self-concept. *Journal of Personality and Social Psychology, 79,* 1022-1038. Retrieved July 28, 2002, from PsycARTICLES database.

Journal article abstracts

If you try to retrieve an article from the Internet, you may be able to retrieve only the article's abstract. If you want to cite that article, you should find and read it. If, however, you can access only the abstract (e.g., your library does not subscribe to the journal and you cannot obtain it from interlibrary loan), cite the abstract using the following format:

General form.

Author, I. N. (year). Article title. *Journal Title Italicized and Capitalized, volume number italicized* (issue number if each issue begins with page 1), start page-finish page. Abstract retrieved from date, comma, and URL or name of source. If the source is a URL, there is not a period at the end of the reference. If the source is a database, there is a period.

Examples.

Greenwald, A.G., & Farnham, S.D. (2000). Using the Implicit Association Test to measure self-esteem and self-concept. *Journal of Personality and Social Psychology, 79,* 1022-1038. Abstract retrieved July 28, 2002, from http://faculty.washington.edu/agg/bytopic.htm

Greenwald, A.G., & Farnham, S.D. (2000). Using the Implicit Association Test to measure self-esteem and self-concept. *Journal of Personality and Social Psychology, 79,* 1022-1038. Abstract retrieved July 28, 2002, from *PsycINFO* database.

4.10 Checklists

4.10.1 Academic Honesty Checklist

___ I did not plagiarize.

    ___ I cited any source from which I got ideas—even if I did not directly quote that source. When I summarized or paraphrased from a source, I cited that source. To minimize the chances that I plagiarized,

        ___ If I had any paragraph without a citation (a) in any section of my term paper or (b) in the Introduction or Discussion sections of my research proposal or report, I went back to my notes to make sure that I had not left out a citation.

        ___ I double-checked my notes and my sources to make sure that I had neither inadvertently quoted someone nor had a paraphrase that was almost identical to the source quotation.

        ___ If I had any doubt about whether to cite a source, I cited it.

    ___ If I took words from a source, I made it clear that I was quoting that source.

    ___ If I got ideas or quotes from an informal source, I cited that source as a personal communication (see 4.3.3).

___ If a source was not the original report of a study, I admitted it.

    ___ When I read a secondary source instead of the original article, I made it clear that I had read only the secondary source by correctly citing (4.3.2) and referencing (4.8.2) that secondary source.

    ___ When I read only the Abstract, I made it clear that I did not read the entire article (4.9.11).

    ___ When I read a theoretical or review article, I made it clear that the article was not an empirical article. In other words, for review articles, I wrote "(for a review, see Smith, 2002)" and for theoretical articles, I wrote "Smith (2002) argued" rather than "Smith found."

4.10.2 Formatting Citations Checklist

___ When citing sources, I did not

    ___ mention authors' first names, professional titles (e.g., "Dr."), or professional affiliations;

    ___ mention article titles; or

    ___ use footnotes.

___ I followed the rules regarding parentheses.

    ___ If I used a name citation, I put only the date in parentheses (e.g., "Jolley and Mitchell (2003) argued that . . .").

___ If I used a parenthetical citation, I put the authors' names and the date in parentheses, and I separated the last author's name from the date with a comma: "Some have argued that . . . (Jolley & Mitchell, 2003)."

___ If I used a name citation for a multiple-author source, I used "and" to connect authors' last names; however, if I used a parenthetical citation for a multiple-author citation, I used "&" to connect authors' last names.

___ When I cited several articles within one set of parentheses,

   ___ I listed the articles in alphabetical order.

   ___ I separated the articles from each other with semicolons: "(Brickner, 1980; Jolley, 2000; Mitchell, 2001; Ostrom, 1965; Pusateri, 1995; Williams, 1992)."

___ I correctly cited multiple-author papers.

   ___ If the paper had more than six authors, I listed only the first author's last name followed immediately (with no comma) by "et al." (e.g., Glick et al., 2002).

   ___ If I discussed a paper with three to five authors, I mentioned all the authors' last names the first time I cited that paper.

   ___ If I discussed a paper with three to five authors and had already cited the paper, I used the first author's last name, followed immediately (with no comma) by et al. (e.g., First et al., 1996).

   ___ I checked all my citations that used the phrase "et al." to make sure that I had (a) correctly used such citations and (b) correctly punctuated such citations.

      ___ I did not overuse "et al." citations.

         ___ I never used "et al." the first time I introduced a paper with fewer than six authors.

         ___ I never used "et al." with a two-author paper.

      ___ I correctly punctuated my "et al." citations.

         ___ I never put a period after "et" (e.g., I wrote "et al." instead of "et. al.").

         ___ I never put a comma between the first author's last name and "et al." (e.g., I wrote "First et al." instead of "First, et al.").

___ I correctly formatted all quotations.

   ___ I listed the page number of the source from which I got the quote. (If there is no page number, as in a web site, see 4.9.12. If it is a quotation from a classic work, see 4.7.)

   ___ I used the short quote format for quotations under 40 words (see 4.7.1), but used the block quote format for quotations of 40 or more words (see 4.7.2).

4.10.3 Finding and Using Sources Checklist

___ I found high-quality sources (see 4.1).

> ___ My citations are recent (most were published within the last two years).

> ___ My citations are from journal articles describing actual research studies rather than from secondhand sources (e.g., textbooks, magazines, newspapers).

> ___ If my professor required the paper to have a certain number of sources, I met that requirement. For example, if my professor required a minimum of five sources, I cited at least five empirical articles published in refereed journals.

___ Rather than quoting, I paraphrased, summarized, interpreted, and critiqued. As a result, I limited quotes to fewer than 50 words for every 950 of my own.

___ I paraphrased and summarized empirical research reports in a way that makes it clear that (a) I read them rather than skimmed their abstracts and that (b) I understood them.

___ I showed, through my paraphrases and summaries of those articles, how the different articles fit together—and how they related to the main point of my paper.

___ I commented on weaknesses I found in published research. If I had trouble finding weaknesses, I consulted Chapter 5.

4.10.4 Reference Page Checklist

___ Margins and spacing

> ___ My reference section starts on a separate page. The centered heading "References" is at the top of that page.

> ___ Everything is double-spaced.

> ___ The first line of each reference is not indented. Instead, it begins at the left margin.

> ___ When a reference takes up more than one line, I indented those additional lines five spaces.

___ My references are listed in alphabetical order (according to the last name of the first author).

___ Each reference begins with the authors' last names and initials, followed by the year of publication (in parentheses), and then a period.

___ Every reference ends with a period—except for (a) those ending with a URL and (b) those ending with a parenthical explanation about the work's original source.

___ If a source had more than one author, I separated authors' names with commas.

___ I italicized only

    ___ book titles,

    ___ names of journals, and

    ___ the volume numbers of journal articles.

___ I capitalized only the following parts of article and book titles:

    ___ the first word of the title,

    ___ the first word following a colon, and

    ___ proper nouns (see 6.1.1).

___ Abbreviations

    ___ When citing journal articles, I avoided both the word "pages" and the abbreviation "pp."

    ___ If a book was published in the United States, I abbreviated, rather than wrote out, the name of the state. I used the same state abbreviations (e.g., PA for Pennsylvania) that the U.S. postal service uses. I remembered that these abbreviations are capitalized and do not contain periods.

___ I appropriately cited and referenced Internet sources.

    ___ I tried to find a print version of any article that I found on the Internet because the print version may be easier for readers to locate and the text of the print version will not change.

    ___ If I did not find a print version, I checked to make sure that the URL worked.

    ___ I turned off the "auto-underline" feature of my word-processing software so the link is not underlined.

___ All the references in this section are also cited in my paper. If a reference was not cited, either I added that citation to the body of my paper or I deleted the reference.

___ All the sources cited in my paper are also listed in this section except for

    ___ "personal communication" citations (see 4.3.3);

    ___ original works that I did not read but instead learned about through a secondary source (see 4.3.2); and

    ___ classical works (e.g., the Bible).

4.11 Summary

1. You need to find good sources to write a good paper. Good sources will usually be research articles published in scientific journals.

2. It is vital to cite and to reference your sources correctly.

3. One source may give you leads to other sources (see 4.1.2).

4. Computerized databases can help you find sources. If you have trouble finding enough sources, consult Table 4.2.

5. When you find a source, read it, reread it, and take notes on it. Your notes should include an APA style reference to the source, your critical comments on the source, and quotations around any words you are copying from the source.

6. When you get an idea from a source, you must cite that source. When you paraphrase from a source, you must cite that source. When you quote a source, you must cite that source. When you are not sure about whether you should cite a source, cite that source.

7. Short quotations (fewer than 40 words) are formatted differently than longer quotations (see 4.7).

8. Use a personal communication citation (4.3.3) to give credit for ideas that you acquired through informal sources. Do not put these personal communications in your reference list.

9. When citing, do not provide any information about the authors except for their last names—unless you have more than one author with the same last name (in that case, see 4.4.5). Do not mention authors' first names, titles, or professional affiliations.

10. There are two types of citations: name citations and parenthetical citations. Use a name citation when you are going to paraphrase extensively from a single source. Use parenthetical citations to show the reader how related studies fit together. Do not use footnotes to cite a source.

11. When using a name citation, put the date in parentheses. When using a name citation for a paper with two authors, connect the last names with the word "and." When using a name citation for a paper with three to five authors, use a comma between all the authors' names and add the word "and" before the last author's name.

12. When using a parenthetical citation for a paper with two authors, connect the last names with the symbol "&" and separate the last name from the date with a comma. When using a parenthetical citation for a paper with three to five authors, use a comma between all the authors' names and add the symbol "&" before the last author's name.

13. When citing several articles within one set of parentheses, (a) put the articles in alphabetical order and (b) separate the articles from each other with semicolons.

14. When citing a source with six or more authors, provide only the primary author's last name followed immediately (with no comma) by "et al." (e.g., Glick et al., 2002).

15. When citing a source with three to five authors that was cited earlier in the paper, use the primary author's last name, followed immediately (with no comma) by et al. (e.g., Lead et al., 1996).

16. The Reference section starts on a separate page titled "References."

17. All the sources listed in the references should be (a) cited in the paper and (b) in alphabetical order according to the last name of the primary author (see 4.9.3).

18. The first line of each reference starts at the left margin. The rest of the reference is indented five spaces.

19. Each reference begins with the authors' last names and initials, followed by the year of publication (in parentheses), and then a period. Separate last names from initials with a comma. Separate initials with a space. Separate different authors' names with a comma. For two or more authors, separate the final name from the rest with a comma then an ampersand (e.g., Burton, G. J., Nagshineh, S., & Ruddock, K. H.).

20. Below is an example of a journal-article reference (for more see 4.9.10):

    Spear, P. D., & Ganz, L. (1975). Effects of visual cortical lesions following recovery from monocular deprivation in the cat. *Experimental Brain Research, 23*, 181-201.

21. Below is an example of a book reference (for more, see 4.9.8):

    Strunk, W., Jr., & White, E. B. (1972). *The elements of style* (2nd ed.). New York: Macmillan.

22. Below is an example of a reference from a book chapter (for more, see 4.9.9):

    Westheimer, G. (1981). Visual hyperacuity. In *Progress in sensory physiology* (Vol. 1) (pp. 1-30). Berlin: Springer.

23. Below is an example of a reference from an Internet source (for more, see 4.9.12):

    Hoffman. W. C. (1998). The topology of wholes, parts and their perception-cognition: Commentary on Latimer & Stevens on Part-Whole-Perception. *Psycoloquy, 9.* Retrieved September 10, 2001, from http://www.ai.univie.ac.at/archives/Psycoloquy/1998.V9/0003.html

CHAPTER

5

Making Your Case: A Guide to Skeptical Reading and Logical Writing

When you read sources that you will use in your paper, you want to know when authors are making claims that do not follow from the evidence. When your professor reads your paper, you do not want your professor to write any of the following comments on your paper: "illogical," "not true," "not fair," "does not follow," "not necessarily," "unsupported assertion," "the evidence does not support that claim," or "that is only one interpretation." Instead, you want your professor to recognize that you have accomplished two competing tasks: (a) making a strong case in support of your claims and (b) acknowledging the case against your claims. In this chapter, we will teach you how to evaluate arguments and interpret evidence so that you will be able to defend your claims fairly and forcefully.

TABLE **5.1** Examples of Legitimate (Although Not Necessarily Correct) Thesis Statements

Human handedness is learned.

There is no intellectual decline in old age.

Situational factors determine more of human behavior than personality.

The research on [this particular topic] is beset with methodological problems preventing any firm conclusion.

Human perception is bottom-up.

IQ tests measure intelligence.

5.1 Theses

In a term paper, your job is to answer a question. Your professor may give you the question (e.g., "Does wisdom increase with age?"), or you may have to generate the question after being given only a general topic (e.g., "Your term paper should deal with an issue related to wisdom."). Your answer to the question, the answer that you believe to be true, is your *thesis*.

In one sense, defending your thesis is like taking one side of a debate. You may remember taking part in school debates in which you defended one side of a question (e.g., "Is it better to be a lion or a lamb?"). Each side of this debate (i.e., "It is better to be a lion than a lamb," and "It is better to be a lamb than a lion.") would constitute a thesis. However, there is an important difference between taking one side in a debate and defending a thesis: In a debate, it does not matter whether the assertion is actually true; in a term paper, the truth does matter. Thus, in a term paper, propose a thesis that, based on your careful examination of the published literature, appears to be true.

Table 5.1 lists some thesis statements that have been used in term papers. To introduce such theses into a paper, precede each thesis with words such as "In this paper, I will argue that."

Although you should believe that your thesis is true, your thesis should be one that some reasonable people might disagree with—before they read your paper. Thus, your thesis statement should not fall into any of the following types of unarguable assertions: (a) a well-documented fact, (b) an extremely vague statement, or (c) a *tautology:* a statement that must, according to rules of logic, be true—often because the statement involves essentially defining a term with itself (e.g., "a reinforcer is something that reinforces"). In Table 5.2, you can see examples of assertions that are not good thesis statements because they fail the test of allowing a reasonable person to disagree with them.

Although your paper's thesis is a statement that some of your readers may disagree with as they start reading the paper, your goal is that all your readers will agree with your thesis by the time they reach the end of the paper. To achieve this goal, you must make a strong argument in support of your thesis statement.

To make a strong argument, you must do two things. First, you must show that your argument is based on premises (statements) that are *sound:* true. You will use cita-

T A B L E **5.2**   Examples of Unacceptable Thesis Statements

Assertion	Problem
Approximately 10% of humans are left-handed.	It is a statement of fact.
Performance on speeded tasks declines in old age.	It is a statement of fact.
Situations are important in human behavior.	All behavior occurs within situations. Consequently, this assertion is too vague to allow disagreement.
IQ tests measure IQ.	This is a tautology.
Some human perception is bottom-up.	This fails on two counts: (a) it is a statement of fact, and (b) it is vague.

tions to show that your premises are probably true. Second, you must show that your argument is *valid:* The conclusion follows logically from your premises.

In the next section, we will focus on helping you use the rules of logic to produce valid arguments. The rules of logic you will use depend on whether you are employing an *inductive* argument or a *deductive* argument.

5.2 Inductive Arguments

Inductive arguments use at least one premise that is stated in relative terms (e.g., "most people are right-handed," "some people are left-handed," "usually, rewards increase behavior"), rather than in absolute terms (e.g., "all babies babble," "every voluntary response can be strengthened by reinforcement"). When making an inductive argument, try to avoid two common errors. First, avoid including a premise that overstates the frequency of an event. For example, if you have evidence that some people have been sexually abused, do not write, "most people have been sexually abused." Second, do not state that you have proved that something is true: Inductive arguments cannot prove that something is true. They can only make a case that something is likely to be true.

To understand induction, examine Induction 1.0. For each row of Induction 1.0, there are three pieces of information. The entry in the first column labels the part of the argument as either a premise or a conclusion. We have given the premises numbers so that when we refer to a premise (e.g., "Premise 1"), you will know which premise we mean. The middle column uses letters (e.g., "A," "B," and "X") to express each part of the argument (e.g., Premise 1, Premise 2, Conclusion) in a general, abstract form. The last column provides a specific, concrete example of each part—an example that you might use in a term paper. As you can see from Induction 1.0, it is possible to pull together enough circumstantial evidence to make it seem that a conclusion is probably true.

Induction 1.0

Premise/Conclusion	General Form	Specific Example
Premise 1:	Some Bs are As.	Phenomena showing acquisition curves (B) are usually learning phenomena (A).
Premise 2:	Some Cs are As.	Phenomena showing situational specificity (C) sometimes are learning phenomena (A).
Premise 3:	Some Ds are As.	Phenomena showing forgetting functions (D) are usually learning phenomena (A).
Premise 4:	Some Es are As.	Phenomena showing spontaneous recovery (E) are usually learning phenomena (A).
Premise 5:	X is B, C, D, and E.	Handedness (X) shows an acquisition curve, situational specificity, a forgetting function, and spontaneous recovery.
Conclusion:	X is probably A.	Handedness is probably a learning phenomenon.

5.3 Deductive Arguments

In deductive arguments, premises are statements couched in absolute terms (e.g., "all," "every," "always") or in unambiguous comparisons (e.g., "A is bigger than B."). The sorts of conclusions that can follow from such premises are determined by the rules of formal logic. The simplest deductive argument is the *syllogism*, in which there are two premises and a conclusion. As you can see from studying Syllogism 1.0, one can construct a sound argument from two sound premises (Premises 6 and 7).

Syllogism 1.0

Premise/Conclusion	Abstract Form	Marble Example	Psychological Example
Premise 6:	All Bs are As.	All the black (B) marbles that either you or your best friend own are in Angie's aquarium. (A).	All learning phenomena show acquisition curves.
Premise 7:	All Xs are Bs.	All your (X) marbles are black.	Handedness is a learning phenomenon.
Conclusion:	All Xs are As.	All your marbles are in Angie's aquarium.	Handedness will show an acquisition curve.

There is, however, more to creating a syllogism than putting two premises together. To illustrate, examine Invalid Syllogism 1.0:

Invalid Syllogism 1.0

Premise/ Conclusion	Abstract Form	Marble Example	Psychological Example
Premise 8:	All Bs are As.	All the black (B) marbles that either you or your best friend own are in Angie's aquarium (A).	All learning phenomena show acquisition curves.
Premise 9:	All Xs are As.	All your marbles are in Angie's aquarium.	Handedness shows an acquisition curve.
Conclusion:	All Xs are Bs.	All of your marbles are black.	Handedness is a learning phenomenon.

Perhaps the easiest way to see that Invalid Syllogism 1.0 is not necessarily valid is to question the conclusion of the marble example. Given that Premises 8 and 9 are true, do all your marbles have to be black? The answer is "no": You could, for example, have some red marbles that are in Angie's aquarium.

Even if an argument is valid, it may be unsound. The soundness of a valid argument depends on the truth of its premises. If either of the premises is incorrect, the argument will be unsound. Syllogism 2.0 is an example of an argument that is valid but unsound.

Syllogism 2.0

Premise 6:	All Bs are As.	All black marbles (B) are white (A).
Premise 7:	All Xs are Bs.	All our marbles (X) are black.
Conclusion:	All Xs are As.	All our marbles are white.

Unfortunately, students commonly introduce unsound premises into their papers. We will briefly mention the two types of unsound premises that are most likely to creep into your paper. The first is stating that a theory makes a certain claim when the theory does not make that claim. The second follows the form "If A, then B" when "B" does not necessarily follow "A" (e.g., "If people had more positive attitudes toward children, child abuse would be eliminated."). If you make this second error, your professor is likely to write something like "does not follow," "illogical," "not necessarily," "I disagree," "non sequitur," or "No!" next to that premise.

When constructing your own syllogism or when reconstructing someone else's syllogism, follow the model presented in Syllogism 3.0. That is, precede premises with the word "If," separate each premise with the word "and," and precede the conclusion with the word "then." Adding "If" to the premises raises the possibility that the premises might be wrong. Adding "and" reminds you that all your premises must be correct to make a sound argument. Careful reading of the literature on a topic will be required to convince yourself, and careful reporting of that literature will be required to convince your reader, that your premises are correct.

Syllogism 3.0   Expressed in Sentences (reading down)

Premise 8:	If all Bs are As, *and*	If all learning phenomena show acquisition curves, *and*
Premise 9:	if all Xs are Bs, *then,*	if handedness is a learning phenomenon, *then,*
Conclusion:	all Xs are As.	handedness will show an acquisition curve.

In conclusion, whether you are writing a term paper or a research paper, you should know about deductive arguments. If you are writing a term paper, you may want to structure your term paper in the form of a syllogism. If you are writing a research paper, you will probably want to use a deductive argument to justify your hypothesis.

5.4 Hypotheses

Your hypothesis should be a prediction about how a measured variable depends on one or more other variables. Table 5.3 provides some examples of hypotheses.

If you think of your hypothesis as the conclusion of a syllogism (see Syllogism 3.0), you will find it easier to write the Introduction of your paper. You will spell out and defend the premises and then explain how the premises lead to the conclusion that your hypothesis should be supported. When you write the discussion section, you will again find it useful to think of your hypothesis as the conclusion of a syllogism. For example, suppose your study shows that your hypothesis—the conclusion of your syllogism—is false. In that case, not only would your conclusion be false, but at least one of your premises would be false as well (provided that your syllogism is valid). Thus, in addition to making the case that your study's results really did disprove the hypothesis, you would also discuss the implications of the study for the validity of the premises. For

TABLE **5.3**   Examples of Hypotheses

Adults over age 65 in good health will score better on the XYZ test of crystallized intelligence than adults between the ages of 25 and 35.

When a person thinks that several others have witnessed an accident, the person will be slower to give help than when the person thinks he or she is alone.

Visual acuity will improve with increases in lighting level.

Performance on the ABC test of IQ will predict school performance.

instance, if your hypothesis was based on Syllogism 3.0, your discussion might make the case that your results also call into question the premise that handedness is learned. Similarly, if one of the premises of your syllogism is a core premise of a theory, you would not only argue that your results disprove your hypothesis, but you would also argue that they challenge the validity of that theory.

5.5 Problems in Making Arguments

As we have pointed out, your paper should make a case for your thesis. In the next sections, we will show you what errors to avoid in arguing for your thesis. Note that you should try to catch these errors both when reading and revising your own paper as well as when reading another person's paper. As you will see, these problems in making arguments can be broken down into three categories: (a) not stating an arguable thesis, (b) not making a fair argument, and (c) failing to consider alternative explanations for the evidence.

5.6 Stating an Unarguable Thesis

As we suggested earlier, people sometimes err by choosing to make a case for an uncontestable claim. For example, their claim is a vague statement ("environment has some effect on behavior"), a statement of a well-documented fact ("some responses can be classically conditioned"), a statement of a feeling or opinion ("I feel that shock treatment is morally wrong"), or a tautology (e.g., "effective behavioral treatments are effective"). The problem with tautologies is that, because they are redundant, they must be true, even though their premises may be questionable. For example, suppose you state the following tautology: "Stereotypes are hateful, inaccurate views of a group held only by extremely prejudiced people. If we stop people from being extremely prejudiced, we will eliminate stereotypes." The reader may disagree with your definitions but, given your definitions, the reader must accept your conclusion.

Sometimes, the reason a reader may disagree with your definitions is that you have defined your terms using a dictionary of English rather than a dictionary of psychology. Your professor, for example, would probably disagree with your definitions if you used a dictionary of English to define any of the following terms: experiment, personality, random, reliable, reinforcement, intelligence, or motivation.

If you find yourself resorting to a dictionary of English to define your argument, stop yourself. Use a reputable dictionary of psychology instead. However, even a psychological dictionary will not always help you make an appropriate argument. If your instructor posed a topic in which the key issue was one of definition (e.g., "Are recovered memories false memories?"), accepting a particular definition because it was stated in your dictionary would be to miss the point of the assignment. For example, if your dictionary defined recovered memories as real memories, accepting this definition would be to miss the point that some memories can be reconstructed. Given your dictionary's definition, the thesis that recovered memories are real would be unarguable.

In conclusion, you should make a strong case for your thesis. However, you should not make a strong case by improperly defining terms or by stating an unarguable thesis. To avoid starting off with an unarguable thesis, ask yourself what evidence would disprove your thesis. If no pattern of results could disprove your thesis, you need a new thesis.

5.7 Substituting Appeals for Reasoning: Nonobjective Thinking

Once you have a thesis that you can argue, the key is to argue using objective evidence and logical reasoning. Unfortunately, sometimes people substitute appeals to emotion, faith, or authority for logical reasoning.

5.7.1 Appeal to Emotion

An appeal to emotion is to set aside one of the major criteria of the scientific method: objectivity. Zechmeister and Johnson (1992) say that appeals to emotion ask the reader to suspend objectivity and to experience either pity or fear. In a paper arguing for the accuracy of recovered memories, pity might be evoked by writing, "The distress shown by clients as they retrieve these painful memories compels us to believe that the memories are real." In such a paper, fear of being considered foolish or insensitive might be evoked by writing, "Only someone devoid of human feelings could doubt clients as they recall these painful memories."

Students commonly use rhetorical questions to make appeal-to-emotion arguments. For example, suppose a student posed the following question: "Who could doubt such clients' experiences?" The question is rhetorical because the writer is convinced that anyone with an ounce of sense will answer, "Nobody could." Rhetorical questions are out of place in scientific discourse; avoid them.

5.7.2 Appeal to Faith

Like appeals to emotion, appeals to faith set aside objectivity. Imagine a writer asserting that there are fairies at the bottom of the garden, but that the fairies will reveal themselves only to those who believe in them. Further, the writer adds, the fairies will refuse to give any evidence of themselves. Such an appeal to faith would probably be ineffective. However, if, instead of appealing to faith in fairies, the writer appealed to faith in a particular religious, political, or theoretical position, the writer would sway some readers.

5.7.3 Appeal to Authority

An appeal to authority is made when a well-respected person's name is cited for a particular position. The assumption underlying appeal-to-authority arguments is that any position associated with someone so wonderful must be a correct position.

Do not rely on appeal-to-authority arguments. At best, arguments made by appeal to authority are weak. For example, it would be weak to write, "In his presidential address to the American Psychological Association, Smith (1993) asserted that most repressed memories of childhood sexual abuse surfacing in therapy are examples of false memories." This citation of Smith is weak because there is nothing in the citation to allow the reader to evaluate Smith's opinion that therapist-elicited repressed memories are false memories. For example, there is no discussion of research demonstrating the falsehood of the memories. Consequently, the only reason to believe Smith's opinion rests on Smith's reputation as president of the APA.

5.8 Unfair Arguments

5.8.1 Ad Hominem Arguments

Ad hominem arguments are, in a sense, the opposite of appeal-to-authority arguments. If, instead of addressing the evidence for a particular position, a writer attacks the character of the person providing the evidence, the writer has committed an ad hominem argument (the English translation of the Latin phrase "ad hominem" is "at the person"). The assumption underlying ad hominem arguments is that any position associated with someone so disreputable cannot be a correct position. For example, let us say that Jones (1990) has shown that some therapists consistently elicit particular sorts of "memories" of childhood sexual abuse (e.g., satanic rituals) from clients randomly assigned to them. Ad hominem arguments would include claims that Jones used cocaine or that Jones was a fascist. Ad hominem arguments would not address the quality of Jones's research. Ad hominem arguments are unfair.

5.8.2 Ignoring Contradictory Evidence

Another unfair way for a writer to favor one position at the expense of opposing positions is to ignore any contradictory evidence. For example, an apparently convincing argument could be mounted that the world is flat by ignoring all the evidence that the world is round. In our example topic, an apparently convincing case for the validity of repressed memories could be mounted by accepting uncritically only papers in which the authors concluded that repressed memories were accurate. Students are often guilty of not citing and discussing contradictory evidence. To avoid making this error, you must (a) read widely enough on a topic to be able to write about the evidence relating to both your position on an issue as well as to the opposing position, and (b) be open-minded enough to be fair to the opposing position.

5.8.3 Straw Man Arguments

If you cannot be fair to the opposing position, you may be guilty of attacking a *straw man*:[1] a description of the opposing position that is designed to be attacked and defeated. By discrediting the opposing position, writers make their own position

---

[1]The original straw man was a soldier's uniform stuffed with straw that was propped on the battlements of a castle. It was designed to draw the arrows of enemy archers, leaving the real soldiers unharmed. As the soldiers were always dressed as men, it is inaccurate, and possibly disrespectful to women, to use the term "straw *person* argument."

appear stronger. For example, suppose that a writer wishes to favor the argument that there have been no reliable demonstrations of repressed memories. The writer could construct a straw man by presenting a weak case for repressed memories. One way to create a weak case would be to build the case using only the most seriously flawed studies the writer could find. The writer would then proceed to demolish the straw man by listing all the methodological flaws.

The straw man argument is likely to surface when students are attacking a theory they do not like. To destroy the theory, they oversimplify it and misstate its premises. Then, the professor, like a referee calling a foul, reprimands the students for attacking a "straw man version" of the theory rather than the theory itself.

Beware of straw man arguments. Students and published writers often make straw man arguments. However, you should avoid making straw man arguments. Indeed, if you want to demolish an argument opposing yours, make sure you demolish the strongest version of the argument, even if you have to strengthen it yourself.

5.9 General Errors in Reasoning from Evidence

Thus far, we have discussed errors caused by ignoring the evidence, such as attacking a caricature of an opposing idea rather than the idea itself, attacking the person who proposed an opposing idea rather than the person's idea, and ignoring evidence that favors an opposing idea. That is, we have discussed errors resulting from passion overriding reason. In the next section, we will discuss errors in which the person looks at the evidence but errs by failing to consider alternative explanations for the evidence. Reading this section will help you evaluate other people's published papers as well as help you evaluate drafts of your own papers.

5.9.1 Inferring Causation from Correlation

If you conduct a correlational study or read a report of one, you learn that two variables are related. Unfortunately, you may also jump to the conclusion that the research has also established that the two variables are causally related. In other words, you may label one variable the "cause" and the other the "effect"—despite the fact that you should not make cause-effect statements from correlational studies.

To understand why you should not draw cause-effect conclusions from correlational studies, imagine reading about a correlational study that found a relationship between television watching and depression. Specifically, suppose that a survey found that people who watched more television were more likely to be depressed. You would be tempted to believe that television viewing caused some of those surveyed to become depressed. Yet to do so would be to commit the error of inferring causation from correlation. The reason we cannot infer causation from correlation is that there are numerous explanations for a correlation between two variables. For example, it may be that television watching, rather than being a cause of depression, may be an effect of depression: Perhaps depressed people watch more television because they are more likely to feel that they do not have the energy to do anything else. Alternatively, both television watching and depression may both be side effects of some other factor: Perhaps people who lose their jobs or who are not getting enough sleep are more likely to (a) become depressed and (b) have more time to watch television.

To make cause-effect statements, you cannot rely on surveys or other correlational studies. Instead, the only studies that allow causation to be inferred correctly are *experiments*[2] embodying three principles:

1. At least two groups of individuals are formed by random assignment.[3]

2. Each group is treated identically except for the *manipulated variable:* the *independent variable.*[4] Sometimes, the experimental group receives a treatment that contains a moderate or high amount of the manipulated variable, whereas another group, a *control* group, gets no treatment. Usually, however, if there is a control group, that group will receive either a treatment that contains a small amount of the manipulated variable or it will receive a *placebo treatment:* a manipulation that does not contain any of the manipulated variable.

3. The groups differ reliably in response to the *measured variable* (also known as the *dependent variable*).

To see how you could do an experiment that incorporated these three principles, imagine that you want to determine whether watching violent television causes children to be aggressive. In that case, you might design the following experiment.

1. Randomly assign children to violent-television-viewing and nonviolent-television-viewing groups. Random assignment might involve flipping a coin for each child: A head means the child goes into the violent-television group, and a tail means the child goes into the nonviolent-television group.

2. Treat the groups identically except that you show one group one television program and the other group a different program (the independent variable manipulation). All children then have an identical session of free play in which an observer counts the number of aggressive acts committed by each child. The number of aggressive acts represents the measured (dependent) variable.

3. Conclude that the difference in the content of the two television programs caused the difference in aggressiveness—if (a) one group commits more aggressive acts than the other, and (b) statistical tests indicate that this difference is reliable.

If any one of the three principles is violated, causation usually cannot be inferred. In the next section, we will show you why the first principle, random assignment, is crucial to making cause-effect statements.

---

[2]We will not discuss small-n research, quasi-experiments or causal modeling because such techniques are beyond the scope of this book.

[3]We will not consider experiments in which people participate in more than a single experimental condition. Such within-subjects (repeated-measures) experiments have their own specialized procedures that allow causation to be inferred.

[4]Experiments can have more than one manipulated variable. However, for simplicity's sake, we will confine ourselves to the simple, single-factor experiment.

If participants are not randomly assigned, the groups may be systematically different even before the treatment is introduced. For example, suppose the researcher decided to assign boys to see the violent program and girls to see the nonviolent program. In that case, skeptics could argue that the difference between the groups' behavior was due to gender rather than to the manipulation. Alternatively, suppose the researcher let all the children who wanted to go first watch the violent program and had the more hesitant children watch the nonviolent program. In that case, skeptics could argue that the difference between groups' behavior was due to personality differences between the groups (e.g., maybe assertive children are more aggressive than reserved children) rather than to the manipulation.

Another form of nonrandom assignment that creates groups that are systematically different before the manipulation is administered is *self-selection:* letting people choose their treatment condition. If the researcher in the television violence study we have been discussing were to let children self-select, the aggressive children might be more likely than less aggressive children to choose to watch the violent television program. Although self-selection might seem far-fetched for the study we are considering, self-selection is a problem with much survey research. For example, suppose that a survey researcher questions children and finds that children who watch more hours of violent television are more aggressive than children who watch fewer hours of violent television (i.e., aggression and watching of violent television are correlated). The researcher should not conclude that watching violent television causes a child to be aggressive because of the problem of self-selection: Aggressive children may simply choose to watch violent television more than less aggressive children.[5]

Any study that uses self-selection is a correlational study and should not be used as the basis of a cause-effect conclusion. For example, in the 1960s, researchers found that people who smoked were more likely to have heart disease than people who did not smoke. However, that finding was not based on randomly assigning people to smoke. Smoking was not even a manipulated variable. Instead, the smoking and nonsmoking groups were formed by self-selection: People chose either to smoke or to not smoke. Thus, the finding that smokers had more heart disease than nonsmokers was a correlational finding. Such a correlational finding did not establish that smoking had any effect on heart disease. Indeed, in the 1960s, when researchers knew only that smokers were more prone to heart disease than nonsmokers, many reasonable people argued that both smoking and heart disease could be side effects of another variable (e.g., stress may cause people to have heart disease as well as cause people to smoke).

---

[5]Note that it is self-selection—not the survey instrument itself—that prevents the survey researcher from making valid cause-effect statements. If a questionnaire is used as the dependent measure in an experiment, the experimenter can make a cause-effect statement. For example, in our television violence experiment, we could have used a questionnaire—rather than observation—to measure aggressiveness. We could make a cause-effect statement because, instead of using self-selection, we randomly assigned participants to receive different manipulations.

5.9.2 Making Something Out of Nothing: Misinterpreting Null Results

The failure to consider alternative explanations for a correlational finding is one of the most common and one of the most serious reasoning errors that students make. The second most common and second most serious reasoning error is the failure to appreciate that there are alternative explanations for null results.

The failure to find a relationship between two variables is not proof that the two variables are unrelated. Admittedly, one reason a study might fail to find a relationship is that there is no relationship to be found. However, there are other reasons for failing to find a relationship. For example, the relationship may be overlooked because the study's measure was not sensitive enough or because, as often occurs in psychological research, the researcher did not study enough participants (Cohen, 1990).

In short, null results are inconclusive. On the one hand, you cannot use them to conclude that your variables are related. On the other hand, you cannot use them to conclude that your variables are unrelated.

5.9.3 Adding Meaning to Significance: Misinterpreting Significant Results

If you observe a relationship between two variables in your study, you need to view that finding with caution. Sometimes, random error makes it appear that two variables are related when, in fact, the variables are not related. Therefore, you need to ask whether the pattern of results you observed is reliable: If you repeated the study, would you get similar results? The best and most direct evidence for reliability is replication: Others have repeated the study and obtained similar results.

For better or worse, the evidence that psychologists have typically used to evaluate reliability is through statistical significance tests. Significance tests tell you the probability of getting the obtained results if the *null hypothesis* (the null hypothesis is that there is no relationship between the variables) is true.[6] Traditionally, if the chances are less than 5 in 100 ("$p < .05$ [or less]") of getting certain results given that the null hypothesis is true, psychologists have considered the null hypothesis to be false, and therefore have considered the results reliable. That is, they declare such results "statistically significant."

Statistically significant results are not necessarily large. Many statistically significant results, based on huge samples, are small and meaningless. In short, realize that if you want to estimate the size of an effect, you must do more than look at the results of a significance test.

---

[6]As Cohen (1994) pointed out, significance tests do not tell us what we really want to know: how likely it is, given these results, that the null hypothesis is true.

5.9.4 Trusting Labels Too Much: Not Questioning Construct Validity

In addition to questioning the relationship between manipulated and measured variables, you should question the labels that the researchers attached to those variables. For example, suppose that the researchers claim to have manipulated the construct "television violence" and claim to have measured the construct "aggression." They could be wrong on both counts.

The researchers' manipulation would not have *construct validity* if the two programs differed in their excitement level. If the violent program was also more exciting than the other program, the increase in aggression may be from the heightened arousal of children who viewed it rather than from the violence.

The researchers' measure would not have construct validity if it did not accurately measure aggression. For example, if their aggression measure consisted of giving children inkblots to look at and then counting the number of times the children thought that the inkblots looked like animals, you should question the construct validity of the aggression measure. The measure does not match up closely with definitions of aggression, and there is no evidence that it correlates with valid measures of aggression. If the measure was how aggressive the researchers thought the inkblot responses were, you would also question the measure's validity on the grounds that it was not objective and therefore allowed the researchers to bias the results.

In many studies, you should be concerned about the potential for *researcher bias:* the researcher behaving differently in different conditions of the study, thereby influencing the behavior of the participants (to favor the researcher's hypothesis). Research has shown researcher bias to be quite subtle and to occur despite the researcher's best intentions (Rosenthal, 1966).

In many studies, you may also need to decide whether the results may be due to *participant bias:* participants guessing the hypothesis and altering their behavior either to favor or to refute the hypothesis. Participant bias is often a problem in research that asks participants to fill out a scale or to answer a question. In such research, it is easy for participants to give a researcher the answers they think the researcher wants to hear.

Researcher bias and participant bias are often serious threats to research in clinical psychology. For example, suppose that people suffering from depression are randomly assigned either to take a particular treatment (e.g., a new drug or a new therapy) or to take a control treatment (a capsule containing an inert substance or an ineffective therapy). If the researcher knows which people are receiving the treatment and which are receiving the control, the researcher might behave more cheerily to those receiving the treatment than to those receiving the control—and that cheeriness might improve the treatment group's mood. In such a case, the study's construct validity would be ruined by researcher bias. If the participants know whether they have received the treatment, those receiving the treatment might cheer up because they expect the treatment to work, whereas those receiving the control might despair. In that case, participant bias would poison the study's construct validity. One popular way to deal with both participant and researcher bias has been to run *double-blind* (also called *double-masked*) studies, in which the experimenter and the participants are kept ignorant of (are blind to) which group is which. For example, in a drug study, the primary investigator might have assigned a code to each bottle of pills. The participants and the research assistants who interacted with the participants would know the pill's code number (e.g., X3987), but would not know whether the pill contained a drug or whether it was only a placebo.

5.9.5 Faulty Generalizations

In addition to questioning the study's construct validity, you should question the study's *external validity:* the degree to which the results of the study can be generalized to different settings and different participants. One clue to the extent to which the results can be generalized will come from the Participants section. If the participants are a large, representative sample (e.g., a large random sample) of a broad population, you can be more confident that the results will generalize to people beyond the participants of that particular study than if the participants were not a representative sample of that population. If, for example, the participants constituted a large, random sample of the population, you could be fairly confident that the same pattern of results would occur if another sample of that population—or if that entire population—were tested. Note, however, that if only two of the participants in this representative sample were Asian Americans, you have little evidence that the results generalize to Asian Americans.

Question generalizations. For example, imagine an experiment in which university students were required to learn lists of words. On each presentation of particular words, the learner was given a mild electric shock. Learning continued until all the words were recalled correctly. Imagine the results showed that, one week later, students recalled fewer shocked words than non-shocked words. Although this study would certainly suggest that repressed memories are possible, if a writer concluded from the experiment that repression of emotionally charged material occurs in children, you should definitely question the writer's generalizations.

In evaluating generalizations, be cautious, but not cynical; you should neither unquestionably accept them nor unquestionably reject them. Be cautious by realizing that any generalization beyond the evidence may be wrong: The only way to be sure that the results generalize to a particular group or setting is to repeat the study with that particular group or setting. However, do not be so cynical that you completely reject any generalization that goes beyond the immediate study. It is often reasonable to make tentative generalizations. For example, given that almost all research results obtained in a lab setting also hold in field settings, it is usually reasonable to generalize from the lab to the field. Similarly, given that most relationships found with one group also can be found with a different group, generalizing the results to a group that was not adequately sampled may be reasonable. To reject such a generalization, you should do more than say that no generalization is possible because the particular group has not been sampled. Instead, you should have a logical explanation of how differences between that particular group and the group studied would prevent the results from applying to that particular group.

5.10   Critical Thinking Checklist

___ I made a suitable claim.
  ___ I did not substitute a tautology for a claim.
  ___ I used accepted definitions of terms.
___ My arguments were logical.
  ___ I identified my premises and, when possible, used evidence to make the case that they were true.
  ___ I made sure that my conclusion followed logically from my premises.
  ___ I avoided appeals to emotion, faith, and authority.
___ I dealt fairly with opposing positions.
  ___ I did not engage in ad hominem attacks on proponents of opposing positions.
  ___ I did not attack a "straw man" version of the opposing position.
  ___ I did not ignore evidence that appeared to support an opposing position: I either showed how that evidence, when properly interpreted, was consistent with my claims, or I qualified my claims to be consistent with that evidence.
___ I considered alternative explanations for findings.
  ___ I did not interpret correlational evidence as proving causality.
  ___ I did not use the fact that studies failed to find differences as proof that differences did not exist.
  ___ I questioned whether the measures and manipulations really reflected the labels that the researcher gave them.
  ___ I considered explanations, other than the ones provided by the authors, for the obtained results.
___ I was careful when accepting generalizations from a study, especially when there was reason to believe that the sample was biased.

5.11 Summary

1. If you are writing a term paper, state an arguable thesis (see 5.1 and 5.6).

2. One step to making a good argument is having sound (accurate) premises. Once you have sound premises, you can focus on demonstrating that your argument is *valid* (the conclusion follows logically from your premises).

3. The simplest deductive argument is the *syllogism*, in which there are two premises and a conclusion. In deductive arguments, premises are statements about the world couched in absolute terms (e.g., "all," "every," "always") or in unambiguous comparisons (e.g., "A is bigger than B.").

4. If you are making a case for a hypothesis, you may want to make your case using a syllogism.

5. Do not appeal to emotion or authority.

6. Do not ignore evidence that contradicts your argument.

7. Do not use unfair tactics, such as ad hominem arguments (5.8.1) or straw man arguments (5.8.3).

8. Common errors in reasoning from evidence include inferring a cause-effect relationship from a correlational study, uncritically generalizing the results from a study that used a biased sample, and uncritically accepting the labels that a researcher gives to the measures and manipulations.

9. Although you cannot safely infer causation from a correlational study, you can reasonably infer causation from an experiment (see 5.9.1).

10. Null results are inconclusive.

11. Statistically significant results are not necessarily large or important.

12. You can be more confident of a study's construct validity if the researcher (a) has used commonly accepted measures and manipulations and (b) has taken steps, such as using "blind" procedures, to decrease both participant bias and researcher bias.

13. Although there is always some risk in generalizing the results of a study, you can be more confident that the results apply to a larger group if the study looked at a large random sample of participants from that group.

CHAPTER

6

Writing the Wrongs: How to Avoid Gruesome Grammar, Putrid Punctuation, and Saggy Style

Writing a paper is like driving passengers to a destination. In addition to knowing where you are going, you should know enough about the

1. components of a car (parts of speech) and how they work together (basic grammar) to get in and start the car;
2. controls (punctuation) to keep the car going, steer, and brake;
3. rules of the road (usage) so you drive on the correct side of the road and respect other road users; and
4. passengers' preferences and the car's handling characteristics (style) to drive with care, and, possibly, flair.

If you spend a little time on this chapter, you will be able to understand most of the comments that the *Publication Manual* makes about writing, as well as the comments that your professor or writing center may make about your paper. If you spend a moderate amount of time with this chapter, you will be able to write competently. If you spend a great deal of time with this chapter, you will be able to express your ideas with style and flair.

6.1 Elements of Grammar

The smallest unit of writing is the word. Types of words include nouns, pronouns, verbs, articles, adjectives, adverbs, prepositions, conjunctions, and relative pronouns. As you will see, the same word can be labeled as one part of speech (e.g., as a noun) in one context and as a different part of speech (e.g., as an adjective) in a different context. To illustrate the different parts of speech, we will analyze a sentence written by McDougall (1914):

> The department of psychology that is of primary importance
> for the social sciences is that which deals with the
> springs of human action. (pp. 2-3)

6.1.1 Nouns

Nouns are names: person names, place names, object names, and concept names (e.g., freedom). Here is McDougall's sentence with the nouns printed in bold italics:

> The ***department*** of ***psychology*** that is of primary ***importance***
> for the social ***sciences*** is that which deals with the
> ***springs*** of human ***action.***

Nouns have a property called *number*, meaning they can be *singular* or *plural*. Singular nouns refer to just one of the named thing (e.g., "department"); plural nouns refer to two or more of the named thing (e.g., "sciences"). Most plurals are formed simply by adding *s*, *es*, or *en* to the end of a singular noun (e.g., "cats," "foxes," "oxen"). However, not all plurals are formed so simply. Nouns derived from Greek or Latin may have singulars ending with *on* or *us* (e.g., criterion, stimulus) and plurals ending with *a* and *i*, respectively (e.g., criteria, stimuli). To use the correct plural form of some nouns, you must memorize the plural form (e.g., geese). The six most misused plurals are listed in Table 6.1. Memorize these six. In addition, when proofing your paper, consult Appendix B to check for other tricky plurals.

Be alert not only to nouns that have unusual plural forms, but also to nouns that are singular even though they refer to more than one person. For example, "everybody," "everyone," and "anyone" are all singular. Similarly, *collective nouns*, nouns that stand for groups (e.g., "team," "university," "family"), are treated as singular—if you are treating the group as a single unit. Thus, you should write, "The family was interviewed together."

Sometimes, students have trouble deciding whether a percentage (e.g., 33%) or fraction (e.g., one in three) is singular or plural. However, the rule is simple: Integers and percentages greater than one are plural (e.g., "One [singular] in three experiences depression some time during life"; "Seventy-five percent [plural] of the population are happy with their lives").

Sometimes, students have trouble deciding what to do when two nouns are connected in a sentence. However, you will not have that problem if you follow two rules. First, when "and" joins two singular nouns, treat the nouns as plural (e.g., "Smith and Brown provide a useful definition"). Second, when "or" or "nor" joins two nouns, use

TABLE **6.1**   Six Tricky Plurals

Singular	Plural	Examples
criterion	criteria	One criterion of good writing is correct use of plural words. There are several other criteria, including correct punctuation and grammar.
datum	data	A datum for each individual was the time taken for his or her first correct response. These data were analyzed using *t* tests.
hypothesis	hypotheses	Hypothesis 1 was supported, but the other hypotheses were not.
medium	media	The most influential medium is television. Other media such as magazines, newspapers, and radio cannot combine moving images and sound.
phenomenon	phenomena	One learning phenomenon is spontaneous recovery. There are three other important learning phenomena.
stimulus	stimuli	Each stimulus was displayed in a circular field. The six stimuli were presented in a random order.

the form required by the noun closer to the verb (e.g., "Either they or I *am* correct," "Neither she nor they *are* correct").

The final problem students have with nouns is that they do not capitalize *proper nouns:* names of particular people, events, organizations, languages, buildings, countries, and racial groups. Remember, proper nouns are always capitalized (e.g., "Jones," "Pennsylvania," "Asian Americans").

6.1.2 Personal and Impersonal Pronouns

Pronouns are words that substitute for nouns. *Personal pronouns* stand for people (e.g., "her," "him"). *Impersonal pronouns* stand for things (e.g., "it," "this," "that," "these," "those," "either," "neither"). Here is McDougall's sentence with its impersonal pronoun printed in bold italics:

> The department of psychology that is of primary importance for the social sciences is *that* which deals with the springs of human action.

The boldfaced and italicized "that" stands for "the department of psychology."

Personal pronouns have three *persons: first person* (referring to the person[s] speaking [e.g., "I," "me"]), *second person* (referring to the person[s] being spoken to [e.g., "you"]), and *third person* (referring to the person[s] being spoken about [e.g., "she," "her"]). In addition, personal pronouns also have three *cases: subjective, objective,* and *possessive.*

- Subjective means the pronoun is the agent, the *subject*, of the sentence (e.g., "*I* calculated"). The subjective pronoun usually comes before the verb. The subjective case is also known as the *nominative* case. "I," "we," "they," "she," and "he," are nominative pronouns. "Who" is also a nominative pronoun: If you can replace the "who" in your sentence with "he" or some other nominative pronoun, you have correctly chosen between "who" and "whom."

- Objective means the pronoun is the *object* acted upon in the sentence (e.g., "The idea [subject] surprised [verb] *me* [object]"). The pronoun following the verb is almost always an objective pronoun[1] (e.g., "I [subject] was surprised *by him* [object]"). "Me," "us," "them," "her," and "him" are objective pronouns. "Whom" is also an objective pronoun: If you can replace the "whom" in your sentence with "him," "her," or some other objective pronoun, you have correctly chosen between "who" and "whom."

- Possessive means the pronoun owns (possesses) something (e.g., "*Our* argument is").

Like nouns, pronouns have number. Table 6.2 shows all the possible combinations of person, case, and number for most of the personal pronouns. Pronouns must agree in number and gender with the nouns they represent:

✘ The technique is best for disciplining the *child* because *they* learn the consequences of *their* actions [unclear because *child* is singular, but *they* and *their* are plural].

✔ The technique is best for disciplining *children* because *they* learn the consequences of *their* actions [now the noun and pronoun are both plural].

The indefinite pronouns "neither" and "either" can bedevil students. For starters, both "neither" and "either" are singular (e.g., "Either is a problem."). Then, there is the problem that "neither" and "either" can be used only when you are referring to two things. Therefore, if you have three items, do not use "either" or "neither." Finally, some students do not understand the intimate relationship between "neither" and "nor." You can use the conjunction "nor" in only two situations: (a) after "neither" or (b) to continue negation started in one clause into the next clause.

✘ There were *neither* colloquialisms, contractions, foreign words, *nor* proper nouns in the list [wrong because *neither* was used to cover more than two things].

✔ There were no colloquialisms, contractions, foreign words, or proper nouns in the list.

✘ Neither Smith (1967) *or* [wrong because *nor* must be used after neither] Jones (1973) explained the phenomenon.

----

[1]The pronoun following a verb will be an objective pronoun except when the verb is "was," "is," "are," "were," or some other form of the verb "to be." In such cases, you would use a subjective pronoun rather than an objective pronoun. Thus, you would write, "It was she" rather than "It was her."

TABLE **6.2** Subjective, Objective, and Possessive Cases of Personal Pronouns by Person and Number

	Person	**Subjective**	**Objective**	**Possessive**
Singular				
	First	I	me	my, mine
	Second	you	you	your, yours
	Third	he, she	him, her	his, her, hers
		who	whom	whose
Plural				
	First	we	us	our, ours
	Second	you	you	your, yours
	Third	they	them	their, theirs
		who	whom	whose

✔ Neither Smith (1967) nor Jones (1973) explained the phenomenon.

✘ Theory Y does not explain paranoia *nor* [*nor* would have been okay if *neither* had come before paranoia] catatonia, *or* [need to use *nor* to show that the theory does *not* deal with mania] deal with mania.

✔ Theory Y does not explain paranoia or catatonia, nor deal with mania ["nor" continues the negation started in the first clause into the last clause].

6.1.3 Verbs

Verbs are words that represent actions; they are the "doers" of the sentence. Here is McDougall's sentence with the verbs italicized (the main verb of the sentence has been printed in bold italic):

The department of psychology that *is* of primary importance for the social sciences *is* that which *deals* with the springs of human action.

Verbs have a property called *tense*. Tense refers to when the action of a verb happened. *Future* tense means the action is going to happen. To form the future tense, put the word "will" before the verb (e.g., will analyze). *Present* tense means the action is happening now. *Past* tense means the action happened some time ago. To form the past tense of regular verbs, put "-ed" onto the end of the verb (e.g., analyzed). *Present perfect tense* means that the event happened in the past at some unknown time and is continuing to occur. To form the present perfect tense, put "have" before your verb (e.g., have analyzed). (To learn more about using the right tense, see 2.10 and 3.11.)

In addition to tenses, verbs also have moods. One mood is the *subjunctive* mood, used to describe something that did not happen. Verbs in the subjunctive mood are often preceded by the word "if" (e.g., "If we were to boil our participants in oil").

A verb, unless it is in the subjunctive mood, must be singular if its subject is singular and must be plural if its subject is plural. If you are using a regular verb in the present tense, finding the verb form that *agrees* with the subject will usually be easy because *regular* verbs have only two forms for the present tense. One form, with an "s" at the end (e.g., "agrees"), covers the third person singular ("he agrees," "she agrees"). The other form, without an "s" at the end, covers the other cases ("I agree," "you agree," "we agree," and "they agree"). Meeting the requirement of subject-verb agreement is more difficult with *irregular* verbs, verbs having more than one form (e.g., the verb "to be" has "I am," "you/we/they are," and "he/she is").

Verbs also have a property called *voice*. There are two voices: *active* and *passive*. In the active voice, the subject acts on the object (e.g., "Smith [subject] discovered [active verb] the phenomenon [object]."). In the passive voice, the subject is acted on by the object (e.g., "The phenomenon [subject] was discovered [passive verb] by Smith [object]."). The active voice is more direct and less wordy. Usually, you should use the active rather than the passive voice. (For more about voice, see 1.3.2.)

Two "almost-verbs" that writers sometimes mistake for verbs are the *infinitive* and the *present participle*. An infinitive always has the word "to" in front of it (e.g., "to be," "to deal"). A present participle is usually produced by adding "-ing" on the end of the verb's infinitive form (e.g., "being," "dealing"). Neither infinitives nor present participles can function as verbs: As you can see from the following examples, trying to use these almost-verbs as verbs will cause you to write incomplete sentences.

✘ To be human. [not a sentence] What does it mean? . . . This theory dealing with motivation. [not a sentence]

✔ What does it mean to be human? . . . This theory deals with motivation.

6.1.4 Articles

Articles come before nouns. There are only three: one *definite* article, "the," and two *indefinite* articles, "a" and "an."

- Use definite articles to (a) refer to a noun you mentioned earlier (e.g., "*The* concept I mentioned earlier") or (b) to indicate that you are referring to one particular noun (e.g., "*The* most important concept for my argument"—there can be only one concept that is most important).

- Indefinite articles indicate that you are not referring to one particular, unique individual entity. Instead, you are referring to one among many possible nouns. Thus, if you write, "*An* important concept for my argument," you are implying that there are other important concepts relating to your argument.

- "An" is usually used for the indefinite article if the word that follows it begins with a vowel sound (e.g., "an apple"); otherwise "a" is used (e.g., "a bed").

However, there are exceptions to this rule. For example, "a" is sometimes used before words beginning with "u" (e.g., "a university"), and "an" is sometimes used before words beginning with "h" (e.g., "an historical event"). You can detect most of the exceptions by reading your sentence aloud: If you have incorrectly applied the rule to an exception (e.g., "an unicorn"), your sentence will probably not sound right.

6.1.5 Adjectives

Adjectives are words that describe nouns and pronouns. Here is McDougall's sentence with the adjectives printed in bold italics:

```
The department of psychology that is of primary importance
for the social sciences is that which deals with the
springs of human action.
```

There are two serious—and avoidable—problems that students have with adjectives. First, students often use too many adjectives because they think that using adjectives will make their writing more powerful. They are wrong. Powerful writing comes from using nouns and verbs that help readers see what you are thinking.

Second, students sometimes use adjectives to label people in ways that are offensive. For example, students may use adjectives such as "elderly" or "retarded" in such a way that the individuals being referred to are not seen as individuals, but rather as members of a group possessing only that one characteristic. In the most extreme cases of focusing on one characteristic to the exclusion of every other characteristic, some students err by using an adjective as a noun (e.g., "the elderly," "the depressed"). Do not make that mistake (for more about using inclusive language, see 1.3.4).

6.1.6 Adverbs

Adverbs are words that modify verbs or adjectives. Adverbs usually are formed from an adjective with "-ly" tacked on the end (e.g., "correctly," "effectively," "largely"). We have changed the first part of McDougall's sentence to include an adverb (the word "primarily"):

```
The department of psychology that primarily deals with the
springs of human action . . .
```

Take care when placing the adverb "only" in a sentence. Usually, that adverb should come after—not before—its verb:

✗ The participant only pressed one button [The participant did nothing else except press one button: The participant did not look at the stimuli, think, or breathe].

✔ The participant pressed only one button.

Be cautious when using adverbs to modify verbs. Sometimes, you can often omit the adverb without losing anything (e.g., "analyze" is not less descriptive than "closely analyze"). Sometimes, rather than looking for an adverb to modify the verb, you should look for a better verb (e.g., instead of adding "closely" to "look at," replace "look at" with "inspect," "examine," or "analyze"). If you must use an adverb to modify the verb, use the "-ly" adverb form rather than the adjective form (e.g., "closely" rather than "close"), and place the adverb close to its verb.

Sometimes, rather than use an adverb to modify a verb, you might use an adverb as a transition word. For example, you might use words such as "consequently," "similarly," or "conversely" at the beginning of a sentence to point out the relationship between that sentence and the previous sentence. Even as transition words, however, adverbs can get you in trouble. Thus, the *Publication Manual* discourages the use of either "importantly" or "interestingly." In addition, the *Manual* points out that it is wrong to use "hopefully" to mean "it is hoped." Most students would be better off if they eliminated "hopefully" from their vocabulary.

6.1.7 Prepositions

Prepositions are words, such as "among," between," "beyond," "during," and "with," that describe the relationship of nouns and pronouns to other words. Some prepositions could be used to describe a cat's location relative to a box (e.g., "in," "on," "near," "behind," "under," "above," "into," and "off"). Many prepositions are short (e.g., "at," "by," "of," "for," and "to"). Here is McDougall's original sentence with the prepositions printed in bold italics:

> The department *of* psychology that is *of* primary importance *for* the social sciences is that which deals *with* the springs *of* human action.

Do not follow prepositions with "I," "she," "he," "we," "they," or "who." If you follow prepositions with a personal pronoun, that pronoun should be "me," "her," "him," "us," "them," or "whom" (e.g., "to *him*," "between *her* and *me*," "give it to *them*").

Secrutinize possessive phrases beginning with the preposition "of" (e.g., "results *of the study*," "origin *of the effect*"). Often, you should reword possessive phrases starting with "of" by adding *apostrophe "s"* ('s) to the key noun or pronoun of the phrase and eliminating the preposition "of" (i.e., "study's results," "effect's origin"). (See also the section on apostrophes [6.2.5].)

Scrutinize prepositional phrases beginning with the preposition "with" that describe a noun. Often, you will want to replace such phrases with an adjective. Using an adjective is more concise and more powerful than using a prepositional phrase. Thus, writing "the *bloody* knife" puts more emphasis on your description of the knife than writing "the knife *with blood on it*")—a prepositional phrase that makes your description of the knife seem like an afterthought. Sometimes, though, you may wish to emphasize the noun rather than the words modifying the noun. For example, the *Publication Manual* recommends using prepositional phrases when describing people who have disabilities (e.g., "a person with a disability" rather than "a disabled person") so that the focus is on the person rather than on a label.

Writers often have trouble with the prepositions "between" and "among." Most of the time, you should use "between" to distinguish two things and use "among" to distinguish more than two (e.g., "Our choice is between Theory X and Theory Y"; "Our choice is among Theory X, Theory Y, and Theory Z"). The exception is when you are discussing differences or variances. Even when you are distinguishing between more than two things, use "between" when you are talking about differences or variances ("There were several differences between our three groups).").

6.1.8 Conjunctions

Conjunctions are words that connect other words, phrases, or clauses. The conjunctions you are most familiar with are coordinating conjunctions such as "and," "but," and "or." However, there are many other conjunctions. To illustrate some of the different types of conjunctions, suppose you had two short sentences that you wanted to connect (e.g., "They talked. I walked."). You could connect the sentences using a coordinating conjunction such as "and" (e.g., "They talked, and I walked."). However, you could also connect the sentences by using either a conjunctive adverb or a subordinating conjunction.

If you use a conjunctive adverb such as "however," "nevertheless," or "moreover" to connect the two sentences, you have two choices. First, you could add the conjunctive adverb to the second sentence (e.g., "They talked. However, I walked."). Second, you could combine the two sentences into one (e.g., "They talked; however, I walked.").

If you use a subordinating conjunction, such as "although" or "as," you must combine the two sentences into one (e.g., "As they talked, I walked.") because you no longer have two independent sentences. If you put a subordinating conjunction in front of the first sentence (e.g., "Although they talked."), your first "sentence" is no longer a complete sentence but instead becomes a sentence fragment. Similarly, if you put a subordinating conjunction in front of the second sentence (e.g., "As I walked."), your second "sentence" would now be a sentence fragment. In short, when using subordinating conjunctions, be careful not to make a sentence fragment.

When using subordinating conjunctions, also be careful not to misuse "while" and "since." Use the subordinate conjunctions "while" and "since" only when referring to time (e.g., "While the experimenter waited, the participant continued with the task"; "Since Freud's seminal works, the idea of the unconscious has gained greater acceptance"). If you are not relating the time sequence of events, do not use "while" or "since". Instead use conjunctions such as "although" and "because" (i.e., "Although the experimenter waited, the participant continued with the task"; "The idea of the unconscious has gained greater acceptance because of Freud's seminal works").

6.1.9 Relative Pronouns

Relative pronouns refer to pronouns such as "that," "which," "who," "whom," and "whose." A relative pronoun introduces text that describes a noun. Here is McDougall's original sentence with the relative pronouns printed in bold italics:

> The department of psychology *that* is of primary importance for the social sciences is that *which* deals with the springs of human action.

Next, we address the most common questions students have about relative pronouns.

■ *"Should I use 'who' or 'that'?"* Although "that" can be used to refer to humans, skilled writers use "who," "whom," and "whose" to refer to humans (e.g., "It was Piaget *who* first showed"; "Freud is the one to *whom* Jung was referring"; "Spock, *whose* ideas shaped the attitudes of a generation of mothers, asserted"). Reserve "that" for referring to animals and objects (e.g., "The animals *that* were in the experimental group"; "The realization *that* changed our approach").

■ *"Should I use 'who' or 'whom'?"* The key is to realize that "who," like "he," "she," and "we," is a nominative pronoun, whereas "whom," like "him," "her," and "us," is an objective pronoun (see Table 6.2). Say your sentence aloud using a nominative personal pronoun (e.g., "he") instead of "who" or "whom." Then, say the sentence again using an objective personal pronoun (e.g., "him"). If the sentence sounds better using the nominative pronoun ("he first showed"), use "who"; if the sentence sounds better using the objective pronoun ("to him"), use "whom."

■ *"Should I use 'which' or 'that'?"* Use "which" when it introduces a parenthetical (nonessential, nonrestrictive) clause (i.e., one that could be left out of the sentence without changing its meaning, one that is set off from the rest of the sentence by commas, or one that could be put in parentheses) (e.g., "This idea, *which* has been promoted on several previous occasions, is again becoming popular"). Also use "which" if you would otherwise have to write "that that" (e.g., In our example passage, McDougall wrote, "sciences is that which" rather than writing, "sciences is that that."). Use "that" when it introduces a clause essential to the meaning of the sentence (e.g., "The stimulus *that* was shown in the intertrial interval was a smiley face.").

6.1.10 Phrases

After the individual word, the next major unit in writing is the phrase. A *phrase* contains more than one word and expresses an element of an idea. *Prepositional phrases* always contain a preposition and either a noun or pronoun. Prepositional phrases may also include an article and an adjective, as you can see from the following examples:

```
The department [phrase] of psychology [prepositional phrase]
that is [phrase] of primary importance [prepositional phrase]
for the social sciences [prepositional phrase] is that [phrase]
which deals [phrase] with the springs [prepositional phrase] of
human action [prepositional phrase].
```

6.1.11 Clauses

After the phrase, the next major unit in writing is the clause. A *clause* contains a subject and a verb. An *independent* clause contains a complete thought and so could stand as a sentence. Note that the first part of the last sentence, *"An independent clause con-*

tains a complete thought," is an independent clause. A *dependent clause,* although it also has a subject and a verb, does not contain a complete thought, and therefore could not stand as a sentence:

> The department of psychology {that is of primary importance for the social sciences} [dependent clause 1] is that {which deals with the springs of human action} [dependent clause 2].

6.1.12 Sentences

The next major unit in writing is the sentence. A *sentence* contains a subject and a verb, expresses a complete thought, begins with a capital letter, and ends with an end mark (usually a period). Often, a sentence is a single independent clause.

In informal writing, the shortest sentences may contain only a single word, a verb. In such sentences, the subject is implicit (e.g., "Observe."). In formal writing, the subject of a sentence should be explicit (e.g., "*You* observe."). Furthermore, in formal writing, if the sentence also contains an object—a recipient of the verb's action—the object should be explicit (e.g., "You can observe *the means and standard deviations* in Figure 3.").

When editing your sentences, try to make sure that you have not committed either of the two most serious errors in sentence construction: (a) writing a sentence that is incomplete (a "fragment") and (b) writing a sentence that is too long. The first error, writing an incomplete sentence, rather than a complete sentence, usually occurs when a student

- leaves out a verb,
- employs an "almost verb" (e.g., "to deal" or "dealing") rather than a verb (e.g., "deals"), or
- turns what would have been an independent sentence (e.g., "I walked.") into a subordinate clause by putting a subordinating conjunction (see 6.1.8) such as "although" or "while" in front of it (e.g., "although I walked.").

The second error, writing a sentence that is too long, often leads to additional problems. At best, such sentences exceed not only the reader's patience but also the reader's short-term memory capacity. Usually, such long sentences also set up the writer to make at least three additional errors.

First, because there are more nouns, more pronouns, and more verbs, the writer has a greater chance of losing track of whether a particular noun, verb, or pronoun is singular or plural. As a result, the writer is more likely to make (a) more subject-verb agreement errors and (b) more pronoun-noun agreement errors.

Second, because there are more words in the sentence, the writer has a greater chance of putting a pronoun too far from its noun and a modifier too far from what it should modify. If your teacher does not know which noun the pronoun refers to, your teacher may circle the pronoun and write "vague referent"; if your teacher does not know what a modifier is supposed to be modifying, your teacher may circle the modifier and write "misplaced modifier."

Third, because there are more clauses, there is greater potential for making errors in joining clauses. For example, the writer may leave out a comma needed to link a dependent clause to an independent clause. Alternatively, the writer may create a "run-on" sentence (see 6.3.4) by (a) trying to join two related independent clauses using only a comma or (b) by trying to join two unrelated independent clauses with a comma and a conjunction (e.g., "The theory has won wide acceptance, and I will consider methodological errors.").

6.1.13 Paragraphs

After the sentence, the next major unit in writing is the paragraph. A *paragraph* expresses one major idea. It must consist of at least two sentences. Although some of your paragraphs may consist of only two sentences, most should be longer: Your average paragraph should consist of about 100 words. If a few of your paragraphs are well under 100 words, do not be concerned. If, on the other hand, any of your paragraphs are well over 100 words (130 words or more), be concerned.[2] Put another way, your paragraphs should usually be shorter than half of a page and should never be longer than one double-spaced page. (To learn more about writing paragraphs, see 6.4.2.)

6.2 Punctuation

6.2.1 End Marks (Periods, Question Marks, Exclamation Points)

In formal writing, you will almost never use an exclamation point to end a sentence. Instead, you will almost always use a period. A period will be the last character of a sentence except

- if the last word of the sentence is in quotation marks, in which case the quotation mark ends the sentence;
- if the entire sentence is in parentheses, in which case the right parenthesis ends the sentence; or
- if your sentence is a question, in which case the question mark ends the sentence.

6.2.2 Commas

Use a comma within a sentence where you would normally pause when speaking. To be more specific, use a comma

- after transition words such as "however," "consequently," and "furthermore";

---

[2]The word count feature of your word processor can tell you how many words are in a paragraph.

- after conjunctions, such as "and," "but," "for," "nor," "or," "so," and "yet" (e.g., "The participants read the instructions, and the researcher read the instructions aloud."), when those conjunctions connect two independent clauses;

- to segregate elements of lists of three or more, including authors' names (e.g., Jones, Smith, and Taylor);

- to set off parenthetical phrases or dependent clauses (e.g., "This idea, which Freud originated, has had enormous influence"); and

- to connect a dependent clause that starts a sentence to the independent clause that follows it (e.g., "Although rewriting is hard work, it should be done.").

6.2.3 Semicolons

There are three main uses for semicolons. First, use a semicolon to separate two or more lists of words. In such cases, the semicolon lets readers know when one list stops and another begins.

```
Here is an example list of related terms: conditioned
response, unconditioned response, conditioned stimulus, and
unconditioned stimulus; milligram, gram, and kilogram; and
intelligence quotient, chronological age, and mental age.
```

Second, use a semicolon to connect closely related, independent clauses without using a coordinating conjunction such as "and." For example, you should write

```
Theory A is popular; theory B is not popular.
```

Note that had you used a comma instead of a semicolon to connect the two independent clauses in the previous example, you would have a "run-on" sentence (see 6.3.4).

Third, use a semicolon to connect highly related independent clauses with linking words such as "consequently," "furthermore," "however," "moreover," "therefore," "nevertheless," "indeed," and "thus." The trick is that the semicolon comes *before* the linking word and a comma comes *after* the linking word (e.g., "; therefore,").

6.2.4 Colons

Use a colon to introduce a list of items (e.g., "There were four conditions: control, auditory, visual, and olfactory") or to emphasize the final element of a sentence (e.g., "Skinner devoted his life to one concept: operant conditioning"). In either case, you can use a colon only if the clause coming before the colon is an independent clause. That is, if you replace the colon with a period, that period should mark the end of a grammatically intact sentence. If the words in front of the period would not make a sentence, you should not use a colon. Thus, you should never use a colon to separate a verb from its direct object (e.g., it is incorrect to write, "Three reasons are:").

6.2.5 Apostrophes

In informal writing, an apostrophe may signal that some letters have been omitted from a word turning that word into a *contraction* (e.g., "wasn't" is a contraction of "was" and "not," the "o" being the omitted letter). In formal writing, an apostrophe may be used for only one purpose: to signify a possessive (e.g., "the experiment's design"). To form the possessive of a singular noun, add *apostrophe "s"* (e.g., "the theory's assumptions," "the stimulus's duration," "Jones's paper"). To form the possessive of a plural noun ending in *s*, add a final apostrophe (e.g., "these theories' assumptions," "The Joneses' [i.e., Fred and Myrtle] contribution"). To form the possessive of a plural noun ending in anything other than *s*, add *apostrophe "s"* (e.g., "children's toys," "the stimuli's origin").

Note that the possessive of "it" is not "it's" ("it's" is the contraction of "it is") but "its." Thus, just as "yours" is the possessive case of the pronoun "you" and "theirs" is the possessive case of the pronoun "their," "its" is the possessive case of the pronoun "it" (see Table 6.2).

In conclusion, the big problem students have with apostrophes is that students use them too much. Do not use apostrophes with dates (e.g., write "1950s," not "1950's"). Do not use contractions (e.g., "don't") in your papers—and especially do not use the contractions "it's," "they're," "who's," and "ain't."

6.2.6 Parentheses

Use parentheses to enclose parenthetical material unnecessary for the meaning of the sentence (e.g., this example). Parentheses signal to the reader that the enclosed material could safely be ignored. Each time you use parentheses, ask yourself if the material is vital to the meaning of the sentence. If the material is vital, build it into the sentence. If it is not vital, consider omitting it: Parenthetical asides may distract the reader from your main point. In short, except for citations, you should probably avoid using parentheses.

6.2.7 Dashes

Use *em dashes*—illustrated here—to enclose parenthetical material. Em dashes—given that name because they are the width of a capital letter "M"—create a form of parenthetical comment intermediate in strength between commas and parentheses. If you cannot make an em dash with your word processor, use two hyphens. Like material set off by parentheses, material set off by an em dash is often material that should be edited or deleted.

6.2.8 Hyphens

Use hyphens in compound words that would otherwise be ambiguous (e.g., compare the meaning of "man chasing woman" with "man-chasing woman"), or to clarify the meaning of words (e.g., "I re-sent the letter"). Do not use hyphens to keep your right margins even. That is, do not use a hyphen to split a word at the end of a line. In short, there are two general rules about hyphens: (a) do not use hyphens for common phrases (e.g. day care center), and (b) try not to use hyphens at all.

6.2.9 Quotation Marks

There are only two reasons to surround words with quotation marks. First, surround words with quotation marks to signal the reader that those words are a brief quotation (see 4.7.1). Second, surround words with quotation marks to signal the reader that you are using the selected word or words in a different way from how the word or words are normally used.

✔ Participants waited in an anteroom with two other "participants" [appropriate only if you had previously explained that these two people were actually confederates of the experimenter].

Keep the latter sort of usage to a minimum. For example, you should not write anything like the following:

✘ the computer "knew" which alternative the participant had chosen.

If you had written the previous sentence, you would be saying to the reader, "I want you to understand the word 'knew' in a way other than you would normally understand it, but I could not be bothered to find a better word. You know what I mean." Rather than telling readers to figure out your unconventional meanings of words, you should make it easy for readers by finding the word you mean:

✔ The computer recorded which alternative the participant had chosen.

Students often make mistakes punctuating material in quotation marks. Fortunately, you can avoid most of these mistakes by following one rule: Put commas and periods inside quotation marks, but put colons, and semicolons outside of quotation marks.

If you are trying to decide where to put question marks in a quoted passage, you need to follow a pair of rules. First, if the question mark is part of the quote (e.g., She said, "What is the rule?"), then put the question mark inside the quotation mark. Second, if the question mark is not part of the quote (e.g., What is "Beetlebom's delight"?), then put the question mark outside the quotation mark.

6.3 Usage

6.3.1 Know What You Mean

Make sure you know the meaning of all words you use. Be careful when using a thesaurus to find synonyms. Check the dictionary definition of any synonym to ensure that it does not have a slightly different meaning from the one you intend.

Sometimes, students see a similarity between two words and end up using the wrong member of that pair. For example, students often use "affects" when they should use "effects"—and vice-versa. To be sure that you are using the right member of these "problem pairs," consult Table 6.3. By consulting Table 6.3, you will avoid common errors such as writing "my analysis infers" and "stress effects memory."

6.3.2 Complete Comparisons

Relational words describe relations between things (e.g., "different [from]," "similar [to]," "bigger [than]," "oldest [of]," "irrelevant [to]"). Unless obvious from the context, each time you use a relational word in a sentence, (a) use the preposition that comes with the relational word and (b) make it clear which two things are being related. If you do not complete your comparisons, you will write ambiguous sentences such as, "*The participants liked the experiment better than the experimenter.*" That sentence is ambiguous because the reader does not know whether (a) participants liked the experiment more than they liked the experimenter or (b) participants liked the experiment more than the experimenter liked the experiment. Note that completing the comparison results in an unambiguous sentence: "The participants liked the experiment more than they liked the experimenter."

6.3.3 Distinguish Comparatives from Superlatives

A *comparative* is an adjective or adverb used to compare two things. It is usually formed by first either adding "-er" to an adjective (e.g., "strong" becomes "stronger") or by placing the word *more* before an adverb (e.g., "strongly" becomes "more strongly") and then adding "than" (e.g., "The mean of group A is *larger than* the mean of group B"; "Participants in the X condition pressed the button *more* strongly *than* participants in the Y.").

Use "less" for uncountable qualities (e.g., less affection); use "fewer" for countable qualities (e.g., fewer hours). The word following "less" must always be singular; the word following "fewer" must always be plural.

✘ Theory A has more applications and *less* problems than Theory B.

✔ Theory A has more applications and fewer problems than Theory B.

Note that "different" is not a comparative, so you should not write, "A is *different than* B." Instead, you should write, "A is different *from* B."

A *superlative* is an adjective or adverb used to compare more than two things. It is usually formed by adding "-est" to an adjective or by placing the word "most" before an adverb (e.g., "Of the three groups, participants in A scored the *fewest* hits"; "Of participants in all four conditions, those in B pressed the button *most* strongly.").

TABLE **6.3** Problem Pairs

Problem Pair	Part of Speech*	Meaning	Example
affect	noun	emotion	The client's *affect* was flat.
affect	verb	influence	Learning the prior list *affected* recall of the test words.
affect	verb	pretend	The client *affected* a cheerful mood.
effect	noun	result	The *effect* of diffusion of responsibility was to delay helping.
effect	verb	bring about	The therapist *effected* a quick recovery in her client.
alternate	verb	change from one to another	The experimenter *alternated* the order in which the stimuli were presented.
alternative	noun	one of two or more possibilities	Choose the correct *alternative*.
	adj	allowing a choice between two or more possibilities	They wanted an *alternative* candidate.
casual	adj	informal	We will be playing outside, so wear *casual* clothes.
causal	adj	relating to the causes of an effect	They found a *causal* relationship between smoking and cancer.
continually	adv	recurring often	The writer was *continually* interrupted by the telephone.
continously	adv	without interruption	The noise level was reduced *continuously* until the observer could hear the tone.
dependent variable	noun	A measure of the participant's behavior	The dependent variable was the participant's score on the measure.
independent variable	noun	The factor that is manipulated in a study	The independent variable was the noise level.
disinterested	adj	impartial, fair, unbiased	Smith, coming from neither side of the controversy, is a *disinterested* judge.
uninterested	adj	without interest, unconcerned	The participant, having just eaten, was *uninterested* in eating more.
experiment	noun	A type of study, usually involving random assignment, that allows researchers to make cause-effect statements	In this experiment, participants were randomly assigned to one of three groups.

Notes: * adj = adjective, adv = adverb

(continued on next page)

T A B L E **6.3** Problem Pairs—*continued*

Problem Pair	Part of Speech*	Meaning	Example
study	noun	Any type of study, including nonexperimental studies, such as survey research.	In this study, participants were asked about their views.
farther	adj	more distant	Observers judged the distance of the *farther* of the landmarks.
	adv	to a more distant point	Maze-bright rats progressed *farther* in the maze than maze-dull rats.
further	adj	additional	With *further* research, the phenomenon might be explained.
	adv	more	Jones developed the theory *further.*
fewer	adj	fewer in terms of how many (refers to a countable quantity)	Participants made fewer errors.
less	adj	less in terms of how much (refers to an uncountable quality)	Participants seemed less anxious.
fortuitous	adj	occurring by chance	The meeting between the mail carrier and the sharp-toothed dog was *fortuitous.*
fortunate	adj	lucky	We are *fortunate* to be living in the information age.
gender	noun	masculine vs. feminine	*Gender* refers to the psychological aspects of being a man or a woman.
sex	noun	boys and men vs. girls and women	*Sex* refers to the biological or sexual aspects of being a man or a woman.
imply	verb	suggest	The author *implied* that previous research was not methodologically sound.
infer	verb	generalize from evidence	From my analysis of the literature, I inferred that much of the previous research was not methodologically sound.
insignificant	adj	unimportant	The effect, although statistically significant, was small and insignificant.

T A B L E **6.3** Problem Pairs—*continued*

Problem Pair	Part of Speech*	Meaning	Example
nonsignificant	adj	not statistically significant	The nonsignificant results may have been due to the study's lack of power.
literally	adv	exactly as written	The patient *literally* threw stones inside a glass house (use *literally* only if readers might otherwise think you were writing figuratively).
figuratively	adv	involving a figure of speech	The comedian *figuratively* died during his act (use *figuratively* only if readers might otherwise think you were not using a figure of speech, e.g., if they might otherwise think that the comedian actually died).
method	noun	procedure, technique	We used Donders's subtraction *method*.
methodology	noun	system, or study, of methods	In one class, we studied the *methodology* of single-case designs.
principal	adj	main, first	The *principal* effect of caffeine is stimulation.
principal	noun	director of a school	The *principal* of the school was fired.
principle	noun	law, tenet, rule	Psychologists should understand the *principles* of reinforcement.
reliable	adj	consistent, replicable	Participants' scores on the retest were similar to their original test scores, suggesting that the test is *reliable*.
valid	adj	accurate	Participants' scores on the test predicted their behavior in a real life situation, suggesting that the test is valid.
significant	adj	unlikely to be due to chance	The effect, although small, was statistically significant.
substantial	adj	large	The difference between carrying 100 pounds and 200 pounds is substantial.
use	noun	purpose	Scientists *use* Theory X to explain Y.
usage	noun	the manner of using	Word *usage* is discussed in this chapter.

6.3.4 Divide Run-On Sentences

There are at least two types of *run-on sentences*. The first occurs when two unrelated independent clauses are fused into one sentence (e.g., "There are problems with classical theories, and Smith proposes a new theory."). Fix such sentences by putting a period at the end of each independent clause. The second, often called a *comma splice*, occurs when two (or more) independent clauses are joined by only a comma. You have three options for fixing comma spliced sentences: (a) replace the comma with a period, (b) replace the comma with a semicolon, (c) add a conjunction (e.g., "and") after the comma.

> ✗   The choice among the classical theories is complicated, there are problems with all of them and Smith proposes a new theory I will discuss.

> ✔   The choice among the classical theories is complicated; there are problems with all of them. Smith proposes a new theory I will discuss.

6.3.5 Specify Nonspecific Referents

All sentences you write should be clear. These provide problems. We hope you have recoiled in horror at the second sentence of this paragraph. You should be wondering what we mean by "These" (a *nonspecific referent*). One possibility is that "these" refers to "All sentences," the subject of the first sentence. However, we were referring to "nonspecific referents," the last part of the heading.

To avoid problems like the ones illustrated by the second sentence of the previous paragraph ("These provide problems."), consider two points whenever you use a nonspecific referent. First, be sure that your sentences stand independently of the previous paragraph, heading, or title. To apply this advice to our troubled second sentence, you would rewrite it as: "Nonspecific referents cause problems." Second, any time you use a pronoun, ensure that the reader knows which noun that pronoun represents. One way to see whether a pronoun ("a pointing word") could mislead or confuse a reader is to draw an arrow from the potentially ambiguous pointing word (e.g., "this," "that," "they," "it," "those") back to the word or idea to which it refers. If, on the way to the word you were trying to refer to, the arrow passes other words that could also fit, you have a problem. Solutions to the problem include

- replacing the ambiguous pronoun with the noun that the pronoun referred to (e.g., change "it is" to "cognitive dissonance theory is"),

- distinguishing the targeted noun from other nearby nouns by making it the only plural (or only singular) noun near your plural (or singular) pronoun (e.g., change "There were several potential causes of these effects. They include" to "There were several potential causes of this effect. They include"),

- using "who" to refer to humans rather than using "that" (e.g., change "the participants that were most influenced" to "the participants who were most influenced"), and

■ adding a word or a descriptive phrase after words such as "this" so the reader knows what "this" refers to (e.g., replace "this is" with "this psychoanalytic idea is").

6.3.6 Attribute Humanity Only to Humans

Only humans do such things as point out, argue, or suggest. Do not attribute human abilities to theories, concepts, data, or other nonhuman entities. To attribute human abilities to nonhuman entities is to commit the error of *anthropomorphism*. Next, we show you some examples of anthropomorphism, followed by solutions:

✗ Smith's (1969) theory suggests an alternative explanation.

✓ Smith (1969) suggests an alternative explanation.

✗ This concept favors a different perspective.

✓ Holders of this concept favor a different perspective.

✗ The data speak to my hypothesis.

✓ Figure 1 shows that the data are consistent with my hypothesis.

✗ The results emphasize the connection between temperature and aggression.

✓ The results indicate that there is a relationship between temperature and aggression.

6.4 Writing with Style

6.4.1 Accentuate the Positive

Research shows that it is easier to understand things expressed positively (i.e., "give a point to all participants numbered 3, 4, 6, or 7") than to understand things expressed negatively (e.g., "give a point to all participants *except for* those numbered 1, 2, 5, 8, or 9"). The following pair of examples will illustrate the benefits of accentuating the positive:

✗ To create a good test, do not use questions worded negatively.

✓ To create a good test, use positively worded questions.

6.4.2 Point the Way Within and Between Paragraphs

The main idea, the punch line, of every paragraph you write should be expressed in a single sentence called the *topic sentence*. If your paragraph does not have a topic sentence, you may be able to generate one for it by either summarizing the paragraph or by referring to your outline. If you cannot generate a topic sentence for a paragraph, you probably should delete that paragraph from your paper.

A paragraph's topic sentence could be the first sentence of the paragraph (e.g., "Smith and Jones (2003) identified three problems with previous research."). In that case, the rest of the paragraph would develop, defend, or explain the topic sentence.

A paragraph's topic sentence will often be the last sentence of the paragraph, especially if you are presenting an argument or a hypothesis (e.g., "Therefore, previous research is flawed in at least three ways."). You will start the paragraph with evidence supporting a position, and hope that the reader will come to your conclusion before coming to your topic sentence stating that conclusion.

The paragraph's topic sentence, regardless of where it is, helps readers navigate within the paragraph. After helping the reader make it through a paragraph, you must help the reader make it through the next one. You must ensure that each paragraph stands independently of others, yet flows logically and gracefully from the one before it and the one after it.

To maintain each paragraph's independence, be cautious about beginning a paragraph with the words "This," "These," or "Those" (such pronouns are known as *nonspecific referents*; see 6.3.5). The problem with using nonspecific referents is that such words are meaningless on their own. As a result, using one of these words to start a paragraph makes that paragraph depend on the previous paragraph for its meaning. Therefore, do not use "this" or a similar word in your paragraph's first sentence as shorthand for a concept, idea, study, or criticism stated in a previous paragraph. Instead, restate the concept, idea, study, or criticism.

Starting a new paragraph by restating an idea from the previous paragraph not only helps the new paragraph stand independently, but it also helps readers see connections between adjoining paragraphs. To further help the reader see connections, you may, occasionally, put connecting words or connecting phrases such as "In addition to," "Next," "Consequently," or "Although" in front of your restatement. However, be selective in your use of connecting words: If most of your paragraphs start with connecting words, it will hurt the flow of your paper.

Often, the smoothest way to ensure that paragraphs flow is to use the concluding sentence of the previous paragraph to set up the next one. Concluding sentences that accomplish flow look like the following.

> `Researchers could use three tactics to overcome these methodological problems.` [The next paragraph would begin with a sentence about the first tactic.]

> `The range must be limited, however, when adaptation phenomena are considered.` [The next paragraph would begin with description of an adaptation phenomenon.]

6.4.3 Use Parallel Construction

You can improve both the flow and the clarity of ideas within a paragraph by using *parallel construction*. Where you have several similar ideas, express them using the same, *parallel*, construction, whether within adjacent phrases, clauses, or sentences:

✗ The participant began each trial with a button press, using the keyboard to give a response, and the trial finished when the participant pressed another button.

✔ The participant began each trial with a button press, gave a response with the keyboard, and finished the trial with another button press.

✔ The participant used keypresses to start each trial, give a response, and end a trial.

✗ The results showed no significant differences in the area of anxiety, or regarding depression; psychoses also did not differ.

✔ The results showed no significant differences in anxiety, depression, or psychosis.

6.4.4 Use a Consistent, Formal Tone

Keep a formal tone; avoid clichés or colloquialisms. Use metaphors sparingly, and carry through any you do use.

✗ When all is said and done [cliché 1], the moral of the story [cliché 2] is that the bottom line [cliché 3] of my study is that children trained with the X technique were literally [cliché 4] out of hand [colloquialism 1], so the results are up the creek [colloquialism 2]. . . . When the results were analyzed with a finer-toothed [metaphor 1] statistical test, the hypothesis still lay bleeding on the ground [mixed metaphor 2].

✗ In conclusion, my study showed that children trained with the X technique misbehaved so badly there were no significant results. . . . When the results were analyzed with a finer-toothed statistical test, the only new results combed out were statistical dandruff. [Although the metaphor has been continued, it is too informal for scientific writing.]

✔ In conclusion, the unruliness of children trained with the X technique obscured any significant results. . . . When the results were analyzed with a higher-powered test, no new meaningful findings emerged.

6.4.5 Use Small Words and Short Sentences

Use concise sentences. If you do not, you may write sentences like the following one. *Obsolescent prolixities are to be eschewed.* Note that if you replaced the previous sentence's unfamiliar words with familiar ones and if you changed the previous sentence's voice from passive to active (for more information about voice, see 6.1.3), you could change the previous sentence to "Avoid unfamiliar words."

Keep sentences shorter than 20 words. A good test of length is to read your assignment aloud, taking a breath only when you find a period. If you find that you are running out of breath and a period still has not come into sight, then the sentence is too long. The solution is to break long sentences into a number of shorter sentences. On the other hand, avoid going to the opposite extreme of using only short sentences; using too many short sentences will make your paper sound choppy and telegraphic.

6.4.6 Be Precise

Do not try to make your sentences sound less telegraphic by adding adjectives and adverbs. Although you may believe that adding adverbs and adjectives makes your writing more dramatic, your writing will be more powerful if you replace your vague adjectives and imprecise adverbs with more precise words. Thus, instead of being dramatic by writing "*numerous* times," be precise by writing "17 times." Similarly, instead of writing things like "a *relatively large* number of participants" and "a *fairly big* effect," be precise by writing "25 participants" and "a 55% increase."

6.4.7 Be Concise

Another problem with using adjectives and adverbs is that such words are often unnecessary. Consequently, adjectives and adverbs can weaken your sentences by making your sentences wordy. Remember, shorter is often more powerful. Thus, rather than writing "a *disastrous* event," save words—and gain power—by writing "a disaster."

In addition to cutting adjectives and adverbs that dilute your prose, you should cut unnecessary paragraphs, sentences, phrases, and expressions. Therefore, when editing your paper, you should

- eliminate paragraphs dealing with material not directly relevant to your paper.
- replace pairs of sentences that restate one another (i.e., sentences beginning explicitly or implicitly with phrases such as "In other words," "To put it another way") with the better of the two.
- replace passive sentences (e.g., "The unconscious *was emphasized by* Freud.") with active sentences (e.g., "Freud *emphasized* the unconscious.").
- replace nouns trying to do a verb's job (e.g., "We did *a modification of*") with verbs (e.g., "we *modified*").
- replace phrases (e.g., "The theory applied *in the context* [phrase 1] *of sensory processes* [phrase 2]") with single words (e.g., "The theory applied to *sensation*").
- replace wordy prepositional phrases referring to time (e.g., "*at the present time*") with single words (e.g., "now").
- replace wordy prepositional phrases for "about" (e.g., "*in relation to*") with "about."
- replace wordy expressions (e.g., "*despite the fact that*") with single words (e.g., "*although*").

T A B L E **6.4** Wordy Expressions to Remove from Your Writing

	Replace This	With This
Prepositional phrases about relationships		
	in terms of	in, on, about
	vis-à-vis	in, on, about
	with respect to	in, on, about
	in relation to	about
Prepositional phrases about time		
	at the present time	now
	at this point in time	now
	in the process of	now
	at that particular time	then
	in the near future	soon
Other wordy expressions		
	be of the opinion	believe
	despite the fact that	although
Double trouble: Redundant pairs		
	actual fact	fact
	close proximity	close
	consensus of opinion	consensus
	final conclusion	conclusion
	future planning	planning
	must necessarily	must
	new innovation	innovation
	reason why	reason

■ replace redundant pairs of words (e.g., "actual fact") with their essential elements (e.g., "fact").

To see examples of redundant pairs and other multi-word expressions that you should replace with single words, see Table 6.4.

6.4.8 Be Cautious

The good writer obeys all the writing rules—even those that most readers would not mind seeing violated. The good writer realizes that obeying all the rules will not offend anyone, whereas disobeying the rules may offend someone. To make reading an agreeable experience for all readers, the good writer tries to obey even those writing rules that most readers ignore, such as not ending sentences with prepositions and not splitting infinitives.

Do not end any sentence with a preposition. For example, do not write a sentence like the following: "This is an impertinence which I will not put up with." Winston Churchill is reputed to have objected to the rule of not ending sentences with prepositions by saying, "This is an impertinence up with which I will not put." Although Churchill's sentence sounds stilted, realize that his sentence can be rewritten in a way that honors the rule, yet sounds natural: "I will not put up with such impertinence."

Keep infinitives intact. Writers *split infinitives* when they put something, usually an adverb, between the *to* and the *verb* part of an infinitive. A famous phrase from the television series "Star Trek" is an example of a split infinitive (and sexist language): "to boldly go where no man has gone before." You could rewrite the phrase to rejoin the infinitive (and to remove the sexist language): "to go boldly into new frontiers."

6.5 Your Own Style

To resume the analogy we made at the start of this chapter, writers ignorant of grammar and punctuation are like drivers who, although they know the way to their destinations, fail to arrive because they drove on flat tires, ran out of gasoline, or crashed into a pole. Writers ignorant of good usage are like drivers who reach their destinations, but only after running over curbs, grinding the gears, and losing their passengers. Writers ignorant of style are like drivers who reach their destinations, but who make some wrong turns and circle some blocks several times. Skilled drivers have their own styles: some drive slowly, admiring the view along the way; others drive fast, showing flair and verve. As you master the skills of driving your words, you can develop your own style. Remember, however, that the point is to arrive at your destination with your passengers still on board.

6.6   Checklists

6.6.1 Parts of Speech

Pronouns

___ I made sure that pronouns pointed to their nouns. Specifically,
  ___ I put pronouns close to their respective nouns.
  ___ I made sure that pronouns agreed with pronouns in number.
  ___ I usually followed the pronoun "this" with a word or phrase that made it clear what the referent was for "this."

___ When referring to humans, I used the pronoun "who" instead of the pronouns "that" or "which."

Verbs

___ The subjects of my sentences agree with the verbs of my sentences. That is, I do not have a plural noun (data) with a singular verb (is). When I was not sure that my subject agreed with my verb,

   ___ I made sure I knew what the subject of the sentence was, even if that meant shortening or simplifying that sentence.

   ___ I remembered that if I had two nouns as subjects and they were joined by the conjunction "and," I used the plural form of the verb. However, if they were joined by the conjunction "or," the noun closest to the verb dictated whether I used the singular or plural form of the verb.

   ___ I checked Appendix B to make sure that the subject of the sentence was in the form (singular or plural) that I intended—unless I was sure I knew what the singular and plural forms were (e.g., dog, dogs).

___ The tense of my verbs is correct.

   ___ If I am referring to either (a) a specific event that occurred in the past or (b) a certain study (including the results of my own study), I use the past tense (e.g., "the study found").

   ___ If I am referring to something that started at some time in the past but continues to the present, I use the present perfect (e.g., "studies have found").

   ___ I usually use the active voice instead of the passive voice.

Adverbs

___ When possible, I eliminated adverbs.

___ If I need an adverb to modify a verb, I made sure that I used the proper "ly" ending for adverbs rather than using the shorter, adjective form. For example, I wrote that participants "worked quickly" rather than "worked quick."

___ If I used an adverb, I put it next to the verb it was modifying.

6.6.2 Punctuation

___ I used commas

   ___ at places where I would pause if I were reading my paper aloud—unless another punctuation mark was more appropriate,

   ___ between a dependent clause that started a sentence and the independent clause that followed it (e.g., "Although I fell, I did not cry."),

   ___ before a conjunction such as "and" that joined two independent clauses, and

   ___ between all lists of three or more items—unless the items contained commas.

___ I used semicolons
  ___ to separate list items when those list items contained commas, and
  ___ to join two independent clauses without a conjunction.
___ I did not overuse apostrophes, quotation marks, parentheses, or hyphens.
  ___ I do not have any contractions in my paper and I have not used apostrophes with the pronoun "its" or with years (e.g., I wrote "1990s" rather than "1990's.").
  ___ I used hyphens only when the meaning of a sentence would be unclear without them. For example, I did not use hyphens merely to make my right margins even.
  ___ I used quotation marks sparingly. I used them only with quotations that were shorter than 40 words or with words that were being used in an unconventional way. Furthermore, I rarely used quotes and I rarely used words in an unconventional way.
___ I put commas and periods inside quotation marks.

6.6.3 Style

___ To prevent my reader from getting lost in my paper,
  ___ I outlined my paper.
  ___ I made sure that all my paragraphs had topic sentences—and I made sure that those topic sentences referred to entries in my outline.
  ___ I used subheadings.
  ___ I built bridges between paragraphs by using transition words or repeating key phrases and ideas.
  ___ I made all my paragraphs shorter than a page, and I kept most of them shorter than half a page.
  ___ I kept most of my sentences under 20 words.
___ To avoid offending readers who have strict views about what is permissible in formal writing, I avoided
  ___ ending sentences with prepositions,
  ___ starting sentences with coordinating conjunctions such as "and," "but," and "or,"
  ___ splitting infinitives,
  ___ using one-word sentences,
  ___ using one-sentence paragraphs,
  ___ using contractions, and
  ___ using exclamation points.

6.7 Summary

1. The main parts of speech are nouns, pronouns, verbs, articles, adjectives, adverbs, prepositions, conjunctions, and relative pronouns.

2. Do not overuse adjectives.

3. Do not overuse adverbs.

4. When you use a pronoun, make sure that the reader can easily tell to which noun it refers.

5. If a plural noun has a pronoun, its pronoun must also be plural; if a singular noun has a pronoun, its pronoun must also be singular.

6. If a subject is plural, its verb must also be plural; if a subject is singular, its verb must also be singular.

7. Most of your sentences should have fewer than 20 words and most of your paragraphs should be less than half a page long.

8. Usually, a period will end your sentence. However, if the last word of your sentence is in quotation marks, the period will be inside the quotation marks.

9. Use apostrophes only to indicate possession (e.g., the participant's score). Do not use apostrophes for contractions (e.g., write "it is" rather than "it's," write "they are" rather than "they're") or to indicate the plural form (e.g., write "1950s" rather than "1950's").

10. An independent clause can stand alone as a sentence. An independent clause must have a verb and must contain a complete thought.

11. If you are using a coordinating conjunction such as "or," "and," or "but" to join two independent clauses, put a comma before the conjunction.

12. If you are combining two independent clauses without a coordinating conjunction, you cannot connect them with a comma. You must use either a semicolon or a colon.

13. Never use a colon unless the words in front of the colon constitute an independent clause.

14. Do not overuse parentheses, hyphens, quotation marks, and dashes.

15. Often, people will write one word when they should write another. If you consult our "Problem Pairs" table (Table 6.3), you will be less likely to make that kind of mistake.

16. All paragraphs should have topic sentences.

17. Obey conventional rules of writing. For example, do not use contractions, do not split infinitives, do not start sentences with coordinating conjunctions, and do not end sentences with prepositions.

18. Try to use the active voice.

19. Try to use parallel structure.

20. Eliminate unnecessary words.

CHAPTER

7

Preparing the Final Draft

7.1 Presentation

7.2 APA Formats

7.3 Conclusions

7.4 Format Checklists

7.5 Summary

7.1 Presentation

Even professors who do not explicitly assign points for how well papers conform to APA format tend to give higher grades to papers that adhere to APA format than to papers that fail to adhere to APA format. If your paper is correctly formatted, your professor will be under the impression that the paper was written by someone who is conscientious and competent—and will tend to evaluate the paper's content accordingly. If, on the other hand, your paper fails to meet even basic formatting requirements, your professor will be under the impression that the paper was written by someone who is careless and incompetent—and will tend to evaluate the paper's content accordingly. In this chapter, we show you how to turn in a paper that will make a good first impression and how to avoid the mistakes that make some students' papers "dead on arrival."

7.1.1 Paper, Margins, Spacing

Use one side of white, bond, letter-sized (8.5 × 11 in. [22 × 28 cm]) paper. Leave margins of at least one in. (2.54 cm) at the top, bottom, left, and right. Double-space all text.

7.1.2 Word Processing Versus Typing

If possible, use a word processor. Word-processing software will format much of your paper for you, as long as you do the following.

- Select a 12-point serif font[1] (such as Courier or Times Roman).
- Select double spacing.
- Deselect "right justify," "auto hyphenation," or anything that would automatically hyphenate words at the end of a line.
- Select the "replace straight quotes with smart quotes" option[2] so that your quotation marks and apostrophes look typeset rather than typewritten ("Jolley's examples" instead of "Jolley's examples").
- Insert spaces only where necessary. Never leave two spaces after a punctuation mark. Do not leave any spaces after (a) hyphens or dashes and (b) periods that are part of an abbreviation (e.g., P.M.). Leave a single space after all other punctuation.[3]
- Italicize where necessary (see 7.2.4).

If you do not have access to a word processor, your professor will probably allow you to use a typewriter. If your typewriter produces 10 characters per inch, set the margins for a maximum of 65 characters per line. If your typewriter produces 12 characters per inch, set the margins for a maximum of 78 characters per line. Do not try to make the right margin perfectly even. Break to a new line if a word would go over the right margin or require a hyphen. Underline material that would normally be italicized. Do not put a space after hyphens and periods that are part of an abbreviation (e.g., P.M.). Leave a single space after all other punctuation marks.

7.2 APA Formats

APA recognizes two formats: copy and final. The first, "copy" style, is a format for authors who are submitting their work for publication. Copy style differs from what the final form of the published work will look like. Copy editors will work with typesetters to convert the submitted document into its final form. The second format,

---

[1]Serifs are the little strokes on the ends of individual letters. Research shows that serif fonts are easier to read than sans serif (without serif) fonts. The *Publication Manual* recommends using either Times Roman or Courier.

[2]You will probably find this option by going to the "Tools" menu and choosing the "AutoCorrect" tool.

[3]You can use a grammar checker program to make sure that you have left only one space after punctuation marks. Alternatively, you can find and remove unnecessary spaces if you select the "find-and-replace" command and put two spaces in the "find" box and one space in the "replace" box.

"final" style, is for authors who are producing the final form of the document themselves. Final style is identical to the format of a published article.

The focus of the *Publication Manual* is on copy style: the format used when submitting an article for publication. Most professors also focus on copy style: They ask students to prepare a paper the same way an author would submit a manuscript to a journal. Therefore, our main emphasis will be on copy style. However, your professor may decide to use the style that is authorized by the American Psychological Association (2001) for final form (if so, see Appendix A). If your professor asks you to use final style (also called "final-form" style), your paper will look like a published article in a recent APA journal (e.g., *Psychological Review*) instead of looking like a manuscript that must be copy-edited and typeset before it looks like an article.

7.2.1 Running Head Versus Short Title

In articles submitted for publication, the first two to three words of the title (the "short title") should appear on the top right-hand corner of each page. Five spaces to the right of the short title is the page number. The title page is numbered "1" and is the first page of the manuscript. If you are using a word processor, put the page number and the short title in the "header" area (If you need help inserting material into the header, specific instructions are available at http://www.writingforpsychology.com).

On the title page, one double-spaced line below the short title, starting on the left margin is the phrase "Running head:" followed by the running head—a two- to six-word phrase, typed in all capital letters, that summarizes the title of the article. The running head has a 50-character limit—and spaces, as well as punctuation, count against that limit. In articles submitted for publication, the running head does not appear on any other page.

In published articles, on the other hand, the phrase "Running head:" followed by the running head does not appear on the title page. Furthermore, the short title does not appear on the title page—or on any page. Instead, the running head is the header that appears on the top of every other page (e.g., on top of page 2, 4, 6, etc.). In final style, headers are centered, rather than being in the top right-hand corner. As was the case with submitted manuscripts, the title page is numbered. However, the page number, rather than being in the right-hand corner, is centered at the bottom of each page.

7.2.2 Paragraphs

The first line of most paragraphs should be indented five characters. To accomplish this press the tab key once. However, there are three exceptions to this indentation rule. Specifically, do not indent the first line of the Abstract, the figure captions, or the table notes. The first line for each of these three should be written flush with the left margin.

7.2.3 Headings

The *Publication Manual* provides five levels of headings. You, however, will probably not need to use more than three levels. The following examples illustrate the three levels of headings that you are most likely to use.[4]

For major sections of your reports, use

A Centered and Capitalized First-Level Heading

For your subheadings under the main headings, use

A Flush Left, Capitalized, Italicized, Second-Level Heading

For your subheadings that split subsections into parts, use

An indented italicized third-level, paragraph heading ending with a period. Text begins immediately after this heading, as shown here.

In a short term paper (fewer than 2,000 words), the first level is the only one you need. You use it to break your paper into its major sections: Abstract, main text (its heading is term paper's title), and References (see 2.2). In a report, you use the first level to head the major sections: Abstract, Introduction (its heading is not "Introduction" but rather the report's title), Method, Results, Discussion, References, and Appendixes (see 3.1). Note that the numbered headings found in this book are inappropriate for APA style; we have used them to help you find the information you need as quickly as possible.

For term papers longer than about 2,000 words, you may need to divide the main text into subsections. If so, use the second level. For research reports, you always use the second level to divide the Method section into subsections. For example, almost all Method sections will have Participants and Procedure subsections. In addition to dividing the Method section, you may choose to divide the Introduction, Results, and Discussion sections. For example, if you had two dependent measures, you could divide the Results section using the second level (e.g., into "Accuracy" and "Reaction Times").

If you need to divide a second-level subsection, use the third level. For example, in a report, if you had five separate tests, all of which required detailed description, you could divide the second-level *Materials* subsection into five, third-level subsections.

7.2.4 Italics or Underlining

In your papers, italicize—or, if you are using a machine that cannot produce italics, underline—only the following items: second- and third-level headings, journal titles, journal volume numbers, book titles, normal (non-Greek) letters used as abbreviations for a statistical term (e.g., *F*, *M*, *p*, and *t*), names of species, words with special meanings (such as linguistic examples, words denoting procedural or experimental

---

[4]If you are writing a multi-study research report (you have conducted two or more studies and are writing up those studies in a single research report), you will need more headings than we describe here. To see how to format your headings for a multi-study paper, see our Web site.

conditions, words serving as labels for rating scale anchors, and the first use of a technical term), and unusual foreign words. Do not italicize commonly used foreign terms such as et al., i.e., e.g., and a posteriori. To better understand how to use italics, study the examples and explanations in the following paragraph.

> Participants in the *hold* and *no hold* conditions [italicize names of experimental conditions] were asked to press the *yes* button [italicize procedural terms] when they heard words containing the *phoneme* [italicize first use of a technical term] /a/ (such as *forgot* and *potty* [italicize linguistic examples]). After the button press, they were asked to rate the subjective strength of the phoneme [technical terms such as "phoneme" are italicized only the first time they are used] on a scale from *weak* (1) to *strong* (5) [italicize rating scale anchors such as "weak" and "strong"]. One participant complained that the task induced feelings of déjà vu [although "déjà vu" is a foreign phrase, it is not italicized because it is not unusual]. The correlation between reaction time and strength rating was found to be *r* = -.40 [italicize *r* because it is an abbreviation for a statistical term].

Do not underline, italicize, boldface, or capitalize words (THUS) that you want to emphasize. To emphasize key points, employ skillful writing—not typographical tricks.

7.2.5 Abbreviations

As a general rule, do not use abbreviations in the main text of your paper. However, there are four major exceptions to this general rule. First, you should abbreviate units of measurement (see 3.6.8). Second, you can use well-accepted abbreviations such as IQ and ESP. Third, you can use an abbreviation for a term after you have properly introduced that abbreviation. To properly introduce an abbreviation, (a) completely write out the term, and then, (b) in parentheses, write its abbreviation in all capital letters. Fourth, you should use certain abbreviations within parentheses. For example, within parentheses, standard Latin abbreviations should be used (cf., e.g., i.e.). Furthermore, within parentheses, an ampersand (&) must be used between two authors' names (see 4.4.2). Punctuate standard abbreviations as if they were spelled-out words or phrases. Thus, you would put a comma after "e.g." (which means for example), but you would not put a comma after "cf." (which means compare). Table 7.1 is a list of the abbreviations that you can use within parentheses.

Keep the abbreviations you define free of periods. For example, "reaction time" becomes "RT," not "R.T." If, as you write, you say the spelled-out version of the abbreviation, you will avoid making some common grammatical errors. For example, you will know to write "a RT" rather than "an RT" because you would never say "an reaction time." Saying the spelled-out version of the abbreviation will also help you avoid silly errors (e.g., you do not refer to "RPMs" because the abbreviation is already pluralized: "revolutions per minute"). If the abbreviation is singular, but you want to make it plural, simply add "s" (e.g., "RTs"). Indicate possession using the

T A B L E **7.1** Abbreviations to Be Used in Parentheses

Abbreviation	Literally	Translation	Usage
&	and per se	and	Between authors' names
c.	*circa*	about	Before a citation date if the date is uncertain
cf.	*confere*	compare	
e.g.	*exempli gratia*	for example	
et al.	*et alii*	and others	For secondary authors' names after first complete citation (see 4.4.3)
etc.	*et cetera*	and so forth	Rare in scientific writing; avoid
i.e.	*id est*	that is	
ibid.	*ibidem*	in the same reference	Rare; avoid by repeating the citation
n.b.	*nota bene*	take notice	
op. cit.	*opere citato*	in the reference already quoted	Rare; avoid by repeating the citation
p.	page	page	
pp.	pages	pages	
viz.	*videlicet*	namely	
vs.	versus	versus	
–	to	to	As in "pp. 22–33"

same principle; usually you simply add apostrophe "s" (e.g., "RT's"; see 6.2.5). To better understand the rules regarding abbreviations, study the following paragraph.

> To test the hypothesis that reaction time (RT) [introduce a lesser known abbreviation by preceding it with unabbreviated term] is related to IQ [do not precede a well-known abbreviation with the unabbreviated term "intelligence quotient"] 200 students were tested on the WAIS [well-known abbreviation] and their RTs [pluralize abbreviations as if not abbreviated] to light onset were determined. Mean RT was 205 ms [abbreviate standard units; see 3.6.8] (cf. [standard abbreviation used within parentheses] Woodworth & [within parentheses, use "&" instead of "and."] Schlosberg, 1954) and the correlation with IQ was .40. It may be that RT's [indicate possession as if not abbreviated] correlation with IQ does not imply a direct relationship, but indicates a third, mediating variable. For example, [abbreviate "for example" as "e.g." only within parentheses] those with high motivation could have tried hard on the IQ test and on the RT task.

7.2.6 Numbers

When should you write out a number ("nine") and when should you express it in digits ("9")? Usually, you should express it in digits. However, there are two cases in which you should write out the number. First, if the number starts a sentence, you write out the number. Second, if the number is a whole number between zero and nine and is not a measurement nor is it directly compared to any number that is 10 or greater, then write out the number. Otherwise, express numbers using digits—and you will be right most of the time.[5] However, use some common sense. For example, if using the numeral "3" makes your sentence easier to read than if you had used "three" (e.g., "3 three-way interactions"), use "3."

What if you are not dealing with integers? Treat percentages as though they were integers, except that you follow them with a percent sign (e.g., 12%). If you are expressing a fraction as a decimal, take it to two decimal places. Put a zero in front of the decimal point for fractions less than 1 that are units of measurement (e.g., 0.1 cm). Never put a zero in front of the decimal point for either correlation coefficients or probability values. Provide as many decimal points as necessary for probability values. For both probability values and correlation coefficients, do not put a zero in front of the decimal point. The examples and explanations in the following paragraph illustrate these rules.

> Twenty [never use numerals to begin a sentence] participants completed three [number less than 10 and not a measurement] tests consisting of 15 [number greater than nine] subscales each. The mean score on the first test was 3.45 [two decimal places for a fraction] $SD = 0.45$ [zero in front of the decimal point for a fraction], but the mode was 5 [integer measure] items correct. The correlation between test A and B was $r = .47$, $p < .001$ [correlation coefficients and probability values never have zeroes before the decimal point].

7.2.7 Tables and Figures

In term papers, avoid using tables and figures. You should be able to communicate the salient points of experiments and theories without resorting to figures or tables. In reports, tables or figures may be appropriate; details and examples are provided in 3.6.5–3.6.7.

7.3 Conclusions

If you have followed the instructions in this chapter, your paper should look professional. To make sure that you have not overlooked any important formatting details, use the following checklists.

---

[5]To be right all of the time, follow the extensive list of rules and examples in the *Publication Manual*.

7.4   Format Checklists

7.4.1 General Appearance Checklist

___ I followed any specific requirements that my professor imposed. For example, if my professor said that unstapled papers would not be accepted, I stapled my paper.

___ I understood whether my professor was requiring APA copy style or APA final-form style.

___ I used white, 8.5 × 11 in. (22 × 28 cm), 20-pound, bond paper.

___ I typed my paper using
   ___ 12-point type,
   ___ Times Roman, Times New Roman, or Courier font,
   ___ black print,
   ___ easy-to-read, dark print,
   ___ one inch (2.54 cm) margins, and
   ___ only one side of the page.

___ I double-spaced everything.

___ I started every paragraph by indenting five spaces with only two exceptions:
   ___ I did not indent the Abstract.
   ___ I did not indent Notes at the bottom of tables.

___ I did not hyphenate words at the end of a line.

___ I did not use boldfacing or any other typographical tricks to emphasize words.

___ I italicized rather than underlined.

___ I italicized (a) letters that served as abbreviations for statistical terms (e.g., "p" as the abbreviation for probability value), (b) second-level headings (see 7.2.3), and (c) book titles, journal titles, and journal volume numbers in the Reference page.

7.4.2 Headings and Headers Checklist

___ If I used APA manuscript style, I put the first two or three words of the title, then five spaces, and then the page number at the top, right-hand corner of every page—except for those pages containing figures.

___ I centered all my first-level headings (e.g., Abstract, Conclusion, References, etc.) in plain (not italicized, not bold-faced) font. I capitalized only the first letters of words of these headings.

___ I italicized all my second-level headings (major subheadings such as Participants, Procedure, etc.) and put them flush against the left margin (I did not indent them). I capitalized only the first letters of words of these subheadings.

7.4.3 Numbers, Tables, and Figures Checklist

___ I tried not to start a sentence with a number. If I started a sentence with a number, I spelled out that number.

___ When I wrote a number above 10, I expressed it in digits.

___ When I wrote a number below 10, I spelled it out unless
    ___ It came right before a unit of measurement (e.g., 3 cm).
    ___ It represented a fraction (e.g., 3/4) or a percentage (e.g., 6%).
    ___ It represented a score (e.g., the mean was 4) or a point on a scale (e.g., a 7-point scale).
    ___ It represented the number of participants (e.g., 3 participants).
    ___ It was being compared to a number greater than 10.

___ I did not put a zero before the decimal point for any correlation coefficients or probability values.

___ I put a zero before the decimal point for fractions (e.g., 0.1 cm).

___ If I used tables or figures, I checked them against the checklist in 3.12.

7.4.4 Citations and References Checklist

___ I used the citation checklist (4.10.2).

___ I used the reference list checklist (4.10.4).

7.4.5 Abbreviations Checklist

___ Within parentheses, I used abbreviations such as "e.g." and "&" only within parentheses.

___ When I used units of measurement, I abbreviated those units and did not add "s" to express their plural forms (e.g., I wrote "5 min" instead of "5 mins").

___ When I used abbreviations outside of parentheses that were not abbreviations for units of measurement, those abbreviations were usually common abbreviations or abbreviations that I had introduced earlier (see 7.2.5), were usually in all capital letters, and were usually punctuated like words (e.g., they did not contain periods, the plural form was created by adding "s," and the possessive form was created by adding "'s").

7.4.6 Title Page Checklist

___ I have a separate title page.

___ At the top right-hand corner, I have
    ___ a short, two- or three-word "mini-title" of my paper. This "mini-title" is the first two or three words of my title.
    ___ the number "1," indicating that it is page 1. The "1" is on the same line as the mini-title, just five spaces to the right of it.

___ One double-spaced line below the short title and the page number,
I have a line that

    ___ starts at the left margin (about an inch from the left edge of the
    page), and

    ___ begins with the words "Running head:" followed by a two- to six-
    word phrase that describes my paper's topic. (Note that the running
    head is *not* the same as the mini-title.)

___ My two- to six-word running head is in all-capital letters and is fewer
than 51 characters and spaces long.

___ I centered the title and capitalized the first letters of each word in the
title (except for words such as "and" and "of").

___ My title is short and to the point.

___ My name (first name, *middle initial*, and last name) is

    ___ one double-spaced line below the title,

    ___ centered, and

    ___ not accompanied by the word "by."

___ My school's name is

    ___ one double-spaced line below my name, and

    ___ centered.

7.5 Summary

1. If possible, use a word processor. Word-processing software will automatically format much of your paper for you.

2. Double space your paper and leave at least one-inch margins.

3. APA recognizes two formats: copy and final-form. Be sure you know which one your professor has assigned.

4. In APA manuscript style, the first two or three words of the title (the "short title") should appear on the top right-hand corner of each page. Five spaces to the right of the short title is the page number. On the title page, one double-spaced line below the short title, starting on the left margin is the phrase: "Running head:" followed by the running head—a two- to six-word phrase, typed in all capital letters, that summarizes the title of the article.

5. Use headings (to see how to format headings, refer to 7.2.3). For term papers longer than 2,000 words, you may need to divide the main text into subsections. If you need to divide a second-level subsection, use third-level headings.

6. If a number starts a sentence, write out the number. If the number is greater than nine, use digits to express that number.

7. Follow any special instructions that your professor gives you.

8. Type your paper using black, 12-point type, and Times Roman, Times New Roman, or Courier font. Type it on to white, 20-pound, bond paper.

REFERENCES

American Psychological Association. (1974). *Publication manual of the American Psychological Association* (2nd ed.). Washington, D.C.: Author.

American Psychological Association. (1992). Ethical principles of psychologists and a code of conduct. *American Psychologist, 47,* 1597–1611.

American Psychological Association. (2001). *Publication manual of the American Psychological Association* (5th ed.). Washington, D.C.: Author.

American Psychological Association. (2002). Ethical principles of psychologists and code of conduct. *American Psychologist, 57,* 1060–1073.

Barkas, J. L. (1985). *How to write like a professional.* New York: Arco.

Clarion University of Pennsylvania. (n.d.). *Plagiarism* [Brochure]. Clarion, PA: Author.

Cohen, J. (1990). Things I have learned (so far). *American Psychologist, 45,* 1304–1312.

Cohen, J. (1994). The earth is round ($p < .05$). *American Psychologist, 49,* 997–1003.

Howard, V. A., & Barton, J. H. (1986). *Thinking on paper.* New York: William Morrow.

Keith-Spiegel, P., Wittig, A. F., Perkins, D. V., Balogh, D. W., & Whitely, B. E., Jr. (1993). *The ethics of teaching: A casebook.* Muncie, IN: Ball State University.

King, S. (2000). *On writing: A memoir of a craft.* New York: Scribner.

McDougall, W. (1914). *An introduction to social psychology* (8th ed.). London: Methuen.

Rosenthal, R. (1966). *Experimenter effects in behavioral research.* New York: Appleton-Century-Crofts.

Zechmeister, E. B., & Johnson, J. E. (1992). *Critical thinking: A functional approach.* Pacific Grove, CA: Brooks/Cole.

APPENDIX A

APA Copy Style Versus APA Final-Form Style

Some of you are reading this Appendix because your teacher is requiring you to use APA final-form style instead of APA copy style. Your teacher, like the third author of this text, probably has excellent reasons for requiring final-form style (to see the third author's reasons, go to http://psy.otago.ac.nz:800/r_oshea/wfp3e/hanging.html). The bad news is that, despite the wisdom of your teacher's decision, most descriptions of APA style focus on copy style. The good news is that, although final-form style is different from copy style, final-form style gives you more freedom than if you had been required to use copy style.

Some of you are reading this Appendix even though your teacher is requiring you to use APA copy style. Your problem is that you want to use a published work as a model, but you realize that there are differences between acceptable format for published work and acceptable format for manuscript. Table A-1 will help you see what you can model and what you should not. As you can see, you should not model single spacing, hyphenation at the end of lines, and the placement of both tables and figures.

TABLE **A.1** APA Copy Versus Final-Form Style

APA Copy Style	APA Final-Form Style
Place tables at end of your paper.	May put a table on the same page as the corresponding text or put it on the following page.
Place figures at end of your paper.	May put the figure on the page immediately following the page where the figure was mentioned.
Place figure captions at end of your paper.	Figure captions may be typed right below the figure.
Short title appears on the top, right-hand corner of each page.	Running head appears centered on every other page (on the pages that do not have the running head, the authors' names replace the running head).
Page numbers are five spaces to the right of the short title.	Page numbers are centered on the bottom of pages.

T A B L E **A.1**   APA Copy Versus Final-Form Style—*continued*

APA Copy Style	APA Final-Form Style
Title page is restricted to short title, page number, title, author's name, and author affiliation.	Title page may contain student information such as course name, assignment name, instructor's name, date submitted, and acknowledgments.
Acknowledgments would usually be put in an author's note that appears on a separate page.	
Double spacing is required.	Single spacing for tables, headings, captions, footnotes is permitted. Some triple or even quadruple spacing is also sometimes allowed.
Right margin is ragged, and you cannot use hyphens at the end of lines.	You can have a justified right margin, and you can use hyphens to keep the right margin even.

Problem Plurals

Singular	Plural	One Brief Definition
alumna	alumnae	female graduate
alumnus	alumni	male graduate
analysis	analyses	a study of
apparatus	apparatus	equipment
appendix	appendixes	supplementary material
bacterium	bacteria	germ
cannula	cannulas	tube used to administer drugs
carcinoma	carcinomas	malignant tumor
chiasm	chiasms	crossing point
continuum	continua	continuous whole
corpus	corpora	body
corpus callosum	corpora callosa	nerve fiber tract joining brain hemispheres
crisis	crises	emergency
curriculum	curricula	course
curriculum vitae	curricula vitae	academic résumé
degree of freedom	degrees of freedom	statistical term
die	dice	dotted cube
emphasis	emphases	importance
erratum	errata	error
focus	foci	central point
formula	formulas	equation
fovea	foveae	retinal area
ganglion	ganglia	group of nerve cells
genus	genera	group of species
hypothesis	hypotheses	conjecture
index	indexes	guide
kudos	kudos	acclaim

Singular	Plural	One Brief Definition
lacuna	lacunae	gap
locus	loci	place
manipulandum	manipulanda	stimulus object
matrix	matrices	array
millennium	millennia	1,000 years
minutia	minutiae	trivial detail
nexus	nexuses	connection, link
nucleus	nuclei	center
octopus	octopuses	eight-armed mollusk
opus	opera	work
parenthesis	parentheses	round bracket, aside
phylum	phyla	taxonomic division
prospectus	prospectuses	summary
quantum	quanta	indivisible amount
radius	radii	distance from center to edge
referendum	referendums	electoral question
retina	retinas	for sensing light
schema	schemas	outline
scotoma	scotomata	hole in visual field
sequela	sequelae	bad outcome of disease
soma	somata	body
spectrum	spectra	range
stratum	strata	layer
sum of squares	sums of squares	The difference between each score and the mean is squared, and then these squared terms are totaled.
syllabus	syllabi	outline
synthesis	syntheses	combination
thalamus	thalami	brain region
thesis	theses	dissertation
vertex	vertices	apex
virus	viruses	germ

INDEX